Andy Wimbush

Still: Samuel Beckett's Quietism

Samuel Beckett in Company

Edited by Paul Stewart ISSN 2365-3809

1   *Llewellyn Brown*
    Beckett, Lacan and the Voice
    With a foreword by Jean-Michel Rabaté
    ISBN 978-3-8382-0819-0 (Paperback edition)
    ISBN 978-3-8382-0939-5 (Hardcover edition)

2   *Robert Reginio, David Houston Jones, and Katherine Weiss (eds.)*
    Samuel Beckett and Contemporary Art
    ISBN 978-3-8382-0849-7

3   *Charlotta P. Einarsson*
    A Theatre of Affect
    The Corporeal Turn in Samuel Beckett's Drama
    ISBN 978-3-8382-1068-1

4   *Rhys Tranter*
    Beckett's Late Stage
    Trauma, Language, and Subjectivity
    ISBN 978-3-8382-1035-3

5   *Llewellyn Brown*
    Beckett, Lacan and the Gaze
    ISBN 978-3-8382-1239-5

6   *Paul Stewart & David Pattie (eds.)*
    Pop Beckett
    Intersections with Popular Culture
    ISBN 978-3-8382-1193-0

7   *Andy Wimbush*
    Still: Samuel Beckett's Quietism
    ISBN 978-3-8382-1369-9

Andy Wimbush

STILL: SAMUEL BECKETT'S QUIETISM

Bibliografische Information der Deutschen Nationalbibliothek
Die Deutsche Nationalbibliothek verzeichnet diese Publikation in der Deutschen Nationalbibliografie; detaillierte bibliografische Daten sind im Internet über http://dnb.d-nb.de abrufbar.

Bibliographic information published by the Deutsche Nationalbibliothek
Die Deutsche Nationalbibliothek lists this publication in the Deutsche Nationalbibliografie; detailed bibliographic data are available in the Internet at http://dnb.d-nb.de.

Cover: Photograph by Dmitri Kasterine

ISBN-13: 978-3-8382-1369-9
© *ibidem*-Verlag, Stuttgart 2020
Alle Rechte vorbehalten

Das Werk einschließlich aller seiner Teile ist urheberrechtlich geschützt. Jede Verwertung außerhalb der engen Grenzen des Urheberrechtsgesetzes ist ohne Zustimmung des Verlages unzulässig und strafbar. Dies gilt insbesondere für Vervielfältigungen, Übersetzungen, Mikroverfilmungen und elektronische Speicherformen sowie die Einspeicherung und Verarbeitung in elektronischen Systemen.

All rights reserved. No part of this publication may be reproduced, stored in or introduced into a retrieval system, or transmitted, in any form, or by any means (electronic, mechanical, photocopying, recording or otherwise) without the prior written permission of the publisher. Any person who does any unauthorized act in relation to this publication may be liable to criminal prosecution and civil claims for damages.

Printed in the EU

> et ego ad nihilum redactus sum et nescivi
>
> Psalm 72:22

> Sedendo et quiescendo anima efficitur sapiens
>
> Aristotle

> Everything is indifferent to me: I cannot will anything any longer: I often do not know whether or not I exist [...] the high noon of glory: a day no longer followed by night; a life that no longer fears death, even in death itself: because death has overcome death, because whoever has suffered the first death will no longer feel the second.
>
> Madame Guyon, quoted in *The World as Will and Representation* by Arthur Schopenhauer

> Pour forth thy Fervours for a healthful Mind,
> Obedient Passions, and a Will resign'd;
>
> Samuel Johnson, The Vanity of Human Wishes

> Perhaps the only happy man is the one who has no enthusiasms: but perhaps that cannot be achieved without having at least an enthusiasm for not having enthusiasms.
>
> B.S. Johnson, *Trawl*

Table of Contents

Acknowledgements 11

Abbreviations and conventions 13
   Published works by Samuel Beckett 13
   Unpublished works by Samuel Beckett 13
   Other works 14
   Reference books 14
   Beckett's correspondents 14

Introduction
La vie très quiétiste 17

Chapter 1
Dereliction into Literature: Quietism and Beckett's 1930s 23
   Quietism in Seventeenth-Century Catholicism 25
   Arthur Schopenhauer's Quietism 30
   Beckett and Schopenhauer 34
   Áskesis, Mysticism, and Belief 37
   André Gide and Dostoevskian Quietism 42
   Christian Mysticism 45
   Quietism and Hellenistic Philosophy 47
   A Basis for Quietism 51
   Humanistic Quietism 57
   Abject Self-Referring Quietism 64
   Geulincx and Quietism? 68
   Quietism continues 73
   Conclusion 76

Chapter 2
A Sufferer of My Pains: *Murphy* and the Little World 79

    Tat tvam asi 84

    The Alyosha Mistake 89

    Luciferian Concentration 95

    The Need for Brotherhood 101

    Into the Big World 108

    Conclusion 114

Chapter 3
Remnants of a Pensum: Decay and quietist aesthetics from *Dream of Fair to Middling Women* to *Molloy* 117

    Moran's Prayer 119

    Molloy and the Contemplative Life 124

    The Thing in Ruins 131

    The Fundamental Unheroic 139

    The Tranquillity of Decomposition 151

    Moran Checks the Rot 154

    Moran's Putrefaction 160

    Quietism, Violence, and Contradiction 166

    Conclusion 169

Chapter 4
The Sage Under the Bo: *How It Is*, Ernst Haeckel and Beckett's (German) Buddhism 170

    Beckett and Buddhism: A Biographical and Critical History 171

    The Western Religious Epic in *How It Is* 182

    Darwin and the Natural Order 186

The Eastern Sage..189

　　Victims and Tormentors..195

　　The End of Suffering?...201

　　Conclusion 210

Chapter 5
**so much short of blessed nothing: Salvation, rebirth
and the late prose** 213

　　Beckett's novel 'series'...215

　　Proustian Rebirth 218

　　Rebirth in the Trilogy..222

　　The Mystic Paradox..226

　　True refuge: from *Ping* to *Lessness*....................................234

　　Unhappily no: *Company*...240

　　The One True End to Time and Grief: *Stirrings Still*...........249

　　Conclusion 256

Afterword...258

Bibliography 265

　　Published works by Samuel Beckett 265

　　Unpublished work by Samuel Beckett..............................266

　　Secondary material on Beckett...267

　　General works...274

Index 281

Acknowledgements

The existence of this book owes a great deal to the generosity, kindness, and insight of many people. In no particular order, I would like to thank: Mary Bryden, Bob Eaglestone, Bharat Tandon, Nicola Jones, Alex Houen, David Trotter, Ann Stillman, Steven Connor, Mark Nixon, Dirk Van Hulle, David Tucker, Jim Knowlson, John Pilling, Lawrence Normand, Alistair Welchman, Ruth Rushworth, John Gallagher, Richard Blakemore, Jan Wilm, Ed Posnett, Patrick Bannister, Graham Riach, Robert Kiely, Valerie Lange, Paul Stewart, Adrian Wimbush, and Moira Wimbush. The research behind this book was made possible by generous grants from the Isaac Newton Trust, Darwin College, and the Faculty of English at the University of Cambridge.

Three people, in particular, require special thanks. Rod Mengham gave me my first proper introduction to Beckett's work as an undergraduate and was patient and encouraging as I found myself, somewhat usually, completely at a loss to write anything at all about these strange texts. It was fitting, therefore, that Rod later supervised the doctoral thesis from which this book grew. Matt Spencer read the entirety of an early version of this manuscript with exacting scrutiny and offered many helpful comments relating to argument, style, and structure. Matthew Feldman has been unstinting in his support of this project and seemed to drop everything to help it find a publisher. I am enormously grateful to all three of them.

Finally, Belinda Sherlock, so patiently and compassionately turned towards the outer world, has supported and encouraged me in more ways than I can express.

Abbreviations and conventions

Published works by Samuel Beckett

PTD	*Proust and Three Dialogues*
Dream	*Dream of Fair to Middling Women*
MPTK	*More Pricks than Kicks*
Mu	*Murphy*
W	*Watt*
MF	*Molloy* (French version)
Mo	*Molloy*
MD	*Malone Dies*
U	*The Unnamable*
CC	*Comment c'est*
HII	*How It Is*
C	*Company*
ISIS	*Ill Seen Ill Said*
WH	*Worstward Ho*
SS	*Stirrings Still*
DN	*Dream Notebook*
Dis	*Disjecta*
CSP	*Complete Short Prose*
CDW	*Complete Dramatic Works*
LSB1	*The Letters of Samuel Beckett, Vol. 1: 1929–1939*
LSB2	*The Letters of Samuel Beckett, Vol. 2: 1941–1956*
LSB3	*The Letters of Samuel Beckett, Vol. 3: 1957–1965*
LSB4	*The Letters of Samuel Beckett, Vol. 4: 1966–1989*

Unpublished works by Samuel Beckett

UoR MS3000	*Whoroscope* notebook
UoR MS5003	Clare Street notebook
TCD MS10967	Notes on philosophy
TCD MS10971/7–8	Notes on psychology
TCD MS10971/1	Notes on German literature
GD	German Diaries

Other works

WWR	*The World as Will and Representation*, by Arthur Schopenhauer, trans. Norman and Welchman
PP	*Parerga and Paralipomena*, by Arthur Schopenhauer, trans. Payne
TCD MIC60	Rachel Burrows's notes from Beckett's lectures on French literature
Dost	*Dostoïevsky : articles et causeries* by André Gide
IC	*The Imitation of Christ* by Thomas à Kempis
CM	*Christian Mysticism* by William Inge
VC	*A Visit to Ceylon* by Ernst Haeckel, trans. Bell
SHD	*A Short History of Decay* by E.M. Cioran, trans. Howard
TE	*The Temptation to Exist* by E.M. Cioran, trans. Howard

Reference books

OED	*The Oxford English Dictionary*
TLFi	*La Trésor de la langue française*

Beckett's correspondents

SB	Samuel Beckett
AA	Avigdor Arikha
AU	Arland Ussher
CP	Charles Prentice
EF	Erich Franzen
HN	Hans Naumann
GD	Georges Duthuit
GR	George Reavey
JHe	Jocelyn Herbert
JHo	Joe Hone
MMH	Mary Manning Howe

MS	Morris 'Sonny' Sinclair
NC	Nuala Costello
SP	Samuel Putnam
TM	Thomas MacGreevy

Unless otherwise stated, biblical references are to the King James Version.

All unreferenced translations are my own. For reasons of space, I have refrained from providing the original quotations from foreign language texts in each and every case. I have included individual words from the original in square brackets where the translation is ambiguous or where the original is particularly relevant.

Elision marks not in square brackets are from the original text. Emphasis in quotations is in the original unless otherwise stated.

Introduction
La vie très quiétiste

While living in London in January 1934, Samuel Beckett wrote one of his typically amusing letters to his teenage cousin Morris 'Sonny' Sinclair. After responding to news of Sonny's health, Beckett turned his attention to a peculiar horse that his cousin kept in a field just outside of Dublin:

> Enchanté d'apprendre que la vie te sourit, nonobstant le climat plutôt vert de tes humanités, et que l'étrange quadrupède aux bosses invertis garde sa sérénité. Cet animal-là, il m'a toujours inspiré d'une [*sic*] certain inquiétude à son égard, c'est que la vie très quiétiste qu'il mène ne la pousse un de ces jours à se précipiter, façon d'un porc biblique, dans la mer.[1] (SB to MS, 27/1/34, *LSB1*, 177)

> [Delighted to hear that life is looking kindly on you, notwithstanding the rather green climate of your humanities, and that that strange quadruped with the inverted humps is keeping up his serenity. That animal has always inspired in me a certain anxiety, which is that the very quietistic life he leads might drive him one of these days to throw himself, like the Biblical swine, into the sea.] (*LSB1*, 180–181)

One wonders what Sonny was supposed to make of Beckett's strange talk of the 'quietistic life'. What kind of life could inspire both serenity *and* despair? And why should the plight of this misshapen horse cause Beckett so much anxiety? Just over a decade later, in *Malone Dies*, Beckett describes another scene of equine dejection: Malone has a photograph of an ass 'at the edge of the ocean' which has been made to wear

---

1   Samuel Beckett, *The Letters of Samuel Beckett: Volume 1, 1929–1940*, ed. by Martha Dow Fehsenfeld and others (Cambridge: Cambridge University Press, 2009). Hereafter, *LSB1*.

a boater hat for the amusement of its human onlookers.² Crass anthropomorphism, we might say, but perhaps no worse than what Beckett does in his letter to Sonny. The quietistic life of serenity and despair that Beckett ascribes to his cousin's horse was, in fact, a reflection of his own personal and artistic concerns at the time. Beckett admires the horse's 'pouting, melancholy attitudes' (*LSB1*, 181); his German diaries from two years later speak of his own 'happy melancholy' and of his plans to write a 'Journal of a Melancholic' (7/11/36).³ And his advice that Sonny urge the horse to be sad and beautiful—in the manner of Baudelaire's 'Madrigal triste' from *Fleurs du Mal*—could be read as a goad to his own artistic aspirations to 'turn this dereliction, profoundly felt, into literature' (GD, 2/2/37).

Quietism, as Beckett presents it to his cousin, is melancholy's symptom and its solution: it is both 'poison and antidote', as *The Unnamable* describes religious instruction.⁴ It holds the promise of serenity of mind, the understanding that 'ennui is the most bearable of ills' (*LSB1*, 181) and the fuel for artistic creation: a way to bring beauty out of sadness, and perhaps even erase the sadness along the way. And yet the quietistic life might also be a demon of sorts, as indicated by Beckett's allusion to the New Testament story of Legion and the herd of pigs (Luke 8:27–33). It might lead to solipsism, loneliness, and despair just as easily as to peace. Having wished the best for Sonny's horse, Beckett re-reads his words, and then decides that he doesn't give a damn about the animal after all—'je m'en fous royalement'—and moves on to a different subject, no doubt turning away from a life that too closely resembled his own.

---

2   Samuel Beckett, *Malone Dies*, ed. by Peter Boxall (London: Faber and Faber, 2010), p. 80. Hereafter, *MD*.

3   Samuel Beckett, 'German Diaries', Unnumbered MS, Beckett International Foundation, Reading University Library. Hereafter, GD. Mark Nixon, *Samuel Beckett's German Diaries 1936–1937* (London: Continuum, 2011), pp. 121–125.

4   Samuel Beckett, *The Unnamable*, ed. by Steven Connor (London: Faber and Faber, 2010), p. 8. Hereafter, *U*.

This strangely beguiling disposition, quietism, seems to have been on Beckett's mind during the 1930s, despite his efforts to turn away. The term appears in a number of his reviews, lectures, and letters, where he connects it to some of his favourite novels, including Thomas Mann's *Buddenbrooks*, Marcel Proust's *À la recherche du temps perdu*, the novels of Dostoevsky, and by extension those of André Gide. He invokes it again to describe the poetry of his friend Thomas MacGreevy, and his reaction to *The Imitation of Christ*, a book that MacGreevy had recommended to him in 1935. Beckett also mentions quietism as one of the themes governing the events of his first novel, *Murphy*. A number of scholars have picked up on these references, notably C.J. Ackerley, Mark Nixon, and Matthew Feldman, all of whom argue that quietism played an important role in Beckett's artistic and personal development, particularly in the 1930s.[5] Despite their important work, however, there has been no book-length study of the place of quietism in Beckett's *oeuvre*, and no consideration of whether and how this early preoccupation leaves its mark on his later writing. Given what we know about Beckett as an obsessive re-writer, combing over his past, his previous texts, and his early notebooks,[6] this latter omission leaves a particularly intriguing gap: one which this book attempts to fill. I will argue that even as the word 'quietism' slips out of usage in Beckett's writing, its preoccupations are still very much apparent in his post-war work. In fact, as his career progresses, it makes less sense to speak about quietism in Beckett than it does to talk about

---

5 C.J. Ackerley, 'Samuel Beckett and Thomas à Kempis: The Roots of Quietism', *Samuel Beckett Today / Aujourd'hui*, 9 (2000), 81–92; Nixon, chap. 3–4; Matthew Feldman, '"Agnostic Quietism" and Samuel Beckett's Early Development', in *Samuel Beckett: History, Memory, Archive*, ed. by Seán Kennedy and Katherine Weiss (New York, NY: Palgrave Macmillan, 2009), pp. 183–200.

6 See for example the accounts in James Knowlson, *Damned to Fame: The Life of Samuel Beckett* (London: Bloomsbury Publishing, 1997); H. Porter Abbott, *Beckett Writing Beckett: The Author in the Autograph* (Ithaca, NY: Cornell University Press, 1996); and Matthew Feldman, *Beckett's Books: A Cultural History of Samuel Beckett's 'Interwar Notes'* (London: Continuum, 2006).

Beckett's quietism. Beckett can be considered an important figure in the recent history of quietism because of the way in which he reinvents the disposition in the pursuit of his own creative ends.

Beckett was himself indebted to another of quietism's innovators: Arthur Schopenhauer. Feldman discerns how Schopenhauer's philosophy left a 'unique and profound legacy in Beckett's art', particularly 'an acceptance of suffering' born of Schopenhauer's own deep admiration for the quietist disposition and the seventeenth-century Christian mystics who advocated it.[7] Feldman acknowledges the limitations of his short study and calls for 'further consideration' of the ways in which Schopenhauerian quietism has informed Beckett's work. This book is my attempt to answer that call. In particular, I will argue that Schopenhauer leaves Beckett with an understanding of quietism as an attitude or temperament, rather than a set of beliefs, a theory, or a metaphysic. In this respect I hope that this study will provide a new perspective on Beckett's much-discussed relationship to matters of religion and theology.

As with any study that tries to tackle one of Beckett's most abiding interests, Molloy's disclaimer must apply: 'if you set out to mention everything you would never be done, and that's what counts, to be done, to have done'.[8] In this book I look to the prose fiction, in the main, with only sideways glances to the poetry and drama. My reasons for doing so will hopefully emerge in what follows, but it will be worth stating them briefly here. Beckett's quietist aesthetic, I argue, develops as part of his reaction against two very different novelists whose approach to writing he could not follow: Honoré de Balzac and James Joyce. While distinguishing his efforts from theirs, Beckett allies himself with a quietist novelistic tradition, which is founded on a poetics of renunciation of self, humility, and the acceptance of textual vicissitudes, and which Beckett sees as exemplified by Dostoevsky, Gide, and, in some instances, Proust. It is also in Beckett's novels where his most salient allusions to quietist philosophies and practices

---

7 Feldman, 'Agnostic Quietism', pp. 190–1.
8 Samuel Beckett, *Molloy*, ed. by Shane Weller (London: Faber and Faber, 2009), p. 39. Hereafter, *Mo*.

occur. Nevertheless, as Martin Thomas has shown, a convincing case can be made for understanding Beckett's stage plays in terms of Schopenhauerian asceticism and the denial of the will-to-live.[9] His study not only confirms my suspicion that the currents of quietism run deep in Beckett's work, but also demonstrates the inevitable incompleteness of what I attempt here.

The book proceeds in a mostly chronological manner through Beckett's writing career. Chapter 1 lays the foundations by defining quietism in relation to its historical usage in Christian mysticism and in philosophy more broadly and outlines the main sources through which Beckett encountered and came to understand the term in the 1930s. It also rehearses Beckett's early interest in quietism and puts into context his uses of the word in those letters and reviews mentioned above. Chapter 2 turns to *Murphy* (1938), the novel that Beckett explicitly linked with quietism. I read the text alongside *The Brothers Karamazov* and understand it as a partial dramatization of Beckett's own tussles with the quietistic impulse and its threat to social relationships. Chapter 3 looks to *Molloy* (1951; translated into English in 1955), the only fictional work by Beckett with an unambiguous reference to quietism in the text. This chapter proposes a hitherto unexamined source for this reference and connects the novel to the quietist aesthetic of decay and incoherence that Beckett drew from his study of Gide and first applied in *Dream of Fair to Middling Women* (written in 1932). Chapter 4 seeks to understand an allusion to Buddhism, often considered a quietistic religion, in *Comment c'est* (1961) and its translation *How It Is* (1964). I propose seeing the novel as an investigation of Buddhist and Schopenhauerian ethics and soteriology. Finally, Chapter 5 examines Beckett's novel 'series' from the perspective of his late work, particularly *Company* (1980) and *Stirrings Still* (1989), and explores the paradoxical nature of quietist salvation.

---

9   Martin Thomas, 'Schopenhauer, Beckett, and the Impoverishment of Knowledge', *Evental Aesthetics*, 2 (2014), 66–91.

Chapter 1
Dereliction into Literature: Quietism and Beckett's 1930s

In this first chapter, I want to lay the groundwork for the rest of the book by setting out the historical, theoretical, and biographical background necessary for understanding quietism, and for tracing it as a theme, an aesthetic, and a personal ethic through Beckett's writing career. My aim in this book is to keep two overlapping definitions of quietism in play. The first and narrower definition of Quietism—with a capital 'Q'—is historical and refers to a controversial approach to contemplative prayer that emerged among Catholic mystics in Spain, Italy, and France during the seventeenth century. These Christian Quietists believed that human effort was a hindrance rather than an aid to spiritual progress, and taught their followers to enter a state of passivity and 'holy indifference', where one's own thoughts, will, and desires were extinguished in total surrender to God.[1] Outward forms of devotion were to be shunned in favour of this inward and silent 'prayer of quiet', which, they believed, would lead the soul to perfection, to union with God, and to a state of tranquil beatitude in this life.[2]

The second, much looser, definition is quietism without the capital, and refers to what Glenn Magee calls a 'perennial standpoint' in religion and philosophy.[3] Here quietism indicates any school of thought or ascetic practice that teaches similar attitudes of interiority, passivity, and resignation of the will. This definition might include the teachings of Christian mystics like Meister Eckhart who predates the

---

1 G. R. Evans, '*Sancta Indifferentia* and *Adiaphora*: "Holy Indifference" and "Things Indifferent"', *Common Knowledge*, 15 (2009), 23–38 (p. 23); R. A. Knox, *Enthusiasm: A Chapter in the History of Religion* (Oxford: Oxford University Press, 1950), pp. 261–2.
2 Evans; Mita Choudhury, 'A Betrayal of Trust: The Jesuits and Quietism in Eighteenth-Century France', *Common Knowledge*, 15 (2009), 164–80.
3 Glenn Alexander Magee, 'Quietism in German Mysticism and Philosophy', *Common Knowledge*, 16 (2010), 457–73 (p. 457).

Quietist controversy of the late seventeenth century but nevertheless anticipated the Quietists' insistence on emptying oneself in complete abandon to God.[4] His watchword was *Gelassenheit*, which literally translates as 'letting-alone-ness', 'allowing-ness', or 'letting-be-ness'.[5] Bernard McGinn even identifies a 'broad quietist tendency' present within Christianity from its beginning, rooted in Jesus's injunctions to forsake one's own life and deny oneself in order to take up the cross (Matthew 16:24), and to seek the Kingdom of God within (Luke 21:10).[6] This broader definition of quietism might also encompass other strands of religion and therapeutic philosophy such as Taoist teachings on *wu wei* ['non-action', 'not-doing'], Buddhist notions of detachment and 'letting go', Stoic indifference and apathy, and Pyrrhonist instructions for the suspension of judgement in the face of epistemic powerlessness.[7] For Beckett, it would certainly be necessary to include writers whose work exemplifies quietism: Hölderlin, Leopardi, Grillparzer, and many others as we shall see. While it might be somewhat reductive and clumsy to lump together such disparate philosophies and distinct individuals under the banner of quietism, both Beckett and his 'dear Arthur' Schopenhauer[8] use 'quietism' in this generalised and ahistorical sense, and so I need at least a working definition that will enable me to follow them.

With these preliminary definitions in place, I will now flesh out my account of Quietism in the seventeenth century and then explain how Schopenhauer gave quietism in the broader sense a central

---

4   Knox, p. 240.
5   Magee, pp. 458–60.
6   Bernard McGinn, 'Miguel de Molinos and the *Spiritual Guide*: A Theological Reappraisal', in *The Spiritual Guide*, by Miguel de Molinos, trans. by Robert P. Baird (Mahwah, NJ: Paulist Press, 2010), pp. 21–39 (p. 23).
7   Stelios Virvidakis and Vasso Kindi, 'Quietism', *Oxford Bibliographies Online: Philosophy*, 2013 <http://www.oxfordbibliographies.com/display/id/obo-9780195396577-0184> [accessed 3 September 2014]; Jacob Raz, '"Kill the Buddha": Quietism in Action and Quietism as Action in Zen Buddhist Thought and Practice', *Common Knowledge*, 16 (2010), 439–56.
8   Samuel Beckett, 'Philosophy Notes', p. 252v, MS10967, Trinity College Dublin. Hereafter, TCD MS10967.

role in his philosophy. The remainder of the chapter will put into context all the references that Beckett made to quietism in the 1930s and chart his understanding of the term through the books that he read during that decade.

Quietism in Seventeenth-Century Catholicism

> Oh, what a happy soul that finds itself thus dead and annihilated! […] Enter truly in your nothingness, and you will be upset by nothing.
>
> —Miguel de Molinos[9]

Any history of Quietism must inevitably begin with Miguel de Molinos (1628–1696), a Spanish priest and member of a religious brotherhood called the School of Christ. In 1675 Molinos published a manual of prayer called *The Spiritual Guide* to great ecclesiastical and popular acclaim. The book was an instant bestseller; it was translated into seven languages, and went through seven editions in Italy, and another three in Spain.[10] *The Spiritual Guide* soon became required reading for monks, nuns, and secular clergy alike. In this book, Molinos argues that the practice of contemplative prayer is superior to that of meditative prayer. Whereas meditative prayer makes use of reflection and thoughts, contemplative prayer is mentally silent: all thoughts and mental imagery, even those concerning God or Jesus, are relinquished in favour of simply resting in the divine presence.[11] 'How happy and how well disposed your soul will be,' Molinos writes, 'if retreating within itself, she there abide in her own nothingness […] without heeding, thinking, or minding any sensible thing'.[12] He adds:

---

9   Miguel de Molinos, *The Spiritual Guide*, trans. by Robert P. Baird (Mahwah, NJ: Paulist Press, 2010), pp. 177–8.
10 Robert P. Baird, 'Miguel de Molinos: Life and Controversy', in *The Spiritual Guide*, by Miguel de Molinos, trans. by Robert P. Baird (Mahwah, NJ: Paulist Press, 2010), pp. 1–20 (p. 7).
11 Molinos, p. 58.
12 Quoted in *The Essential Writings of Christian Mysticism*, ed. by Bernard McGinn (New York, NY: Modern Library, 2006), p. 146.

> Come to prayer surrendering the whole of yourself into the divine hands with perfect resignation. Make an act of faith that you are in the divine presence. Keep yourself in that holy leisure with quietude, silence, and calm.[13]

Effort and striving are supposed to fall away in this practice, which Molinos, following the example of St John of the Cross and St Teresa of Ávila, calls 'the prayer of quiet'.[14] Through this act of silent surrender and after enduring various stages of purgation, the soul would be raised to a state of equanimity and mental stillness. Passivity and resignation would become so all-consuming, that even the wish for salvation would disappear and the soul would begin to feel that it would gladly go to hell, if that were God's wish.[15] The final step is 'annihilation' of the soul, the self, and the will, and union with God.[16] The soul, Molinos explains, 'passes into the state of nothingness [*la nada*] where it scorns itself, abhors itself, and confounds itself, knowing that it is nothing, that it can do nothing, and that it is worth nothing.'[17]

Molinos was, however, hardly 'nothing' at the peak of his career. As well as his publishing success, he had a large following, and could count Pope Innocent XI and the royalty of several nations among his admirers.[18] In the end, however, it was Molinos's popularity that led to his downfall. Gilbert Burnet, later the Bishop of Salisbury, visited Italy in 1685 and reported that most of the nuns in Rome were laying aside their traditional practices, such as saying the rosary, to focus on Quietist contemplative prayer alone.[19] Quietism, Burnet observed, was dissuading not just monastics but also lay people from 'zeal in their whole deportment as to the exterior parts of the religion of that Church' (quoted in *CM*, 233). This brought Molinos into a

---

13 Molinos, p. 86.
14 McGinn, 'Miguel de Molinos and the *Spiritual Guide*', p. 23.
15 Molinos, p. 168.
16 McGinn, 'Miguel de Molinos and the *Spiritual Guide*', p. 38.
17 Molinos, p. 177.
18 Baird, 'Miguel de Molinos', pp. 1–2.
19 William Ralph Inge, *Christian Mysticism* (London: Methuen, 1899), p. 233. Hereafter, *CM*.

heated conflict with the Jesuits, whose *Spiritual Exercises* relied on effortful, mentally discursive meditative prayer, devotional practices, and the guidance of a spiritual director, all of which they felt were marginalised or excluded in Molinos's form of mentally silent contemplative prayer.[20] After trying and failing to get Molinos indicted by the Inquisition in 1681, the Jesuits persuaded Louis XIV, the French king, to intervene and voice his own concerns to Rome.[21] In 1685, the Inquisition went knocking on Molinos's door a second time. He was arrested on suspicion of heresy, along with many of his friends and followers, and in 1687 the pope condemned his writings. Under threat of torture, Molinos confessed to heresy, and also to charges of sexual misconduct with his penitents, and was confined to a prison in Rome, where he died on 29 December 1696.[22]

Quietism's popularity proved hard to uproot, however. Jeanne Marie Bouvier de La Mothe Guyon (1648–1717), a French laywoman, began teaching a similar practice to that of Molinos in the 1680s. Madame Guyon, as she is more commonly known, had entered a life of prayer after the death of her husband in 1679. While she had no direct contact with Molinos, her own spiritual director François La Combe may have been influenced by *The Spiritual Guide*.[23] Whereas Molinos had retained a role for meditative prayer as a first step towards contemplative prayer, Guyon thought that everyone—'princes, kings, prelates, priests and magistrates, soldiers and children, tradesmen, labourers, women and sick persons'[24]—could practice contemplative prayer without much preparation.[25] Reason and learning were hindrances in this practice, which Guyon called the 'prayer of the

---

20 Baird, 'Miguel de Molinos'; Choudhury; In reality, Molinos had high regard for spiritual directors. See McGinn, 'Miguel de Molinos and the *Spiritual Guide*', p. 34.
21 Evans, p. 27.
22 Baird, 'Miguel de Molinos', pp. 19–20.
23 McGinn, The Essential Writings of Christian Mysticism, p. 505.
24 Guyon, quoted in Nancy C. James, *The Spiritual Teachings of Madame Guyon, Including Translations into English from Her Writings* (Lewiston, NY: Edwin Mellen Press, 2007), p. 30.
25 Richard Parish, *Catholic Particularity in Seventeenth-Century French Writing: 'Christianity Is Strange'* (Oxford: Oxford University Press, 2011), p. 165.

heart'.²⁶ Like Molinos, she believed that the soul would annihilate itself through passive contemplative prayer and become unified with God: a 'happy nothingness' born of complete 'abandonment' to the divine will. Unsurprisingly, given the similarities of her teachings to those of Molinos and her status as a laywoman, Guyon was viewed suspiciously by the church hierarchy. François Fénelon (1651–1715), the Archbishop of Cambrai, came to her aid and protection, much to the irritation of the Bishop of Meaux, Jacques-Bénigne Bossuet (1627–1704). Bossuet and Fénelon held a long public debate on the orthodoxy of Guyon's teachings in a series of mutually antagonistic books. Eventually, Fénelon had his writing condemned, and Guyon was held prisoner for eighteen years. She was eventually released and continued her teaching and writing until her death in 1717.²⁷

As McGinn points out, 'Quietism' was never really a sect or a movement, but rather an entity created by those who opposed it, much like Pelagianism, in which Beckett also had a passing interest.²⁸ Molinos felt that he was continuing a tradition that already existed within Catholic mysticism, as shown by his frequent appeals to the authority of St Thomas Aquinas, St Teresa of Ávila, St Bernard, St Augustine, and St Bonaventure.²⁹ In truth, Molinos had few ideas that had not been mooted before by canonised contemplatives. As Gershom Scholem suggests, the downfall of the Quietists may have simply been a matter of bad timing.³⁰ Molinos was unlucky enough to have provoked the Jesuits at a time when they were hugely influential, while Guyon and Fénelon had the misfortune to be arraigned by Bossuet, a man hostile to all mysticism who would have poured just as much

---

26 Patricia A. Ward, 'Madame Guyon (1648–1717)', in *The Pietist Theologians: An Introduction to Theology in the Seventeenth and Eighteenth Centuries*, ed. by Carter Lindberg (Oxford: Blackwell, 2008), pp. 161–2.
27 *Guyon* (Oxford: Oxford University Press, 2012), pp. 16–18.
28 McGinn, 'Miguel de Molinos and the *Spiritual Guide*', p. 23. Pelagianism was the 'most amiable heresy' according to Beckett's 'Notes on Augustine of Hippo and Porphyry on Plotinus', p. 11r, MS10968, Trinity College Dublin.
29 McGinn, 'Miguel de Molinos and the *Spiritual Guide*', p. 23.
30 Gershom Scholem, *On the Kabbalah and Its Symbolism* (New York, NY: Random House, 1996), p. 25.

scorn on St John of the Cross and St Teresa had he lived in their day.[31] Furthermore, in the seventeenth century, Protestantism threatened the Catholic Church and its sacraments; the iconoclastic and individualistic tendencies of Quietism therefore seemed all the more subversive.[32] In 1682, the Archbishop of Naples reported that certain Quietist devotees in his flock were not only refusing to make the Sign of the Cross and engage in vocal or meditative prayer, but also believed that they were receiving direct inspiration from God without a priestly intermediary.[33] At its extremes, Quietism was seen to resemble something like deism or even atheism:[34] Innocent XI's 'Caelestis Pater' condemned Molinos for having taught 'forgetfulness of any particular and distinct thought of the attributes of God and the Trinity,'[35] a heresy that I will revisit in my discussion of *Molloy*. Fénelon admitted that Quietism had such tendencies and was liable to 'confound God with *néant*' (quoted in *CM*, 238).

Thanks to this history, 'quietism' has remained a pejorative term, a 'heretical buzzword'.[36] As Leibniz pointed out, you need only invoke the 'hateful name' of quietism to have an excuse to bother a suspected heresiarch.[37] The American psychologist and philosopher William James was therefore fairly unusual in praising seventeenth-century Quietism as a 'healthy-minded' philosophy and Molinos as a

---

31 Knox, p. 254.
32 Bernard McGinn, '"Evil-Sounding, Rash, and Suspect of Heresy": Tensions between Mysticism and Magisterium in the History of the Church', *The Catholic Historical Review*, 90 (2004), 193–212.
33 Baird, 'Miguel de Molinos', p. 15.
34 Parish, *Catholic Particularity*, p. 181.
35 'The Errors of Miguel de Molinos: Apostolic Constitution "Caelestis Pater" Issued by Innocent XI', in *The Spiritual Guide*, by Miguel de Molinos, ed. by Robert P. Baird, trans. by Bernard McGinn (Mahwah, NJ: Paulist Press, 2010), pp. 185–93 (p. 187).
36 Nancy C. James, 'Introduction', in *The Complete Madame Guyon*, by Jeanne Marie Bouvier de La Motte Guyon, trans. by Nancy C. James (Brewster, MA: Paraclete Press, 2011), pp. 3–35 (p. 16).
37 Daniel J. Cook, 'Leibniz on Enthusiasm', in *Leibniz, Mysticism and Religion*, ed. by Allison P. Coudert, Richard H. Popkin, and Gordon M. Weiner (Dordrecht: Springer Netherlands, 1998), pp. 107–35 (p. 117).

'spiritual genius' in his *Varieties of Religious Experience*.[38] In 1911, the Anglo-Catholic writer Evelyn Underhill sought to distance Teresa of Ávila, John of Ruysbroeck, and even Madame Guyon from the charge of quietism, which she calls a 'morbid perversion' of 'the true and healthy mystic state of "Quiet"'.[39] Aldous Huxley, despite his inclusive and syncretic perspective on world religions, found it necessary to warn about the dangers of quietism, which he deemed 'inadequate', 'uncaring', and 'false' in *The Perennial Philosophy* (1945) and dismissed as 'mere self-indulgence' in *Eyeless in Gaza* (1934).[40] In 1946, Jean-Paul Sartre distinguished Existentialism from the 'quietism of despair', which leads to 'inaction' and 'abandon'.[41] By using the word 'quietism' Beckett was therefore adopting a tarnished term, a word of outsiders and heretics, and making it his own.

Arthur Schopenhauer's Quietism

> In a conversation about philosophy,
> I admitted that my system takes a quietist form.
>
> —Arthur Schopenhauer,
> Handschriftlichem Nachlass[42]

In 1930, aged 24, Beckett began research for an essay on Marcel Proust's *À la recherche du temps perdu* that he was hoping to have published in the Dolphin Books series from Chatto & Windus.[43] Having

---

38 William James, *The Varieties of Religious Experience: A Study in Human Nature* (London: Routledge, 2008), p. 95.
39 Evelyn Underhill, *Mysticism: A Study in Nature and Development of Spiritual Consciousness* (Mineola, NY: Dover Publications, 2002), p. 322.
40 Aldous Huxley, *The Perennial Philosophy* (New York, NY: Harper Perennial Modern Classics, 2009), pp. 23, 65, 104; Aldous Huxley, *Eyeless in Gaza* (London: Vintage, 2004), p. 408.
41 Jean-Paul Sartre, 'Existentialism Is a Humanism', in *Existentialism from Dostoevsky to Sartre*, ed. by Walter Kaufmann, Revised and Expanded Edition (London: Penguin, 1975), pp. 345–68 (pp. 345, 352, 358).
42 Arthur Schopenhauer, *Aus Arthur Schopenhauer's handschriftlichen Nachlass: Abhandlungen, Anmerkungen, Aphorismen und Fragmente*, ed. by Julius Frauenstädt (Leipzig: F.A. Brockhaus, 1864), p. 18.
43 Knowlson, p. 113.

learnt that Proust was influenced by the German idealist philosopher Arthur Schopenhauer, Beckett started reading *The World as Will and Representation*.⁴⁴ He wrote to his friend Thomas MacGreevy:

> I am reading Schopenhauer. Everyone laughs at that. [...] But I am not reading philosophy, nor caring whether he is right or wrong or a good or worthless metaphysician. An intellectual justification of unhappiness—the greatest that has ever been attempted—is worth the examination of one who is interested in Leopardi & Proust rather than Carducci & Barrès. (SB to TM, n.d. [c. 18–25/7/30]; *LSB1*, 33)

Schopenhauer provides plenty of reasons why our unhappiness might be justified, given the wretched state of the world. According to his metaphysics, the world and all of its particular objects are part of an illusion and the true 'inner nature' of reality—the Thing-In-Itself—is a monistic and sourceless will (*WWR*, I.2.29, 187). This will is an 'endless striving' that can never be satisfied (I.2.29, 188). It is the 'inner working' behind the instincts and urges of living creatures, the movements of inanimate nature, and, most noticeably, the behaviour of human beings (I.2.18, 124). We crave pleasure, we strive to keep ourselves in good health, we strenuously avoid death, we compete with one another over resources, and we give in to our urge to procreate. All this, for Schopenhauer, is simply the will, the essence of reality, manifesting itself. And because this will cannot be satisfied, neither can we:

---

44 Later in his life, Beckett read Schopenhauer in German, but at this point probably turned to a French translation or the English one by Haldane and Kemp, entitled *The World as Will and Idea*. (See C.J. Ackerley, *Demented Particulars: The Annotated Murphy* (Edinburgh: Edinburgh University Press, 2010), p. 18.) Throughout this book I will cite the most recent English translation: *The World as Will and Representation: Volume 1* and *Volume 2*, ed. by Christopher Janaway, trans. by Judith Norman and Alistair Welchman (Cambridge: Cambridge University Press, 2014 and 2018). Hereafter, *WWR*.

> All striving comes from lack, from a dissatisfaction with one's condition, and is thus suffering as long as it is not satisfied; but no satisfaction is lasting; instead, it is only the beginning of a new striving. We see striving everywhere inhibited in many ways, struggling everywhere; and thus always as suffering; there is no final goal of striving, and therefore no bounds or end to suffering. (I.4.56, 336)

Schopenhauer concludes that existence is a mistake, an evil, and perhaps even a punishment, and Beckett, an admirer of the pessimism he found in Proust's novels and the poetry of Leopardi, found in him an intellectual ally.

Schopenhauer has far more to offer than unrelenting pessimism, however. The other side of his philosophy is an ethics rooted in compassion, a therapeutic theory of aesthetics, and a path to salvation that he calls 'quietism'.[45] Even though the blind striving of the will cannot be satisfied, Schopenhauer thought that it was possible for human beings to escape its clutches and consequently transcend suffering. He argued that temporary relief can be obtained through the contemplation of beautiful artworks and sublime natural phenomena, whereby the observer is lifted out of their individuality and into a state of pure will-less knowledge where there is no suffering. A more permanent solution is also possible for certain rare and talented souls who have learnt to silence the will through practices of self-denial and renunciation. These people are called 'holy souls, sometimes pietists, quietists, pious enthusiasts, etc' (*WWR*, I.4.68, 411) and through their ascetic practices they gain insight that acts as a '*Quietiv*'—a tranquillizer or sedative—of the will-to-live. Denying the will enables the quietist

---

45 A thorough overview of Schopenhauer's relationship to quietism can be found in Raymond B. Marcin, *In Search of Schopenhauer's Cat: Arthur Schopenhauer's Quantum-Mystical Theory of Justice* (Washington, DC: Catholic University of America Press, 2006), chap. 13; See also the entry for 'Quietism' in David E. Cartwright, *Historical Dictionary Of Schopenhauer's Philosophy* (Oxford: Scarecrow Press, 2005), pp. 143–4.

or ascetic to see through the illusory nature of the world as representation—what Schopenhauer often refers to as piercing the veil of Maya—and understand that reality is really just one substance, one will, free of distinctions. Breaking through the illusion of separateness—the *principium individuationis*—not only brings 'salvation', that is a state of will-less blessedness and bliss, but also unbounded compassion for suffering creatures still caught in egoistic delusion.

At several points in *The World as Will and Representation*, Schopenhauer refers directly to the Christian Quietists. Although he thought of himself as an atheist and was dismissive of popular piety, Schopenhauer had great respect for what he called the 'beautiful souls' (*WWR*, I.4.68, 409): the saints, ascetics, and mystics of religion. His ideas have far more in common with those of Molinos and Guyon than with any of his contemporaries or fellow atheists. He recommends Guyon's *Autobiography* as 'a particular, carefully detailed example and factual description of the concepts I am advancing' and adds that the 'memory of this great and beautiful soul always fills me with awe' (I.4.68, 411). Later on, he refers his reader to her 'wonderful work', *Spiritual Torrents* (II.4.48, 627). To understand the 'complete forgetting of one's own person and absorption into the intuition of the divine', Schopenhauer recommends Fénelon's *Explanations of the Maxims of the Saints Concerning the Inner Life* (*WWR*, I.4.68, 413). He also points to the writings of Molinos, along with those of several other Christian mystics including Tauler, Meister Eckhart, and even 'the Englishman Bunyan' (II.4.48, 630) as means of becoming acquainted with quietism. Schopenhauer felt that his own philosophy was in 'unexampled agreement [...] with quietism and asceticism', and challenged his contemporaries, particularly in 'the *Protestant* universities', to investigate quietism, since it is 'identical to all of metaphysics and ethics, with respect to content' (II.4.48, 630–1).

Schopenhauer was convinced that quietism is not something confined to Molinos, Guyon, and Fénelon, nor even their coreligionists. It is rather a disposition that can be found in any truly transformative school of religion and philosophy. Quietism, he argues, 'weaves its way through all the works of Brahmanism and Buddhism' (*WWR*,

II.4.48, 630), and it appears in the Upanishads, the Tamil Thirukkural, and the writings of Islamic mystics and Neo-Platonists (II.4.48, 628–9). Schopenhauer was interested in quietism not as a moment in Christian history, but in the broader sense as a perennial standpoint, which he defined as a 'cessation of all willing, asceticism' and the 'intentional extirpation of one's own will' (*WWR*, II.4.48, 628). And because this quietist disposition can be found in so many different—and theologically incompatible—religions, that must mean that it is not dependent on belief, metaphysics, or doctrine. Schopenhauer points out how all ascetics—whether Buddhist, Hindu, Christian, or from some other religion—follow a similar path of self-denial so that the will-to-live may be stilled. 'Despite the vast differences in the dogmas imprinted on their reason,' Schopenhauer writes, 'these people conducted their lives in ways that gave identical expression to the inner, immediate, intuitive cognition from which all virtue and holiness spring' (I.4.68, 409). When he was mocked by a Hegelian for his fondness for the Christian Quietists, Schopenhauer replied that he did not admire them for their theoretical achievements or philosophical prowess, but rather solely on a practical basis, for their conduct and their actions.[46] In *The World as Will and Representation*, he warns that when reading the books of Madame Guyon it is necessary 'to do justice to her *disposition*, allowing for the superstitions of her reason' (*WWR*, I.4.68, 412, my emphasis). The quietists and ascetics are valuable insofar as they provide examples of a resigned will; they are absolutely *not* to be relied on as metaphysicians. It is worth noting that this is exactly how Beckett said he wanted to approach Schopenhauer himself: not for his metaphysics, but for his disposition and attitude towards the world.

Beckett and Schopenhauer

Beckett's encounter with *The World as Will and Representation* in July 1930 was the beginning of a lifelong interest in Schopenhauer. As Ulrich Pothast comments,

---

46 Schopenhauer, Handschriftlichen Nachlass, p. 18.

there probably was on Beckett's part, from the first intellectual contact with Schopenhauer, a strong feeling of kinship with that philosopher's description of life and human relationships, of everyday reality as a will-dominated illusion, of true reality as a wretched realm of pain. [... It is a] closeness of feeling and experience between two individuals separated by more than a century, rather than [...] an 'influence' as traditional history of literature would have it.[47]

Pothast points to the fact that Beckett took the trouble to read Schopenhauer's doctoral dissertation—by no means an easy or entertaining read—as evidence of Beckett's dedication to the philosopher, surpassing the interest of the many other artists and writers who were drawn to *The World as Will and Representation*. Recent research has also shown that Beckett owned at least one volume of Schopenhauer's handwritten notebooks.[48] Beckett's *Whoroscope* notebook contains a list of 'Books Sent Home' from his German trip of 1936: the first entry, duly ticked, is 'Schopenhauer: Werke'.[49] These six volumes of Julius Frauenstädt's edition of Schopenhauer's *Sämmtliche Werke* remained in Beckett's library until his death.[50]

Schopenhauer often advises his reader that whatever they have before them is likely to be unintelligible unless they have already absorbed his previous work. Beckett was one of the few readers who seems to have taken this to heart: almost straight away he began looking to lesser-known texts. In late July or early August 1930, he made a start on Schopenhauer's sizeable 'appendix' of miscellaneous essays, *Parerga and Paralipomena*. Beckett writes to MacGreevy, 'Schopenhauer says de-

---

47 Ulrich Pothast, *The Metaphysical Vision: Arthur Schopenhauer's Philosophy of Art and Life and Samuel Beckett's Own Way to Make Use of It* (New York, NY: Peter Lang, 2008), p. 6.
48 Mark Nixon and Dirk Van Hulle, *Samuel Beckett's Library* (Cambridge: Cambridge University Press, 2013), p. 148.
49 Samuel Beckett, 'Whoroscope Notebook', p. 17v, MS3000, Beckett International Foundation, Reading University Library. Hereafter, UoR MS3000.
50 Nixon and Van Hulle, p. 144.

functus is a beautiful word—as long as one does not suicide' (n.d. [before 5/7/30]; *LSB1*, 36). Beckett is referring to the essay 'On the Sufferings of the World': 'Das Leben ist ein Pensum zum Abarbeiten: in diesem Sinne ist *defunctus* ein schöner Ausdruck'[51] [Life is a task to be worked off: in that sense 'defunctus' is a beautiful expression[52]]. He paraphrases it again, this time without acknowledgement, in *Proust*: 'the 'invisible reality' that damns the life of the body on earth as a pensum and reveals the meaning of the word: "defunctus"'.[53]

Beckett's philosophy notes, compiled in the early 1930s, also pay close attention to the account of Schopenhauer's ideas given in Wilhelm Windelband's *A History of Philosophy*.[54] As Feldman observes, Beckett's notes on Schopenhauer suggest 'both personal affinity and prior understanding of his philosophy':[55] in the midst of his faithful transcriptions from Windelband, Beckett refers to Schopenhauer as 'dear Arthur' and sums up his pessimism by concluding that 'it must be a balls aching world' (TCD MS10967, 252v). Feldman adds that such personal touches are not granted to other philosophers, not even Descartes, who was once presumed to be Beckett's favourite thinker.[56]

On 25 August 1930, Beckett wrote again to MacGreevy from Paris:

> Schopenhauer has a nice explanation of the temptation to write one[']s nominative letters across the frieze-fesses. Stimulation of the will. Since the fesses as fesses as Platonic Idea— have no action on the Thing in Itself (God help it!), they will bloody well have a reaction. (*LSB1*, 43)

---

51 Arthur Schopenhauer, *Parerga und Paralipomena*, 2 vols. (Leipzig: F.A. Brockhaus, 1874), p. 321.
52 Arthur Schopenhauer, *Parerga and Paralipomena: Short Philosophical Essays*, trans. by E.F.J. Payne, 2 vols. (Oxford: Oxford University Press, 1974), vol. II, p. 300. Hereafter, *PP*.
53 Samuel Beckett, *Proust and Three Dialogues with Georges Duthuit* (London: Calder Publications, 1969), p. 93. Hereafter, *PTD*.
54 Wilhelm Windelband, *A History Of Philosophy* (New York, NY: Macmillan, 1901), pp. 572, 620ff.
55 Feldman, *Beckett's Books*, p. 50.
56 Feldman, *Beckett's Books*, pp. 44–47.

This means that by this point Beckett is well into *The World as Will and Representation*, up to the fourth book of the first volume, entitled 'With the achievement of self-knowledge, affirmation and negation of the will to life'. There Schopenhauer describes how the vast majority of people are 'quite incapable of the joys which lie in pure knowledge' and are therefore unable to take pleasure in something without it stimulating their will. As an example, he suggests:

> people write their names on popular sites that they visit, in order to react to the place and have an effect on it since it does not have an effect on them. (*WWR*, I.4.57, 341)

Volume I, Book 4 is also where Schopenhauer begins his discussion of quietism, asceticism, and the denial of the will.

Áskesis, Mysticism, and Belief

The lasting impact of Schopenhauer's quietism on Beckett's work is one of the main subjects of this book, and I will turn to Schopenhauer's writing frequently in what follows. At this stage I would like to reiterate the point I made at the end of the last section but one—namely that for Schopenhauer quietism is both perennial and practical—as this is particularly important for Beckett and the way I want to read him. Schopenhauer understands quietism as an attitude of renunciation that is not tied down to any particular doctrine or theology. Indeed, it can exist by itself without any form of religious belief. Schopenhauer claims that 'the inner nature of holiness, self-denial, asceticism, and mortification of one's own will' can just as easily be 'expressed abstractly, cleansed of all mythology, as the *negation of the will to life*' (*WWR*, I.4.68, 410). Beckett, who claimed 'never to have had the least faculty or disposition for the supernatural' (SB to TM, 10/3/35; *LSB1*, 257), would have appreciated this aspect of Schopenhauer's thought.

The importance of practice and attitude in Schopenhauer's quietism has consequences for the way we might approach the abundance of religious material in Beckett's own work. Studies of Beckett's religiosity are legion, but, as Steven Connor helpfully points out, it is possible to discern three dominant ways of interpreting Beckett's attitude to religion:

The first is cryptic belief—where the belief, though straightforward and even orthodox in form, is nevertheless fugitive and uncertain. This kind of religious belief remains what it is or traditionally has been, but almost terminally diminished, like so many other things in Beckett. Then there is repudiated belief, in which religion is there to be sighed over, signed off, or sent up. Finally, there is the religion beyond belief. In this form of belief, belief is actually beside the point. The very form of religious negation is what guarantees it as religious.[57]

Given what I have already said about quietism not being primarily concerned with belief, it might seem that this study would have the most in common with the third and final strand. But, as Connor explains, and as his word 'beyond' suggests, this third way of interpreting Beckett's work is usually dependent on a sophisticated mystical theology. Connor's examples of studies in this group include Hélène Baldwin's *Samuel Beckett's Real Silence*[58] and Marius Buning's essay 'Samuel Beckett's Negative Way', which invoke Simone Weil and Meister Eckhart respectively in order to unlock a theology in Beckett that is able to move beyond belief through apophatic negation. As I mentioned at the start of this chapter, Meister Eckhart had plenty in common with the Quietists and so I agree with Buning when he finds in Beckett's writing something akin to

> successive descents into the Dark Night of the Soul, […] the ablation of desires, the dying to the body and its functions, the annihilation of the self, and the emptying of the mind of all preconceived notions.[59]

---

57 Steven Connor, *Beckett, Modernism and the Material Imagination* (Cambridge: Cambridge University Press, 2014), p. 136.
58 Hélène L. Baldwin, *Samuel Beckett's Real Silence* (London: Pennsylvania State University Press, 1981).
59 Marius Buning, 'Samuel Beckett's Negative Way: Intimations of the *Via Negativa* in His Late Plays.', in *European Literature and Theology in the Twentieth Century: Ends of Time*, ed. by David Jasper and Colin Crowder (London: Macmillan, 1990), pp. 129–42 (p. 136).

Buning also mentions that Eckhart demands 'not only abandoning the self and all things, but also God himself', and again this seems applicable enough to some of Beckett's work. As I will argue in Chapter 3, Beckett depicts precisely this in Molloy's meditations on the biblical story of the flight into Egypt. But there comes a point when Buning, again following Eckhart, wants to admit God by the backdoor, disguised as 'emptiness', 'detachment itself', or 'being without becoming'. He suggests that intimations of this Eckhartian Godhead can be found in *Not I*, *That Time*, and *Footfalls*. His argument, in other words, ends up being a theological one, which reaches for metaphysics rather than remaining at the level of those ascetic attitudes of abandon, annihilation, and ablation.

I want to do things slightly differently. Quietism, I am arguing, is not theology but *áskesis*. It is practical rather than theoretical. This is true not only of Schopenhauer's perennial quietism, but also of Christian Quietism. Ronald Knox, writing about the seventeenth century only, calls Quietism 'a direction of the human mind, not a bunch of conclusions'.[60] Quietists like Guyon, according to Yves Krumenacker, had lost confidence in theological discourse, and their response was to 'renounce theology'.[61] They aspired to 'universality, but without dogmatic rigour'.[62] In his essay on Beckett's quietism, Ackerley speculates that Beckett may have known something of this tendency. In the *Dream* notebook, compiled in the early thirties, there are several phrases which Beckett lifted from the entry on mysticism in the 1929 *Encyclopaedia Britannica*.[63] Ackerley notes how the *Britannica* describes how mysticism 'is marked on its speculative side by even an overweening confidence in human reason.'[64] He contrasts this quotation with the entry for Quietism, which describes how the Quietists

---

60 Knox, p. 260.
61 Quoted in Parish, *Catholic Particularity*, p. 182.
62 Parish, *Catholic Particularity*, p. 181.
63 *Beckett's Dream Notebook*, ed. by John Pilling (Reading: Beckett International Foundation, 1999), p. 88. Hereafter, *DN*.
64 Andrew Seth Pringle-Pattison and Evelyn Underhill, 'Mysticism', ed. by J.L. Garvin, *The Encyclopædia Britannica: A new survey of universal knowledge*

rejected any 'sense of proprietorship' in their thoughts and actions: 'the first duty of the Quietist was to be "passive."'[65] There is something triumphant, even heroic, about Eckhart's efforts in mystical theology, through which he deftly reconfigures our understanding of God. Quietism, by contrast, remains deflated, dejected, ignorant, passive, and abandoned.

With Beckett's own admission that his artistic project was about impotence and not-knowing, in contrast to Joyce's 'heroic' and 'omnipotent' achievement,[66] it is easy to imagine Beckett cleaving closer to the simplicity of the quietist attitude than to its more theological and transcendent sister, mysticism. In *Dream of Fair to Middling Women*, Belacqua is called a 'dud mystic' and a 'mystique raté'.[67] During the First World War, the term 'dud'—which previously had meant counterfeit—began to be applied to shells that failed to detonate (*OED*). The French term 'raté' means misfired, aborted, and failed. Being a dud mystic or *mystique raté*, then, might mean having all the appearance and workings of a mystic—the attitude of renunciation and will-lessness—but none of the metaphysical, theological, or transcendental results.

Molinos himself was explicit about his rejection of theoretical flourishes: 'This is,' he writes in his address to the reader of *The Spiritual Guide*, 'a science of practice, not theory, in which experience surpasses even the most prudent and quick-witted speculation by the highest degree'.[68] Quietism's focus on the pragmatics of the contemplative life and its potentially life-changing consequences might ac-

---

(London: The Encyclopædia Britannica Company, Ltd., 1929), 51–55 (p. 52).
65 J.L. Garvin, 'Quietism', ed. by J.L. Garvin, *The Encyclopædia Britannica: A new survey of universal knowledge* (London: The Encyclopædia Britannica Company, Ltd., 1929), 850 (p. 850).
66 Beckett, quoted in Knowlson, p. 352.
67 Samuel Beckett, *Dream of Fair to Middling Women* (New York, NY: Arcade Publishing, 1993), p. 186. Hereafter, *Dream*.
68 Molinos, p. 52.

count for William James's otherwise unexplained attribution of 'genius' to Molinos in *The Varieties of Religious Experience*.⁶⁹ James and Schopenhauer were both primarily interested in the great mystics for the way they approach and experience the world, not for what they have to say about metaphysics. While Meister Eckhart may have much to offer a theologically-inclined critic like Buning, Schopenhauer turns to Eckhart's sermons to admire his denial of the will (I.4.64, 414), his inwardness (II.4.48, 627), his disregard of external forms (II.4.48, 629), his embrace of suffering (II.4.48, 649), and his indifference to earthly goods and ills (II.4.49, 656). Schopenhauer even dismisses Eckhart's Christianity, and hence his theology, as a mere 'garb' that he was obliged to wear in order to avoid persecution by the Church authorities (II.4.48, 629).

A paper by Robert Kiely shows how it is even possible to approach Beckett's use of mysticism without needing to appeal to theology in the way that Buning and Baldwin do. Kiely argues that Beckett's mystical references, particularly those found in *Dream of Fair to Middling Women*, are best understood as a reaction to his reading of Max Nordau's *Degeneration* in 1930–1.⁷⁰ As Beckett records in his *Dream* notebook, Nordau attacks mysticism as an 'uncontrolled association of ideas' (*DN*, 91). Kiely points out that many of the habits of the mystics that Nordau attacks were either things that Beckett already did or that he adopted in order to rebel against Nordau's view of art. Beckett embraces vagueness, contradiction, and nothingness in his writing, and these are precisely the things that Nordau abhors in the 'mystics', a category in which he places the Symbolist poets. Kiely's analysis suggests that Beckett was predominantly interested in a disposition that could contribute to his aesthetic, rather than theology and doctrine.

---

69   William James, p. 95.
70   Robert Kiely, 'Beckett and Nordau's Pathologized Mysticism' (presented at the London Beckett Seminar, Birkbeck College, University of London, 2013) <http://www.academia.edu/3409239/Beckett_and_Max_Nordaus_pathologized_mysticism> [accessed 16 July 2013].

André Gide and Dostoevskian Quietism

After Schopenhauer, the next most important influence on Beckett's quietism was the French novelist André Gide. During the academic year 1930–1, Beckett worked as a lecturer on French literature at Trinity College Dublin, where he himself had recently studied, and one of his lectures was entitled 'Gide and the Modern Novel'.[71] The notes of his student Rachel Burrows show that Beckett had relied heavily on Gide's 1922 book *Dostoïevsky: articles et causeries* in which Gide argues that Dostoevsky should be understood as a quietist novelist. Burrows writes:

> Tolstoy followed European tradition while Dost. remained Russian. cf. <u>Stendhal on Dost</u>—St.'s gospel of energy results from union of St John Evangelist—R.C. Orthodoxy. Dost's quietism—St. J. Greek church almost Buddhism. Lack of anger in Dost. no sense of insult.[72]

At this point in the lecture, Beckett was either quoting or paraphrasing Gide's book. In the original, Gide describes how 'Dostoevsky leads us to a sort of Buddhism, or at least quietism'.[73] Gide also associates Dostoevsky with Schopenhauer's philosophy on several occasions, and finds in Dostoevsky's life and work a host of quietist attitudes, such as 'gentle and total resignation', 'the renunciation of self, the abandonment of self', and 'abnegation' (*Dost*, 261, 144, 117). According to Gide, these quietist traits enabled Dostoevsky to discern that the mind is mostly discordant and unruly, that the self is unstable and always in flux, and—most importantly—to write novels that could accommodate 'the most contrary sentiments' and an 'extraordinary wealth of antagonisms' (*Dost*, 117). Gide argues that Dostoevsky's quietist attitude prevented him

---

71 For an overview of Beckett's lecture see Brigitte Le Juez, *Beckett before Beckett*, trans. by Ros Schwartz (London: Souvenir Press, 2008), pp. 33–48.

72 Rachel Burrows, 'Notes on Beckett's Lectures at Trinity College Dublin', p. 24, MIC60, Trinity College Dublin Hereafter, TCD MIC60.

73 André Gide, *Dostoïevsky: articles et causeries* (Paris: Librairie Plon, 1923), pp. 226–227. Hereafter, *Dost*.

from succumbing—as the classical realist writers did—to the urge to smooth over the cracks in his characters, language, and plot.

In the lecture, Beckett quotes Gide's analysis and then applies it to Gide himself: Burrows's notes show that Beckett saw the attitude of renunciation in Gide's *La Porte étroite, Les Cahiers d'André Walter*, and *Les Faux-monnayeurs* (TCD MIC60, 12, 23).[74] Alissa in *La Porte étroite* tells Jérôme that she admires those souls who 'would be hard pressed to say whether they are Jansenists, Quietists, or whatever else'.[75] She shrugs off the label, but the attitude of quietism permeates the novel. Those souls she looks up to, for instance, are described in the humble and passive terms of quietism:

> They bow down before God like grass bent by the wind, with no spite, no trouble, no beauty. They hold themselves of little worth, and believe that their only value lies in their effacement before God.[76]

Alissa too lives a life of renunciation: she repeatedly sabotages her chances of a loving relationship with Jérôme because she believes it incompatible with her love for God. 'We are not', she tells Jérôme, 'made for happiness'.[77] It was perhaps passages like these that made Beckett feel that Gide's analysis of Dostoevsky's novels was equally a commentary on Gide's own practices as a novelist. Beckett told his students to 'read Gide on Dostoevsky for Gide himself' (TCD MIC60, 8). Indeed Gide admits that 'Dostoevsky has often just been an excuse to express my own ideas' (*Dost*, 252).

Beckett clearly knew Gide's work well and admired it greatly. His lecture mentions most of Gide's creative works, and also quotes from his diaries. Burrows records that Beckett had claimed that *Les Faux-monnayeurs* was the 'greatest book since Proust' (TCD MIC60,

---

74 Le Juez, p. 33.
75 André Gide, *La Porte étroite* (Paris: Éditions Mercure de France, 1959), p. 138.
76 Gide, *La Porte étroite*, p. 139.
77 Gide, *La Porte étroite*, p. 128.

43). In early 1932, he suggested to Charles Prentice at Chatto & Windus that he might follow *Proust* with another Dolphin Book, this time on Gide, and when that failed he tried to get an essay published on Gide in the *New Statesman* (SB to TM, 18[/8/32]; *LSB1*, 118). He abandoned the project, but not from a lack of knowledge about Gide's writing: 'I have all the notes & quotations I want without opening a text', he told MacGreevy (SB to TM, 3/9/32; quoted in *LSB1*, 123). Gide also seems to have inspired Beckett to go off and read Dostoevsky: around about the same time as he was lecturing on Gide at Trinity, Beckett read *Les Possédés* in a 'foul translation' by Victor Derély. Although he complains about the 'clichés & journalese' that he presumes are there in the original Russian, he admires 'the movement, the transitions' of Dostoevsky's prose. 'No one,' he adds, 'moves about like Dostoievski. No one ever caught the insanity of dialogue like he did' (SB to TM, 29/5/31; *LSB1*, 79). Beckett suggested to Prentice that he might expand his essay on Proust with a further five or six pages, so that he could 'develop the parallel with Dostoievski' (SB to CP, 4/10/30; *LSB1*, 52). He also proposed a book on Dostoevsky to Prentice, but admitted to MacGreevy that this was just 'for the sake of something to say more than anything else & knowing bloody well I would (could) never do it' (SB to TM, [undated, after 15/8/1931]; *LSB1*, 82). *Le Crime et le châtiment*, translated by Derély again, *La Confession de Stravroguine*, translated by Ely Halpérine-Kaminsky, and *Souvenirs de la maison des morts*, translated by M. Neyroud, remained in Beckett's library after his death.[78]

Gide, then, was a significant influence on Beckett's critical thinking, his reading habits, and his writing style. But there have only been a handful of studies on the relationship between the two men. Angela Moorjani has proposed that the influence of Gide's *Les Fauxmonnayeurs* can be felt in *Murphy*,[79] while John Bolin, in his recent book *Beckett and the Modern Novel*, makes a sustained and convincing case for

---

78 Nixon and Van Hulle, p. 268.
79 Angela Moorjani, 'André Gide among the Parisian Ghosts in the "Anglo-Irish" *Murphy*', *Samuel Beckett Today / Aujourd'hui*, 21 (2010), 209–22.

seeing Gide as one of Beckett's most important novelistic precursors.[80] In this book, I argue that Gide is also one of the most important figures for Beckett's quietism, not least because he demonstrated how the philosophical ideal of quietism, which both Gide and Beckett drew in part from Schopenhauer, might be transformed into an aesthetic. Such is the importance of Gide that I will save most of my discussion of his writing and Beckett's lecture for later, particularly Chapter 3, in which I argue that Gide's reading of Dostoevsky influenced the disintegrating aesthetic of *Molloy*.

Christian Mysticism

Another important book that Beckett read in the early 1930s was *Christian Mysticism* by William Inge. This was undoubtedly the main source of his knowledge of mysticism. Inge's book is quoted over several pages of the *Dream* notebook, in which Beckett listed material for interpolation into *Dream of Fair to Middling Women*, written in 1932. Although Beckett recorded no details about Molinos or Guyon, *Christian Mysticism* does discuss them at length. Inge notes the similarities between St Teresa of Ávila and Molinos in their 'prayer of quiet', quotes Bishop Burnet's account of the popularity of *The Spiritual Guide*, and recounts the story of Fénelon and Guyon. Most importantly, Inge describes Molinos's approach to prayer:

> The "interior road," the goal of which is union with God, consists in complete resignation to the will of God, annihilation of all self-will, and an unruffled tranquillity or passivity of soul, until the mystical grace is supernaturally "infused." Then "we shall sink and lose ourselves in the immeasurable sea of God's infinite goodness, and rest there steadfast and immovable." [Molinos] gives a list of tokens by which we may know that we are called from meditation to contemplation; and enumerates four means, which lead to perfection and inward peace—

---

80 John Bolin, *Beckett and the Modern Novel* (Cambridge: Cambridge University Press, 2012).

> prayer, obedience, frequent communions, and inner mortification. The best kind of prayer is the prayer of silence; and there are three silences, that of words, that of desires, and that of thought. In the last and highest the mind is a blank, and God alone speaks to the soul. (*CM*, 231)

Inge also quotes in full a poem by Madame Guyon, translated by William Cowper as 'The Acquiescence of Pure Love', which demonstrates her indifference—'To me 'tis equal, whether Love ordain / My life or death, appoint me pain or ease'—and the uncompromising goal of quietism: 'Die to the world, and live to self no more' (*CM*, 235).

Inge has a mostly positive view of Molinos, Fénelon, and Guyon, and concludes that they were treated unfairly. Nevertheless, he uses the term 'quietism' in a largely pejorative sense, associating it with 'self-simplification', 'passive expectancy', 'distrust of reason', annihilation of the self and the will, detachment from worldly pursuits, the eradication of desire, rejection of vocal prayer, self-mortification, and self-absorption, all of which he deems 'errors' compared to true mysticism (*CM*, 159, 229, 187). Inge finds that the 'most consistent quietists' are the 'hesychasts [*sic*] of Mount Athos', the contemplatives of the Eastern Orthodox Church (*CM*, 243). 'Hesychast' literally means 'quietist', and it was on account of their prostrated, almost foetal position of prayer that the derogatory terms 'navel-gazer' and 'omphalopsychite' were coined. Inge also observes tendencies towards quietism in St John of the Cross, St Francis of Sales, the Lutheran pastor Valentine Weigel, certain neo-Platonists and 'debased Oriental type[s]', pseudo-Hierotheus, Meister Eckhart, Tauler, and even parts of the Psalms (*CM*, 224, 230–1, 276, 287, 103, 159, 187, 43). Although not as favourable towards quietism as Schopenhauer, Inge's account of the phenomenon is more or less consistent with that in *The World as Will and Representation*. Like Schopenhauer, Inge presents quietism not as a fixed sect but rather as a tendency or attitude that can be found in a number of mystical writers.

Quietism and Hellenistic Philosophy

According to Inge, the 'Atomists, from Epicurus downwards, have been especially odious to the mystics' (*CM*, 22). The incompatibility of mysticism with atomism would cause some problems for Beckett, an admirer of that 'little wearish old man, / Democritus',[81] the father of atomism. Schopenhauer, however, is happy to reference atomist Epicureanism when discussing the goal of his quietist path to the denial of the will:

> It is the painless state that Epicurus prized as the highest good and the state of the gods: for that moment we are freed from the terrible pressure of the will, we celebrate the Sabbath of the penal servitude of willing, the wheel of Ixion stands still. (*WWR*, I.3.38, 220)

Epicurus called the painless state *ataraxia*: imperturbability of mind. Beckett's philosophy notes record how this goal was shared by the two other schools of Hellenistic philosophy, Stoicism and Pyrrhonian Scepticism:

> Epicureans, Stoics & Sceptics are at one in praising <u>imperturbability, ataraxy, independence of the world</u>, as most prominent characteristics of the wise man. For this period the normal man is he who finds his happiness in himself alone. Since this implies <u>overcoming the outer world</u> over which he has no power, he must overcome it <u>within himself</u>; he must become master of the effects which it exercises upon him, Wisdom resides therefore in the relation of man to his passions (<u>perturbations animi</u>). Wisdom is <u>emotionless, apathy</u>. (TCD MS10967, 120r)

---

[81] 'Enueg I' in Samuel Beckett, *The Collected Poems of Samuel Beckett*, ed. by John Pilling and Seán Lawlor (London: Faber and Faber, 2012), p. 7.

Beckett's notes on Pyrrhonism sound especially quietistic, emphasising as they do inwardness, passivity, and resignation:

> Happiness the highest good zwar, but happiness presupposes a knowledge of the nature of things which cannot be acquired. Hence happiness is not possible or only possible in a non-committal condition of suspense, suspension of judgement, reserve of opinion. Only possible happiness <u>ataraxy</u>. Our faculties cannot furnish us with information concerning the essence of phenomena and our relations to them, but only concerning the relations of phenomena to one another. Sujet detient [*sic*] sur l'objet. Doctrine which leads to absolute inaction. Pyrrhonism. (TCD MS10967, 122r)

Beckett revealed his allegiances to something very like Pyrrhonism in a remarkable letter to Mary Manning Howe from 1937:

> There is an ecstasy of <u>accidia</u>—willless in a grey tumult of <u>idées obscures</u>. There is an end to the temptation of light, its polite scorchings & consolations. It is good for children & insects. There is an end to making up one[']s mind, like a pound of tea, an end of patting the butter of consciousness into opinions. The real consciousness is the chaos, a grey commotion of mind, a fullness of mental self-aesthesia that is entirely useless. The monad without the conflict, lightless & darkless. I used to pretend to work, I do so no longer. I used to dig about in the mental sand for the lugworms of likes & dislikes, I do so no longer. The lugworms of understanding.
> Do not envy me, do not pity me. (30/8/37; *LSB1*, 546)

The end of opinions and making up one's mind is precisely what a Pyrrhonist would recommend, and Beckett goes on to invoke the vocabulary of quietism—'willless'—to describe the results. 'Accidia', or variously accidie or acedia, means sloth and indolence, a deadly sin and one to which monks were supposed to be particularly prone thanks to their solitary and silent lifestyle.[82] Beckett's beloved Samuel Johnson also suggests the connection between Pyrrhonism and quietism in his *Dictionary*, where the entry for 'Quietism' is illustrated by a quotation from William Temple:

> What is called by the poets apathy or dispassion, by the scepticks indisturbance, by the Molinists *quietism*, by common men peace of conscience, seems all to mean but great tranquility of mind.[83]

Schopenhauer recognised that the Stoics were in pursuit of 'an important and salutary end, namely that of raising us above the suffering and pain that every life encounters' (*WWR*, I.1.16, 117), but he felt that their recommendation of trying to remain equanimous in the face of suffering did not go nearly far enough. While the Stoic tries to adjust his wishes to fit with the way of the world through the use of reason, the Buddhist ascetic or Christian Quietist attempts to totally abandon desire through unremitting surrender of the will (*WWR*, II.1.16, 628). Charles Taylor puts it well when he says that Buddhists and Christians are called to 'detach themselves from their own flourishing': they renounce ordinary flourishing, while the Stoic merely revises its definition.[84] Beckett, however, had at least a passing interest in the Stoics. They have a prominent role in his notes on philosophy (TCD MS 10967 114r–118r) and his Clare Street notebook contains an attempt at a German translation of a section of the *Enchiridion* of Epictetus.[85] The passage discusses the imperative to retain 'peace of mind' when your possessions are broken or stolen, or your servants

---

82 *The Nature of Melancholy: From Aristotle to Kristeva*, ed. by Jennifer Radden (Oxford: Oxford University Press, 2002), pp. 69–70.
83 Samuel Johnson, *A Dictionary of the English Language* (London: J & P Knapton, 1755), p. 1623.
84 Charles Taylor, *A Secular Age* (London: Belknap Press, 2007), p. 17.
85 Samuel Beckett, 'Clare Street Notebook', pp. 39–40, MS5003, Beckett International Foundation, Reading University Library. Hereafter, UoR MS5003.

misbehave. In the *Whoroscope* notebook, Beckett records how 'The Stoics aspired to Apathia the repression of all emotion, & the Epicurean to ataraxia, freedom from all disturbance' (UoR MS3000, 82v). Beckett took this phrase from W.H.D. Rouse's introduction to the Everyman edition of the *Meditations* of Marcus Aurelius, the Roman Emperor and Stoic philosopher.[86] Rouse compares the *Meditations* to *The Imitation of Christ*, a book that became important to Beckett's relationship with quietism, as we shall see. Both books, Rouse writes, promise that in 'withstanding passions standeth very peace of heart'.[87] In the translation itself, the Stoic is frequently advised to be 'still and quiet',[88] two words that become increasingly important in Beckett's late prose work.

Stoic philosophy can be found in the intellectual ancestry of Christian Quietism: the goal of 'holy indifference' descends from the Stoics' *adiaphora*, via the *Spiritual Exercises* of St Ignatius of Loyola, who also used the term.[89] Beckett similarly mixes Hellenistic vocabulary with theological language: Lucky, in *Waiting for Godot*, speaks of 'divine apathia divine athambia divine aphasia'.[90] *Athambia* was Democritus's term for 'rest' or 'imperturbability',[91] and 'aphasia' signifies silence and wordlessness: in other words, the holy indifference, stillness, and silence of quietism. In his later work, Beckett turns to the Hellenistic philosophers in ways that seem integral to his own brand of quietism; contravening Inge, Beckett blends *ataraxia* with tropes from the Christian mystical tradition. In Chapter 5, I will show how Beckett blends Pyrrhonist terms with the imagery of German mysticism in a line of thought that can be traced from *The Unnamable* through *Company* to *Stirrings Still*.

---

86   W.H.D. Rouse, 'Introduction', in *Meditations*, by Marcus Aurelius, ed. by Ernest Rhys, trans. by Méric Casaubon (London: J.M. Dent & Sons Ltd, 1906), pp. ix–xxii (p. xiii).
87   Rouse, p. xvii.
88   Marcus Aurelius, *Meditations*, ed. by Ernest Rhys, trans. by Méric Casaubon (London: J.M. Dent & Sons Ltd, 1906), pp. 29, 40, 140, 141.
89   Evans, pp. 23–26.
90   Samuel Beckett, *The Complete Dramatic Works* (London: Faber and Faber, 1986), p. 42. Hereafter, *CDW*.
91   Windelband, p. 116.

A Basis for Quietism

In May 1934, Beckett wrote to his friend A.J. Leventhal:

> There's a good passage in Buddenbrooks where [Thomas] Mann speaks of happiness, success etc., as analogous with light from a star, its foyer abolished when it most bright [*sic*], & that brightness its own knell. So please God it is with unhappiness, if it can be bright, & with the bells rung in the distant heart … It's a basis for quietism anyhow, if basis be needed. (7/5/34)[92]

Mann was another literary admirer of Schopenhauer, and *Buddenbrooks* grants his philosophy a brief but important role when Thomas Buddenbrook discovers an unfamiliar book in his father's library. He opens it at a chapter entitled 'On Death, and its Relation to our Inner Nature', which identifies the volume as the supplementary material to *The World as Will and Representation*. After reading just a few words of the text, Thomas loses himself in an ecstatic mystical experience.[93] It is not, however, this moment that Beckett mentions to Leventhal, but rather a passage from Chapter 6 of Part 7, when Thomas has just been elected Senator and has moved to a new house with his wife and son. He tells his younger sister Antonie:

> I know, from life and from history, something you have not thought of: often, the outward and visible material signs and symbols of happiness and success only show themselves when the process of decline has already set in. The outer manifestations take time—like the light of that star up there, which may in reality be already quenched, when it looks to us to be shining its brightest.[94]

---

92 Quoted in Nixon, p. 55.
93 For more analysis of this passage and its relation to Beckett's aesthetics, see Nixon, pp. 171–2.
94 Thomas Mann, *Buddenbrooks: The Decline of a Family*, trans. by H.T. Lowe-Porter (London: Vintage, 1999), p. 352.

Thomas implies that although he may appear happy in a worldly sense—he has property, a good family, and a coveted political position—the real source of those outward signs has faded, and therefore he is in fact unhappy. If Beckett suggests that the same psychological mechanics are at work with unhappiness, he is saying that his own moodiness and melancholy are only the delayed reaction of a cause of sorrow long-since passed, those 'bells rung in the distant heart'. Quietism, in this instance, might mean being resigned and indifferent to these shifts in one's emotional weather, over which one has little to no control.

This is a good point to pause and ask why Beckett felt he might have 'needed' a basis for quietism. The image of the bells wrung in the distant heart provides a clue. Since the age of 20, Beckett had suffered from anxiety attacks which set his heart racing in panic. James Knowlson describes the first of these attacks which happened in April 1926:

> During the night his heart started to race faster and faster, fast enough to keep him awake. At first, this caused him relatively little anxiety. But, later, the attacks were to become more frequent and far more distressing. Soon they were accompanied by dreadful night sweats and feelings of panic that eventually became so serious that Beckett felt he was being paralysed by them and was forced to seek medical help. The problem was to plague him for very many years.[95]

Beckett's problem was poised between the mind and the body, clustered around that most psychosomatic of organs: the heart. On the one hand, the heart has an uncomplicated role as a pump for moving blood around the body. But it has also been associated with a range of abstract psycho-spiritual qualities. The *OED* gives a long list which includes: 'one's inmost thoughts and secret feelings', 'the depths of the soul', will and purpose, character and identity, 'the emotional nature', affection and love, mercy, courage, enthusiasm and energy, memory, conscience and morality. The word 'heart', as Beckett said in relation

---

95 Knowlson, p. 64.

to Goethe's use of it, is a 'flabby' one (SB to TM, 29/5/31; *LSB1*, 79). And as Beckett would have known from his reading of *Christian Mysticism* and Windelband's *History of Philosophy*, 'purity of heart' was what countless Christian mystics, as well as numerous passages in the Bible, demanded as the prerequisite for a life of faith.[96] A revealing entry in Beckett's Clare Street notebook, from 11 August 1936, shows just how much he felt his problem to sit at the intersection between psychology, physical medicine, and spirituality:

> So fängt die Angst wieder zu steigen an, und in den alten wohlbekannten körperlichen Schmerz überzugehen. [...] So mag der Neurotische, d.h. Jedermann, mit dem grössten Ernst u. mit aller Ehrfurcht behaupten, dass zwischen Gott in Himmel u. Schmerz im Bauch der Unterschied bloss minimal ist. (UoR MS5003, 5–7)

> [This is how angst starts growing and to be transformed into the old familiar physical pain. [...] Thus the neurotic, i.e. Everyman, may declare in all seriousness that there is only a marginal difference between God in heaven and a pain in the stomach.[97]]

With an affliction so ambiguously poised between body and mind, Beckett took himself to both physicians and psychologists in search of a solution. Dr Geoffrey Thompson, a heart specialist in Dublin, could find nothing physically wrong with him and so recommended he try psychoanalysis.[98] Since this was unavailable in Ireland, Beckett

---

96 Windelband, p. 365; Inge, pp. 145, 290, 304, and 312.
97 Translation from Feldman, *Beckett's Books*, p. 112.
98 *Beckett Remembering, Remembering Beckett: Uncollected Interviews with Samuel Beckett and Memories of Those Who Knew Him*, ed. by Elizabeth Knowlson and James Knowlson (New York, NY: Arcade Publishing, 2006), p. 68. Thompson's wife, Ursula, recalls Beckett suffering from a 'kind of psychosomatic illness', p. 71.

went to London and began psychotherapeutic (but not psychoanalytic) treatment with Dr Wilfred Bion at the Tavistock Clinic in 1934.[99]

Beckett's heart problem made its way into his unpublished and published writing from this period. In letters he called it 'the old internal combustion heart' (SB to TM, 31/8/35),[100] 'my old Grillen' (SB to TM, 10/3/35; *LSB1*, 256)[101], 'my bitch of a heart' (SB to TM, 24/2/31; *LSB1*, 69) and a 'demon' that wanted to 'disable' him 'with sweats & shudders & panics & rages & rigors & heart burstings' (SB to TM, 10/3/35; *LSB1*, 258). In *Dream of Fair to Middling Women*, Belacqua suffers from 'palpitations' in the 'pulsing snowball of his little heart that went pit-a-pat' (140–141). He has a 'bitch of a heart' that 'knocks hell out of his bosom three or four nights in the week' (73). In Beckett's 1934 short story 'A Case in a Thousand', Dr Nye has a 'heart that knocked and misfired for no reason known to the medical profession'.[102] And Murphy too has 'such an irrational heart that no physician could get to the root of it', one moment prone to 'seizing', the next to 'bursting'.[103] Murphy's one-time philosophical-cum-spiritual mentor, Neary, however, 'could stop his heart more or less whenever he liked and keep it stopped, within reasonable limits, for as long as he liked.' Murphy decides against learning this skill, hoping instead for a taste of Pythagorean *armonia (αρμονια)*, a healthy attunement of the soul.

Matthew Feldman has argued that Beckett's 'Psychology Notes', compiled between 1932 and 1935, roughly the time he was in

---

99 Knowlson, p. 175. Bion only later trained as a psychoanalyst. See Feldman, *Beckett's Books*, p. 88.
100 Quoted in Nixon, p. 38.
101 Beckett took the word *Grillen* from Goethe, who used it to 'denote his moodiness and troubles', according to Nixon, p. 76.
102 Samuel Beckett, *The Complete Short Prose, 1929–1989*, ed. by S.E. Gontarski (New York, NY: Grove Books, 1995), pp. 18–19. Hereafter, *CSP*.
103 Samuel Beckett, *Murphy*, ed. by J.C.C. Mays (London: Faber and Faber, 2009), p. 4. Hereafter, *Mu*.

therapy with Bion,[104] represent an attempt at self-diagnosis.[105] In that notebook, Beckett writes out Karin Stephen's list of the characteristics of a neurotic, copies down what Ernest Jones has to say about melancholy and angst, and notes Otto Rank's theories of 'primal anxiety'.[106] Beckett's notes from literary, philosophical, and historical sources could be seen to serve a similar purpose. In the *Dream* notebook, Beckett notes down 'gravidum cor, fetum caput' from Robert Burton's *Anatomy of Melancholy* (*DN*, 104), which turns into 'gravid heart' and a 'fetid head' in *Dream of Fair to Middling Women* (17). Beckett also records how St Augustine 'turned to God with a pain in his chest' and how Martin Luther is described, in Thomas Carlyle's *On Heroes and Hero Worship*, as 'heartily weary of living' (*DN*, 23, 39). Beckett wrote the phrase 'my psychic and somatic stigmata' based on a line from Nordau's *Degeneration* (95). And Ecclesiastes 2:23 was particularly appropriate: 'His heart taketh not rest in the night' (*DN*, 82). Beckett also wrote out and memorised Leopardi's poem 'A se stesso' [To himself] in the early 1930s,[107] no doubt attracted to it because the speaker has a similarly troublesome heart: 'Or poserai per sempre, / Stanco mio cor' [Now you will rest forever, my weary heart], 'Assai / Palpitasti' [You have beaten enough].[108] Belacqua, in *Dream*, can recite 'A se stesso' from memory (62).

Beckett's heart condition and panic attacks, then, exerted a strong influence over his reading habits and his written work during this period. It would stand to reason that quietism should somehow

---

104 Everett Frost and Jane Maxwell, 'Catalogues of Beckett's Reading Notes and Other Manuscripts at Trinity College Dublin', *Samuel Beckett Today / Aujourd'hui*, 16 (2006), 15–199 (p. 158).
105 Feldman, *Beckett's Books*, pp. 110–1.
106 Samuel Beckett, 'Psychology Notes', pp. 4, 6, 15, 34, MS10971/7–8, Trinity College Dublin. Hereafter, TCD MS10971/7–8.
107 Nixon, p. 54.
108 Giacomo Leopardi, *Canti: Bilingual Edition*, trans. by Jonathan Galassi (New York, NY: Farrar Straus Giroux, 2010), p. 234. I have adjusted Galassi's translations here.

fit into this overarching concern. *Dream of Fair to Middling Women* suggests as much when Belacqua 'lay lapped in a beatitude of indolence […] in a Limbo purged of desire':

> If that is what is meant by going back into one's heart, could anything be better, in this world or the next? The mind, dim and hushed like a sick-room, like a chapelle ardente, thronged with shades; the mind at last its own asylum, disinterested, indifferent, its miserable erethisms and discriminations and futile sallies suppressed; the mind suddenly reprieved, ceasing to be an annex of the restless body, the glare of understanding switched off. (44)

Disinterest and indifference were, of course, the aims of quietism, and are seen as the solution to Belacqua's mental and physical woes. As John Pilling has shown,[109] 'erethism' was cribbed from Pierre Garnier's *Onanisme*.

> In virtue of its etymology, onanism has gradually and logically broadened to include all acts and abuses, vices and depravations which have the effect of engendering erethism and venereal pleasure, without the resulting generation.[110]

Mental erethisms then would suggest a kind of issueless perturbation, spasms of thought with no useful consequence and therefore the opposite of a mind that has been quietened and emptied. According to the *OED*, 'erethism' means 'Excitement of an organ or tissue in an unusual degree'. This would certainly apply to Beckett's heart at this period and yet in *Dream* it is applied to the mind. As with the quotation from the Clare Street notebook, Beckett makes it clear this affliction

---

109 Pilling, Beckett's *Dream Notebook*, p. 60.
110 Pierre Garnier, *Onanisme, seul et à deux sous toutes ses formes et leurs conséquences* (Paris: Garnier Frères, 1894), p. 20.

was deeply psychosomatic. A similar point is made by the phrase 'paroxysm of gratuitous thoughts' on the following page (*Dream*, 45): a paroxysm is a severe fit or attack.

The vital point of connection between the heart and quietism comes, I suspect, from Beckett's reading of Schopenhauer. Molinos, Guyon, and all the other mystics quoted by Inge agree that quietism consists of the resignation of the will, but it is only Schopenhauer who connects this with Beckett's 'bitch of a heart':

> It is entirely accurate for the heart, this first mover of animal life, to be chosen as the symbol, indeed synonym for the *will*, the primal core of our appearance, and that it should signify this in contrast to the *intellect*, which is identical with the *head*. Everything that in the broadest sense is the business of the will, such as wishes, passion, joy, pain, goodness, evil, as well as what people tend to understand by 'someone's nature' and what Homer expresses as *'ƒõilon htor'* [beloved spirit] is attributed to the heart. (*WWR*, II.2.19, 249–250)

Heart and will are treated as synonyms throughout *The World as Will and Representation*: wherever Schopenhauer discusses the heart, he will often put 'the will' in brackets afterwards (e.g. *WWR*, II.3, 468, 473). If quietism in all its forms was about resigning the will, then—through Schopenhauer—that also means calming the heart, the source of Beckett's anxieties. This is why a 'basis for quietism' might be needed: to silence or at least endure those bells rung in the distant heart.

Humanistic Quietism

1934 was a significant year in Beckett's tussles with his heart and anxiety problems, and it is also the year when most of his references to quietism appear. In addition to the letter to Sonny about his quietistic horse, and the letter to Leventhal about *Buddenbrooks*, Beckett also wrote about the 'conflict between intervention and quietism' as one of the things 'that constitute the essence of Proust's originality' in a review of Albert Feuillerat's *Comment Marcel Proust a composé son roman*, which appeared in the June edition of the *Spectator*.[111] Whereas 'intervention' refers to the way that Proust brings 'critical analysis' into his novel, 'quietism' means letting the text stand without too much explanatory interference, with all its 'perturbations and dislocations' (*Dis*, 64). In this review Beckett was once again drawing on his reading of Gide's *Dostoïevsky*, where 'quietism' stands for an aesthetic of incoherence and contradiction, and against realist clarity. Unsurprisingly, Beckett says that this quietist and dislocated Proust is the one 'esteemed by Gide' (*Dis*, 64). I will say more about this in Chapter 3. For now, it is also worth noting that Proust, like Gide, Dostoevsky, and Beckett himself, was often quietist in theme, as well as form. This passage from *La Fugitive* seems indebted to Schopenhauer:

> The more desire advances, the more true possession recedes. So that if it is possible to obtain happiness, or at least freedom from suffering, what we should see is not the satisfaction, but the gradual reductions and final elimination of desire.[112]

This is the side of *À la recherche* that Beckett picks up on in *Proust*, referring to 'the wisdom of all the sages, from Brahma to Leopardi, the wisdom that consists not in the satisfaction but in the ablation of desire' (*PTD*, 18).

Another important mention of quietism from 1934 is Beckett's essay 'Humanistic Quietism', a review of *Poems*[113] by his friend Thomas MacGreevy, which appeared in the July–September edition of *The Dublin Magazine*.[114] That Beckett should attribute a qualified quietism to MacGreevy's poems suggests that, as with his comments on

---

111 Samuel Beckett, *Disjecta: Miscellaneous Writings and a Dramatic Fragment*, ed. by Ruby Cohn (New York, NY: Grove Press, 1984), p. 65. Hereafter, *Dis*.
112 Marcel Proust, *In Search of Lost Time, Vol. 5: The Prisoner and the Fugitive*, trans. by Carol Clark (London: Penguin, 2003), pp. 417–8.
113 Thomas MacGreevy, *Poems* (London: William Heinemann, 1934).
114 An expanded version of this section can be found in Andy Wimbush, 'Humility, Self-Awareness, and Religious Ambivalence: Another Look at Beckett's "Humanistic Quietism"', *Journal of Beckett Studies*, 23 (2014), 202–21.

Proust, he continued to think about quietism in aesthetic terms, drawing on Gide, as well as a disposition related to his heart problems. In this review, however, the main concern is not that 'wealth of antagonisms' that Gide found in Dostoevsky's writing, but rather the attitude of humility and introspection that might provide the foundation of a quietist poetics. Beckett describes how MacGreevy 'evolves his poems' from a 'nucleus of endopsychic clarity' (*Dis*, 69). 'Endopsychic' literally means 'in the mind' and Beckett probably took the term from Ernest Jones's *Papers on Psycho-Analysis* that he was reading and taking notes on at the time (TCD MS10971/7–8, 1–20). Another reference to inwardness comes towards the end of the review when Beckett writes that 'For the intelligent Amiel there is only one landscape'. Here he implicitly compares MacGreevy to the Swiss poet and philosopher Henri-Frédéric Amiel (1821–1881), best known for his *Journal intime*. The 'landscape', then, is the terrain of the mind and the self, perhaps what Amiel referred to as the 'consciousness of consciousness'.[115]

While most critics have assumed that Beckett's review contains either genuine praise or warm words born of friendly obligation,[116] Seán Kennedy has argued that 'Humanistic Quietism' is really a carefully veiled attack on MacGreevy's poetics, and particularly its religious foundations. MacGreevy was a devout Catholic with Irish nationalist leanings, whereas Beckett described himself as a 'dirty low-church P[rotestant] even in poetry' (SB to TM, 18/10/32; *LSB1*, 134). Kennedy thinks that where other critics see Beckett praising MacGreevy for his self-awareness, he was really criticising his friend for an inward-looking and irrationally humble faith and for basing

---

115 Henri-Frédéric Amiel, *Journal intime*, ed. by Bernard Gagnebin and Philippe M. Monnier, 12 vols. (Paris: Éditions L'Âge d'Homme, 1976), vol. II, p. 441.
116 See for example Sinéad Mooney, '"Integrity in a Surplice": Beckett's (Post-)Protestant Poetics', *Samuel Beckett Today / Aujourd'hui*, 9 (2000), 223–38; Ackerley, 'The Roots of Quietism'; Susan Schriebmann, 'Introduction', in *Collected Poems of Thomas MacGreevy* (Washington, DC: Catholic University of America Press, 1991), pp. ix–xxxviii.

his aesthetic on religious sectarianism. I want to argue that the situation is more complicated, and that Beckett was both drawn to humility and inwardness as part of his allegiance to the quietist aesthetic, but also increasingly suspicious that these monkish virtues might be the cause, and not the cure, of his heart problems. As the letter to Sonny Sinclair suggests, quietism brings serenity only for the price of eventual despair.

Kennedy cites the following sentence from the review, in which Beckett is developing his comparison of poetry and prayer:

> To the mind that has raised itself to the grace of humility 'founded'—to quote from Mr McGreevy's *T. S. Eliot*—'not on misanthropy but on hope', prayer is no more (no less) than an act of recognition. (*Dis*, 68)

As Kennedy points out, the full quotation from MacGreevy's *Thomas Stearns Eliot: A Study* is an attack on a particular kind of Protestantism:

> even in [Eliot's] early poems there were traces of a capacity for self-criticism, for humility, that penitential Catholic virtue, founded not on misanthropy but on hope, that is so utterly alien to the puritanical mind.[117]

According to Kennedy, Beckett quotes this passage in order to take 'a subtle swipe at the sectarian discriminations on which MacGreevy's aesthetic is based'.[118] He also concludes that Beckett rejects MacGreevy's Catholic virtue of humility in order to replace it in his aesthetics and ethics with a 'new, more avowedly Protestant, priority—"integrity"' which is 'synonymous with self-reliance'.[119]

---

117 Thomas MacGreevy, *Thomas Stearns Eliot: A Study*, The Dolphin Books (London: Chatto & Windus, 1931), p. 16.
118 Seán Kennedy, 'Beckett Reviewing MacGreevy: A Reconsideration', *Irish University Review*, 35 (2005), 273–87 (p. 277).
119 Kennedy, p. 283.

But even if Beckett had problems with Catholicism, he still had a number of 'low church' models of humility at his disposal, not least from his reading of Gide's *Dostoïevsky*. In his lecture, Beckett explained how Gide was particularly influenced by the 'Humilité of Dost[oevsky]' and his 'Renouncement' which 'accommodate[s] complexity with humility' (TCD MIC60, 23). Burrows's notes show that Beckett was particularly pained to emphasise Gide's Protestant upbringing:

> Protestant background which has endured, encouraged by Dost[oevsky]. Renunciation. (TCD MIC60, 14)
> Protestant & iconoclast (31)
> Influenced by Protestantism (37)
> Protestantism explains most of his characters (42)
> Summary ① Protestant & ② Iconoclast—Prot in all that Fr. Prot^{ism} implies (44)

Gide himself stresses Dostoevsky's vehement dislike of the Catholic Church—all too apparent to any reader of *The Brothers Karamazov*—and says that humility is so embedded in the Russian psyche that it can be found even among souls who lack the Christian faith (*Dost*, 226, 15). So despite the arguments of Kennedy—and indeed MacGreevy—humility need not be incompatible with Protestantism or even atheism, nor is humility something which Beckett necessarily scorns. In fact, he seems to appreciate the way in which humility leads Gide to a 'quality of inconclusiveness' and 'integrity of incoherence' (TCD MIC60, 43, 37). Precisely what Kennedy sees as a replacement for humility—integrity—appears in Beckett's lecture as a product of it.

It is also worth noting that Beckett does not criticise Gide for basing his aesthetic on a religious position. In fact, he seems to admire how Protestantism informs Gide's work, and how the 'quietism' of Eastern Orthodoxy shapes Dostoevsky's. This makes it unlikely that he would want to criticise MacGreevy for his reliance on a sectarian poetics. In fact, Beckett's title—'Humanistic Quietism'—may have been coined as a tribute to MacGreevy's own religious interests. Although Ackerley thinks the idea of a humanistic quietism is a contradiction in terms,[120] Beckett may have been thinking of the life and work of St Francis of Sales, who was both one of the founders of Christian humanism[121] and a mystic whose emphasis on indifference and resignation anticipated the teachings of the Quietists.[122] In *Christian Mysticism*, Inge notes that the 'errors of the quietists certainly receive some countenance from parts of [Francis's] writings' and he chooses a phrase from Francis—'the disinterested heart is like wax in the hands of its God'—to illustrate quietist indifference (*CM*, 231, 237). Molinos, Guyon, and Fénelon all considered Francis an important precursor.[123] MacGreevy was an admirer of the saint: the poem 'Arrangement in Gray and Black', included within the 1934 collection, is dedicated to *'the memory of a student of François de Sales'*.[124] Years later, MacGreevy wrote an essay in which he discussed how Francis's humanist upbringing informed his thinking even after he became a bishop. Francis was a humanist 'by instinct and training', according to MacGreevy, but his humanism was now 'a Christianised humanism and all the more humane for accepting the implications of the Kingdom of God that is within every human being'.[125] Beckett's admiration for the Protestant-inspired quietism of Gide, and the quasi-Buddhist, eastern quietism of Dostoevsky means that he probably appreciated MacGreevy's Catholic-inspired humanistic quietism more than Kennedy acknowledges.

Kennedy follows J.C.C. Mays in concluding that Beckett's comparison of MacGreevy to Amiel was not intended as praise. According to Mays, it suggests Beckett thought MacGreevy's poetry 'was

---

[120] Ackerley, 'The Roots of Quietism', p. 88.
[121] Eunan McDonnell, *The Concept of Freedom in the Writings of St. Francis de Sales* (Bern: Peter Lang, 2009), pp. 27–55.
[122] Knox, pp. 254, 258.
[123] Richard Parish, 'Introduction', in *Dialogues posthumes sur le quiétisme*, by Jean de La Bruyère, ed. by Richard Parish (Grenoble: Éditions Jérôme Millon, 2005), pp. 5–44 (p. 15); Molinos, pp. 114, 150.
[124] MacGreevy, *Poems*, p. 55.
[125] Thomas MacGreevy, 'Saint Francis de Sales', *Father Mathew Record*, June 1943, 2 (p. 2).

relatively colourless; that it drove towards a vacant, nameless consciousness'.[126] But it is not certain that Beckett thought that this exploration of consciousness was a worthless enterprise. In the *Dream* notebook he records a phrase which seems to be of his own coinage: 'plung[e] à la Amiel into the Encyclopaedia of my subject' (*DN*, 132). Rather than being colourless and dull, the inner landscape of the aspiring Amiel might be as rich and fascinating as an encyclopaedia (Beckett was an avid reader of encyclopaedias in the 1930s and beyond). Beckett suggests as much several years later in his 1947 poem, 'bon bon il est un pays' [all right all right it is a country]: the mind is compared to 'un pays sans traces' [a trackless land] where 'la tête est muette' [the head is silent] and 'il n'y a rien à pleurer' [there is nothing to lament].[127] Ackerley is surely right to say that this poem is both 'a celebration of the realm of the mind and a grumble against the lack of time to explore it fully'.[128] We cannot, therefore, unambiguously assume that Beckett is being critical of MacGreevy when he describes his poetry as inward or even solipsistic. It was, after all, the 'Celtic drill of extraversion' and the 'flight from self-awareness' in the poetry of the Irish Literary Revival that Beckett really despised (*Dis*, 73).

Kennedy is, I think, wrong to cast Beckett as straightforwardly unsympathetic with MacGreevy's inward and humble poetics. Although Beckett had little taste for his friend's nationalism or Catholicism, his allegiance to Gide's quietist aesthetic meant that he was unlikely to have completely rejected an approach to poetry born of religious renunciation. Nevertheless, another of Beckett's reviews from the same year makes it clear how easy it is to go wrong in this enterprise. Beckett is contemptuous of the poetry of Rainer Maria Rilke, which he dismisses as a 'turmoil of self-deception and naif discontent' (*Dis*, 67). Beckett says that Rilke 'changes his ground without ceasing, like Gide, though for very different reasons; not in order to save his bacon (oh in the very highest sense), but because he cannot stay still' (*Dis*, 67). Rilke's error is

---

126 J.C.C. Mays, 'How Is MacGreevy a Modernist?', in *Modernism and Ireland: The Poetry of the 1930s*, ed. by Patricia Coughlan and Alex Davis (Cork: Cork University Press, 1995), pp. 103–28 (p. 115).
127 Beckett, *Collected Poems*, p. 115.
128 Ackerley, 'The Roots of Quietism', p. 89.

to take his 'fidgets' and 'disorder' and give them lofty titles: 'God, Ego, Orpheus and the rest'. This 'interchangeability of Rilke and God'—what Rilke calls the *Ichgott*—is mere 'childishness' according to Beckett. It is worth noting here that the conflation of God and ego is precisely what Kennedy thinks Beckett is accusing MacGreevy of doing in his solipsistic Catholicism. But Beckett clearly differentiates Rilke's efforts from MacGreevy's: Rilke is childish, while MacGreevy attains to an 'adult mode of prayer'. Beckett probably recognised that he was actually far more prone to Rilke's delusions than MacGreevy was. He aspired to change his ground and move about in his writing like Gide and Dostoevsky did, and he suffered from his own 'fidgets': those heart problems that afflicted him for so long. And whereas MacGreevy had the saving grace of religious belief, Beckett, like Rilke, was an apostate, and therefore more liable to replace self with God in his quietistic exploration of the inner world. The following year Beckett admitted as much to MacGreevy, and was forced to confront his doubts about the value of quietism as a viable philosophy of life.

Abject Self-Referring Quietism

> She had not perceived—how could she until she had lived longer?—the inmost truth of the old monk's out-pourings, that renunciation remains sorrow, though a sorrow borne willingly.
>
> —George Eliot, The Mill on the Floss[129]

In March 1935, MacGreevy wrote to Beckett and suggested that he might find some solace from his anxieties and heart problems by reading Thomas à Kempis's *Imitation of Christ*, a fifteenth-century devotional manual for monks and nuns. Beckett had actually read the text before, in 1931, when looking for material that he could appropriate for use in *Dream of Fair to Middling Women*. He read the text in both English and Latin; Ackerley and Pilling both propose that the former

---

129 George Eliot, *The Mill on the Floss*, ed. by Gordon S. Haight (Oxford: Oxford University Press, 2008), p. 291.

was John Ingram's edition,[130] which collates the earliest translations of the *Imitation*.[131] They note that Beckett veers from the Ingram edition at certain points, and suggest that he was paraphrasing or changing certain words. A more elegant solution to this mismatch is that Beckett did not use Ingram's text but rather the softly modernised version in the 1910 Everyman edition, which was reprinted several times.[132] Pilling points out that Beckett's transcription 'Be ye sorry in your chambers',[133] does not match Ingram's 'Be ye compuncte in your pryue couches'.[134] It does, however, match the Everyman text perfectly, as do Beckett's other English quotations in the *Dream* notebook and the letter to MacGreevy. I will therefore use the Everyman edition in this book.

MacGreevy was aware of his friend's lack of faith, and so suggested that if Beckett objected to the theistic language of the *Imitation*, he could replace the word 'God' with 'goodness & disinterestedness'. But Beckett replied to say that he was already familiar with the text, and ambivalent about its usefulness.

> I found quantities of phrases like <u>qui melius scit pati majorem tenebit pacem</u>, [he who knows how to suffer well shall find the most peace] or, <u>Nolle consolari ab aliqua creatura magnae puritatis signum est</u> [to refuse comfort from any creature is a sign of great faith], or the lovely <u>per viam pacis, ad patriam perpetuae claritatis</u> [by the way of peace to the country of everlasting clearness] that seemed to be made for me and which I have never forgotten. Amg many others. (SB to TM, 10/3/35; *LSB1*, 257)

---

130 Ackerley, 'The Roots of Quietism', p. 82; Pilling, *Beckett's Dream Notebook*, p. 80.
131 Thomas à Kempis, *The Earliest English Translation of the First Three Books of the De Imitatione Christi*, ed. by John K. Ingram (London: Kegan Paul, Trench, Trübner & Co. Ltd, 1893).
132 Thomas à Kempis, *The Imitation of Christ* (London: J.M. Dent & Sons Ltd, 1910). Hereafter, *IC*.
133 John Pilling, *Beckett before Godot* (Cambridge: Cambridge University Press, 2004), p. 82.
134 Thomas à Kempis, *The Earliest English Translation of the First Three Books of the De Imitatione Christi*, p. 25.

The phrases that Beckett admired resonate perfectly well with the quietism of Schopenhauer. Thomas à Kempis also has a number of things in common with the seventeenth-century Quietists, and the *Imitation* was an important influence on the writing of Madame Guyon.[135] But whereas Schopenhauer's quietism is supposed to lead to compassionate interest in others, the quietism of the *Imitation* has other priorities, according to Beckett:

> if certain forms of contact [with other people] are commended by the way, it is very much by the way, and incidental & secondary to the fundamental contact—for him with "God". So that to read "goodness & disinterestedness" every time for God, would seem the accidental for the essential with a vengeance & a mining of the text; whereas to allow the sceptical position [...] & replace a principle of faith, absolute & infinite, by one personal & finite of fact, would be to preserve its magnificent basis of distinction between primary & secondary, in the interests of a very baroque solipsism if you like. (*LSB1*, 258)

In this passage, Beckett is saying that there are three options for reading the text, none of which he finds particularly satisfying. The first is to accept it on its own terms and take it in faith. This would have been impossible for Beckett, since he was not a Christian and in his own words seemed 'never to have had the least faculty or disposition for the supernatural' (*LSB1*, 257). The second is to read it as MacGreevy suggests, replacing God with goodness and disinterestedness, and thereby turning it into a predominantly ethical work. But as Beckett points out, this goes against the *Imitation*'s relegation of the interpersonal to a secondary concern. The third option is to replace God with one's 'own feathers or entrails' (257) and put Thomas's exercises to a different use: instead of drawing closer to God, Beckett will delve into himself. In other words, he admits to having done the very thing that he damned Rilke for doing the previous year. This approach maintains

---

[135] Nancy C. James, 'Introduction', p. 23.

the distinction between a primary goal of God / self, and secondary goal of the interpersonal and ethical. But even this last option proves fruitless. Beckett knows this because he had previously 'twisted' the advice of Thomas à Kempis 'into a programme of self-sufficiency', and found that such inwardness promoted only 'isolationism', 'an index of a superiority', a 'feeling of arrogant "otherness"', and 'a crescendo of disparagement of others & myself' (*LSB1*, 258). Again, this is not so far from Rilke's 'turmoil of self-deception and naif discontent' in the 'privacies' of his *Ichgott*. Beckett also implies that this isolationism was what eventually led to the 'terrifying physical symptoms' that he is now enduring: heart palpitations, night sweats, and all the rest. As Beckett suggested in his letter to Sonny about the horse, the serenity of quietism can easily turn into a demon of despair. Even the parts of the *Imitation* that Beckett liked 'conduced to the isolationism that was not to prove very splendid'. He goes on:

> What is one to make of "seldom we come home without hurting of conscience" and "the glad going out & sorrowful coming home" and "be ye sorry in your chambers" but a quietism of the sparrow alone upon the housetop & the solitary bird under the eaves? An abject self-referring quietism indeed. (*LSB1*, 257)

Beckett does not mention Schopenhauer in this letter, but his reply to MacGreevy constitutes a rejection of Schopenhauer's insistence that ascetic temperament can be successfully amputated from religious beliefs, expressed in his advice about how to read Madame Guyon. Beckett was trying to do something similar with Thomas à Kempis, and yet ended up in a melancholy solipsism rather than a peaceful state of willlessness. Gide is also not mentioned, but was perhaps in the background of Beckett's thoughts. His lectures had, after all, mentioned Gide's claim that Dostoevsky's novels—like the *Imitation*—are more interested in the 'inner life' than 'social connections' (TCD MIC60, 60,

70). Gide's own novel of renunciation, *La Porte étroite*, is, as Gide himself admitted, a critique of these priorities:[136] Alissa turns away from a life of earthly happiness with Jérôme, expecting a spiritual happiness that never materialises. Whatever value quietism had at an artistic level could not efface the dangers it posed to interpersonal relationships. In the next chapter, I will show how Beckett makes this last point the central concern of *Murphy*.

Geulincx and Quietism?

Beckett's misgivings about *The Imitation of Christ* suggests that 1935 marked a rueful but irrevocable rejection of the quietist ethic. While he had aspired to that humility and abnegation that he admired in the life and work of Gide and Dostoevsky, he had ended up in Rilke's self-absorbed turmoil. It would seem that one of Beckett's withering comments about Rilke applies just as much to himself: in his writing there is 'the overstatement of the solitude which he cannot make his element' (*Dis*, 67). But just over a year after his letter to MacGreevy in which *The Imitation of Christ*, and with it quietism, had been dismissed, Beckett signed off a letter to his friend Arland Ussher with Thomas à Kempis's words 'Humiliter, Simpliciter, Fideliter' (SB to AU, 25/3/36; *LSB1*, 329). Did this mean that some sort of reconciliation had taken place, and that he was now interested in quietism again? And if so, how had he got to this point so soon after seeing quietism as 'a way of living that tried to be a solution & failed' and the *Imitation* as something he was utterly incapable of 'approaching [...] "meekly, simply & truly"'? (SB to TM, 10/3/35; *LSB1*, 257)

The contents of the letter to Ussher may provide the answer: in the final paragraph Beckett enthuses about the Flemish Occasionalist philosopher Arnold Geulincx (1624–1669) whose work he had been studying 'without knowing why exactly' at Trinity College Dublin (SB to TM, 5/3/36; *LSB1*, 318). Geulincx, like Schopenhauer, was a

---

136 André Gide, 'Feuillets', in *Oeuvres Complètes*, ed. by Louis Martin-Chauffier, 15 vols. (Paris: Nouvelle Revue Française, 1932), 439–40.

thinker whose metaphysics were tied up with his ethics. Just as Schopenhauer's account of the insatiable will driving living beings towards craving, violence, and suffering demands an ethic of renunciation, compassion, and quietism, Geulincx's philosophy of Occasionalism—wherein a human being has no power to act in the outer world, but is moved only by God—demands an ethic of humility and religious obligation. Beckett's outspoken admiration for yet another low church advocate of humility again suggests that Seán Kennedy is wrong to think that Beckett rejects the virtue as a solely Catholic trait in 'Humanistic Quietism'. Beckett writes to Ussher:

> I am obliged to read in Trinity College Library, as Arnoldus Geulincx is not available elsewhere. I recommend him to you most heartily, especially his <u>Ethica</u>, and above all the second section of the second chapter of the first tractate, where he disquires on <u>his</u> fourth cardinal virtue, Humility, <u>contemptus negativus sui ipsius</u> [to comprise its own contemptible negation] (25/3/36; *LSB1*, 329)

As David Tucker points out in his definitive study, Beckett's turn to Geulincx was 'also a turning back' towards several of the themes he was thinking about in 1934 and 1935.[137] Geulincx seems to have taken him back to whatever he found admirable about the quietist humility of the *Imitation* and Gide's account of Dostoevsky. The fact that Beckett recommends Geulincx 'heartily' even suggests that the *Ethica* had restored his hope of finding a solution to his anxieties through reading, and he implies as much when he tells MacGreevy about his Geulincx studies:

> my instinct is right & the work worth doing, because of its [i.e. Geulincx's *Ethica*] saturation in the conviction that the <u>sub specie aeternitatis</u> [from the perspective of eternity] vision is the only excuse for remaining alive. (5/3/36; *LSB1*, 319)

---

137 David Tucker, *Samuel Beckett and Arnold Geulincx: Tracing 'a Literary Fantasia'* (London: Continuum, 2012), p. 45.

Psychotherapy had, at least in 1935, failed 'to render the business of remaining alive tolerable' (SB to TM, 10/3/35; *LSB1*, 259), but Geulincx provides an 'excuse' for it, perhaps as Schopenhauer had provided 'justification' previously. But was this Geulingian vision a return to quietism, as Beckett's quotation from *The Imitation of Christ* suggests, or was it something else entirely?

In his transcriptions from the *Ethica* in the first three months of 1936, Beckett records several phrases from Geulincx's work that might easily be included in the loose definition of quietism that I have explored so far. For example:

> Humility is *Disregard of Oneself* ... The Disregard consists in the abandonment of myself, altogether relinquishing, transferring, and yielding of myself to God[138]
> I cannot get beyond *I do not know*, there is nothing I can add to this *I do not know*. I do not know how I came to this condition. *I shall remain here on God's orders; without his orders I shall not depart. Let all the hatred,* **etc** ... *of the world befall me* ... [...] *Yet still I am certain that I should not want to prevent death, or slay myself, but stay calm* ...
> Where there is no *Me*, there also there is no *My*.
> To *believe* (that is, to opine, to conceive and cherish opinions) *is not for the Wise Man* (not for the sage or philosopher) in the vicissitudes of one's mode of life (where the strange and the unaccustomed disturb and alarm, afflicting the mind with a thousand anxieties) [...] the mind has to stay calm
> one should *frequently relax the mind, lest it become jaded by incessant business*
> Happiness is like a shadow: it flees from you when you pursue it; but pursues you when you flee from it. [...] A truly humble mind, having not only submitted to, but immersed itself in its Obligations ... beyond concern ... is capable of Happiness.[139]

---

138 Samuel Beckett, 'Notes on Geulincx', in *Arnold Geulincx' Ethics: With Samuel Beckett's Notes*, by Arnold Geulincx, ed. by Han Van Ruler and Anthony Uhlmann, trans. by Martin Wilson (Leiden: Brill, 2006), pp. 311–54 (p. 337).

139 Beckett, 'Notes on Geulincx', pp. 334, 341, 344, 348, 345, 348, 348, 353. Italics and bold in original.

In Geulincx's *Ethica*, Beckett finds self-abandonment, ablation of desire, endurance of vicissitudes, mental quiet, unknowing, humility, and the recognition of the fickleness of happiness: all of which would not be out of place in a text by Schopenhauer or Molinos, and which complement Beckett's interest in Proust, Leopardi, and Gide. Geulincx's signature motto, which Beckett was fond of quoting when talking about his own work, also has a kind of quietist ring to it: *ubi nihil vales, ibi nihil velis*, variously translated as 'wherein you have no power, therein you should not will' and 'where you are worth nothing, there you should want nothing'. Beckett knew this motto before his research trip to Trinity, having read it in Windelband's *A History of Philosophy* in the early 1930s. In his notes on Windelband, Geulincx's philosophy is summarised as follows: 'Man has nothing to do with the outer world' (TCD MS10967, 189v). This suggests precisely the kind of resignation and inwardness that can be found in quietism.

But as Tucker points out, Geulincx's position was far more nuanced than the account in Windelband's book implies.[140] The motto '*ubi nihil vales, ibi nihil velis*' has less to do with quietist passivity than with acting responsibly and in accordance with divine will. Geulincx recommends finding a decent steady job, maintaining good friendships, feeding oneself moderately, and starting a family. Later Beckett would reflect, in a letter to Georges Duthuit, that he was 'a little hasty' in linking Geulincx's motto with Murphy's little world of self-absorption. Rather, he admitted, the phrase was 'not in the least little bit metaphysical or mystical' and just 'common sense, good and round' ([n.d., between 30/4 and 26/5/49]; *LSB1*, 148–50).

There is one particular aspect of Geulincx's ethics of common sense which Beckett would not have been able to reconcile with Schopenhauerian pessimistic quietism. In *Proust* (67), Beckett quotes Calderón's maxim—'el delito mayor / Del hombre es haber nacido' [the greatest sin of man is to have been born]—which he had found in *The World as Will and Representation*. In his essay 'The Doctrine of the Suf-

---

140 Tucker, p. 17.

fering of the World', Schopenhauer repeats this idea: 'everyone is punished for his existence and indeed each in his own way' (*PP*, II.303). Beckett's own work contains many echoes of this pessimistic anti-natalism. Point 6 of the outline of *Murphy* in the *Whoroscope* notebook includes the phrase 'individual existence as atonement' (UoR MS3000, 1r). Neary, upon learning that the pub is not yet open, 'cursed, first the day in which he was born, then—in a bold flash-back—the night in which he was conceived' (*Mu*, 30). Echoing both Calderón and Schopenhauer, Malone describes Macmann's feelings on existence:

> without knowing exactly what his sin was he felt full well that living was not a sufficient atonement for it or that this atonement was in itself a sin, calling for more atonement and so on (*MD*, 67)

But Geulincx cannot countenance the proposal that it would have been better not to have been born or that life is a kind of punishment. He says, and Beckett records: 'I should look upon my birth as a good, never detest it, and never lament it. I must not rage with madness and impotence that I am punished by having been born.'[141]

Beckett seems to have realised that Geulincx could not keep step with Schopenhauer and the quietists on every matter and appreciated him all the more as a result. In a letter to MacGreevy, Beckett describes Geulincx as 'patiently turned outward, & without Schwärmerei turned in-ward' (5/3/36; *LSB1*, 319). The term *Schwärmerei*, which literally means 'enthusiasm' or 'effusiveness', usually denotes religious fanatics of some kind. Luther coined the phrase to denounce the subversive theology of the peasants' revolt of 1524–5, and Kant adopted it over two centuries later to refer to anyone claiming religious knowledge which depended on emotionalism or extremism.[142] Beckett, however, was no doubt thinking of Schopenhauer, who mentions,

---

141 Beckett, 'Notes on Geulincx', p. 350.
142 Alberto Toscano, *Fanaticism: On the Uses of an Idea* (London: Verso, 2010), pp. xiv–xv, and chapter 3, passim.

in the same breath, 'Quietisten' and 'fromme Schwärmer'[143] ['quietists, pious enthusiasts' (*WWR*, I.4.68, 411)]. The quietists are those who had 'turned in-ward' with too much *Schwärmerei* and who perhaps arrived at the same 'baroque solipsism' that Beckett had 'twisted' out of *The Imitation of Christ* a year before (SB to TM, 10/3/35; *LSB1*, 257).[144] Rilke too 'cannot hold his emotion', according to Beckett (*Dis*, 66). It is possible that Geulincx's Protestant pragmatism and patient outward turn softened the edges of the 'negation of living' that he had drawn from quietism (*LSB1*, 259). Tucker surmises that Beckett's encounter with Geulincx 'rekindled the faint hope'[145] of finding 'some way of devoting pain & monstrosity & incapacitation to the service of a deserving cause' (SB to TM, 10/3/35; *LSB1*, 259). In other words, he was able to resume his quietist literary project, drawing on his own suffering, but without the fanatical negativity and 'isolationism' he had previously adopted.

Quietism continues

After the spring of 1935, Beckett does not mention quietism again in any of the extant texts that we have, with one important exception: Moran's 'pretty quietist Pater' (*Mo*, 175) which I treat in detail in Chapter 3. But whatever reconciliation with quietism that took place during psychotherapy or the Geulincx research seems to have been enough for Beckett to pursue reading and writing which, if not explicitly quietist, still presents a similar attitude. Samuel Johnson, particularly in *Prayers and Meditations*, provided another example of the quietist endurance that Gide found in Dostoevsky and Beckett found in *The Imitation of Christ*: 'Where there is nothing to be done,' Johnson said, 'something must be endured.'[146] But, as Mark Nixon has shown, it was mostly in the work of

---

143 Arthur Schopenhauer, *Die Welt als Wille und Vorstellung* (München: Dt. Taschenbuch-Verl., 1998), p. 495.
144 See also Knox, chap. 12.
145 Tucker, p. 45.
146 Samuel Johnson, *Johnsonian Miscellanies*, ed. by George Birkbeck Norman Hill, 2 vols. (Oxford: Clarendon Press, 1897), I, p. 26; Quoted in Nixon, p. 57.

German language writers where Beckett found quietist themes. Earlier in the decade, Beckett read and admired the Austrian dramatist Franz Grillparzer, having recorded his phrase 'Des Innern stiller Frieden' [The quiet inner peace] in his 1934 notes on German literature.[147] The phrase was taken from George Robertson's *History of German Literature*, in which Grillparzer's work is described in terms of 'renunciation'.[148] Nixon also points out how Goethe, despite his *Vorwärtsstreben* [striving forward], may have provided some quietist inspiration, particularly in his invocation of Ixion, Tantalus and Sisyphus—all doomed to futile and repetitive toil in Hades—as 'saints'.[149] In 1938–9, Beckett undertook a sustained study of the life and work of Friedrich Hölderlin, and marked up the following passage in his copy of *Hyperion*:

> There is a forgetting of all existence, a silencing of our being, when we feel as if we had found everything. There is a silencing, a forgetting of all existence, when we feel as if we had lost everything, a night of our soul, in which no glimmer from a star nor even a rotting log gives us light. I had now become quiet. Now nothing drove me up around midnight. Now I no longer scorched myself in my own flame.[150]

Nixon and Van Hulle note that this passage 'stages a Schopenhauerian renunciation of the will, a quietist refusal of the self'.[151] As with Beckett's earlier transcription of 'unanxious repose' from St Augustine's *Confessions* (*DN*, 28), this annotation demonstrates his appreciation of descriptions of mental quiet. Beckett's own work, despite its ambivalent relationship to soteriological 'solutions' (which I discuss in Chapters 4 and 5), abounds with similar moments of peace, from Belacqua's

---

147 Samuel Beckett, 'Notes on German Literature', p. 42v, MS10971/1, Trinity College Dublin. Hereafter, TCD MS10971/1.
148 John G. Robertson, *A History of German Literature* (London: William Blackwood and Sons, 1902), p. 537.
149 Nixon, p. 77.
150 Translation from Nixon, p. 83.
151 Nixon and Van Hulle, p. 92.

'mind abode serene', 'sweet aboulia' and 'Limbo and wombtomb alive with the unanxious spirits of quiet cerebration' (*Dream*, 5, 47, 121), Celia's 'amnion about her own disquiet' and Murphy's 'Belacqua bliss' and 'unparalleled beatitude' (*Mu*, 44, 71, 72), through Molloy's 'old ataraxy' (*Mo*, 40), Malone's 'great calm, and a great indifference' (*MD*, 24) to the final striving for stillness in the late prose texts. These fleeting moments of peace are often undercut by humour or contradiction and yet their presence throughout Beckett's work suggests another enduring and ambivalently held fascination.

Further evidence of Beckett's continued interest in quietism, after his encounter with Geulincx, is his return to Schopenhauer in 1937. 'I have been insulting myself with Belloc on Milton & diverting the surviving attention with Schopenhauer on women' (SB to JHo, 3/7/37; *LSB1*, 509). Beckett told MacGreevy

> When I was ill I found the only thing I could read was Schopenhauer. Everything else I tried only confirmed the feeling of sickness. It was very curious. Like suddenly a window opened on a fug. I always knew he was one of the ones that mattered most to me, and it is a pleasure more real than any pleasure for a long time to begin to understand now why it is so. And it is a pleasure also to find a philosopher that can be read like a poet, with an entire indifference to the apriori forms of verification. Although it is a fact that judged by them his generalisations show fewer cracks than most generalisations. (21/9/37; *LSB1*, 550)

As in 1930, Schopenhauer appeals to Beckett not because of his metaphysics, but because he provides a sense of personal relief. Beckett's image of a window opening through the fug recalls Schopenhauer's description of salvation as piercing the veil of Maya and also Thomas Buddenbrook's feeling that 'the whole wall of dark had parted wide' after his own encounter with *The World as Will and Representation*.[152] Yet again, reading Schopenhauer has a kind of soteriological function for

---

152 Mann, *Buddenbrooks*, p. 526.

Beckett, which suggests that his interest in quietism was not yet spent. Around 1938, Beckett read *Der Pessimismus in Vergangenheit und Gegenwart* by Olga Plümacher, an 1888 account of pessimistic philosophy through the ages with special attention to Schopenhauer and the psychologist Eduard von Hartman.[153] According to Nixon and Van Hulle, Beckett read this book in an intensive way: he inserted blank pages for notes and heavily annotated the text itself until the book was so dilapidated that it needed to be taped back together. Plümacher mentions quietism and asceticism in connection with Schopenhauer's soteriology, and with an attitude of 'laissez faire, laissez aller'.[154]

Conclusion

In his notes on German literature, compiled around 1934, Beckett copied out Goethe's artistic credo, from his autobiography *Dichtung und Wahrheit*:

> Und so begann diejenige Richtung[,] von der ich mein ganzes Leben über nicht abweichen konnte, nämlich dasjenige was mich erfreute oder quälte, oder sonst beschäftigte, in ein Bild, ein Gedicht zu verwandeln und darüber mit mir selbst abzuschliessen, um sowohl meine Begriffe von den äussern Dingen zu berichtigen, als mich im Innern desshalb zu beruhigen. (TCD MS10971/1, 54v–55r)

> [And thus began that tendency from which I could not deviate my whole life through; namely, the tendency to turn into an image, into a poem, everything that delighted or troubled me, or otherwise occupied me, and to come to some certain understanding with myself upon it, that I might both rectify my conceptions of external things, and set my mind at rest about them.[155]]

---

153 Nixon and Van Hulle, pp. 152, 156.
154 Olga Plümacher, *Der Pessimismus in Vergangenheit und Gegenwart* (Heidelberg: George Weiss, 1888), p. 267.
155 Johann Wolfgang von Goethe, *The Autobiography of Goethe: Truth and Fiction Relating to My Life*, trans. by John Oxenford, 2 vols. (Boston, MA: Estes and Lauriat, 1883), I, pp. 234–5.

The remainder of the decade saw Beckett trying to find his own solution to Goethe's problem: the difficulty of turning personal affliction into literature, and in such a manner that the affliction might be healed. As I have argued, Beckett's interest in quietism was caught up in this struggle, since it provided an aesthetic, a theme for writing, and an imperfect personal solution for his own woes. From the references that I explored in this chapter, it seems that Beckett understood quietism primarily as a disposition that can calmly accept vicissitudes. Translated into the sphere of literary aesthetics, this means the ability to accommodate textual incoherence and humbly recognise the inconsistencies of the inner world, something which Beckett saw exemplified in the work of Dostoevsky, Gide, and Proust. I will say much more about this in Chapter 3. Such a calm, humble inner gaze is also what Beckett admired about MacGreevy's poetry. The danger arises when such calm detachment mutates into aloof isolationism, as Beckett suggests it might in his letters about Sonny's horse and *The Imitation of Christ*, and his review of Rilke's poetry.

In Germany in 1937, Beckett wrote of his desire to turn 'this dereliction profoundly felt, into literature' (GD, 2/2/37). Just as Goethe evoked a kind of quietism in his desire to calm his inner world, Beckett takes the term 'dereliction' from St Teresa of Ávila, an advocate of the 'prayer of quiet' who through fortune or good sense managed to stay on the right side of heterodoxy.[156] Beckett had recorded Teresa's 'Great Dereliction' from Inge's *Christian Mysticism* in the *Dream* notebook and bestowed it twice on Belacqua in *Dream of Fair to Middling Women* (6, 185). Whereas for Teresa dereliction was 'a sense of ineffable loneliness and desolation, which nevertheless is the path to incomparable happiness' (*CM*, 221), Beckett, like Goethe, hoped it would also lead to literary creation. This would become Beckett's task, or more properly his Schopenhauerian pensum, which would occupy his literary efforts until the very end of his life.

---

156 Teresa of Ávila, 'The Four Stages of Prayer', in McGinn, *The Essential Writings of Christian Mysticism*, pp. 113–4.

Chapter 2
A Sufferer of My Pains:
Murphy and the Little World

> For a man never to feel trouble nor suffer no heaviness in body nor in soul, is not the state of this world but the state of everlasting quiet.
>
> —Thomas à Kempis,
> *The Imitation of Christ* (III.xxix, 151)

> une culte ascétique du moi
>
> —Bishop Bossuet on Quietism[1]

Beckett's first published novel, *Murphy*, written between August 1935 and June 1936,[2] is encyclopaedic in its points of reference: as C.J. Ackerley rightly observes, a truly exhaustive study would need to take into account 'music and theatre, semiotics of the London scene, spiritualism, astrology, kites, dogs, chess, and mathematics' and probably much more besides.[3] We know, however, that quietism was at the forefront of Beckett's mind when he began writing: in the *Whoroscope* notebook, he jotted down the following in Point 3 of an outline of his projected novel:

> H.[oroscope] any old oracle to begin with. If corpus of motives after stichomancy had given quietism oder was [or what]. But <u>gradually ratified by its</u> <u>own refutation</u>. Till it acquires authority of fatality. No longer a guide to be consulted but a force to be obeyed. Dutiful death of <u>both</u>! (UoR MS3000, 1r)

The 'corpus of motives' is the horoscope: in the finished novel, Murphy refers to it as his 'corpus of incentives' (16). In Point 1 of the

---

1   Quoted in Knox, p. 248.
2   J.C.C. Mays, 'Preface', in *Murphy*, by Samuel Beckett (London: Faber and Faber, 2009), pp. vii–xix (p. viii).
3   Ackerley, *Demented Particulars*, p. 20.

Whoroscope outline, Beckett notes that the main character—who is not yet Murphy, but merely 'X'—has 'no motives', and therefore has to rely on the horoscope to provide him with some. It becomes a corpus of motives 'after stichomancy', that is, after it has been used for divination by selecting from its lines at random. Quietism seems to be what results from this exercise, which would be somewhat ironic if Beckett was still following Schopenhauer's account of it. Schopenhauer gives motives quite a prominent role in *The World as Will and Representation*, and sees them as closely related to willing. Although contact with everything in the world produces motives, Schopenhauer explains that knowledge of the Thing-In-Itself, reality as it really is, produces no motives, and instead acts as *'tranquillizer [Quietiv]* of all willing, from which complete resignation (which is the innermost spirit of both Christian as well as Indian wisdom)' proceeds (*WWR*, I.3.48, 259). 'X' seemingly seeks motives from his horoscope, but then lapses back into quietism—the position of having no motives. In *Murphy*, Celia despairs of such backsliding when she hears Murphy reel off reasons why the horoscope is, after all, counselling him to passivity, at least for the time being. His corpus of motives has quickly become a 'corpus of deterrents' (24), an excuse for maintaining his life of inaction, sitting in his rocking chair, living inside his mind, and 'apperceiving himself into an early grave', in the fond hope that he is somehow not of this world (*Mu*, 15, 3).

Mark Nixon dates the outline of *Murphy* in the *Whoroscope* notebook to the spring of 1935, precisely the time when Beckett was discussing the quietism of Thomas à Kempis with MacGreevy.[4] This might account for the rather blasé German expression 'oder was' added after 'quietism', which could mean 'or something like that' or 'if anything'. As we saw in the last chapter, the letter to MacGreevy marks a moment of deep ambivalence towards quietism on Beckett's part, when he rejected the 'abject self-referring quietism' that emerged from his solipsistic misreading of *The Imitation of Christ*, but still felt drawn to some of its sentiments. The letter constitutes Beckett's dismissal of

---

4 Nixon, p. 55.

that particular oracle, and yet also an admission that he was, on occasions, tempted to approach certain books in this soteriological, even devotional, manner. Beckett had tried to find a 'solution' in the *Imitation*, just as he had approached Schopenhauer's books as a 'justification', Geulincx's as an 'excuse for remaining alive', and Spinoza's as a 'solution & a salvation' (*LSB1*, 257, 33, 319, 371). While not quite seeing each book as 'any old oracle', he was remarkably ecumenical in his search for textual solace and guidance. The 'oder was' also hints at this inclusive approach to quietism, no doubt inspired by Schopenhauer's broad definition of the term. As I have argued, Beckett's quietism was as much literary as it was philosophical, and could come as readily from Leopardi, Epicurus, Hölderlin, Pyrrho, St Teresa, and Goethe.

These aspects of Beckett's personal experiments with quietism seep into the finished novel. Neary, Murphy's former philosophical-cum-spiritual master, is ecumenical to the point of dilettantism. He dabbled in Hindu asceticism 'somewhere north of the Nerbudda', and Murphy duly comes to sit at his feet, a gesture which imitates the name of the Upanishads (*upa* means 'near', *nishad* means 'sitting down').[5] But by the time Murphy submits to Neary's guidance, the master has already moved on to a mystical form of Pythagoreanism, but cannot make up his mind about what to call its highest beatitude: 'When he got sick of calling it the Apmonia he called it the Isonomy. When he got sick of the sound of Isonomy he called it the Attunement' (*Mu*, 4). The narrator's description of 'Neary, at that time a Pythagorean' suggests he has since moved on to newer philosophical pastures. Murphy is also rather fickle with his spiritual and philosophical allegiances, calling on Democritean atomism, Geulincx's Occasionalism, William of Champeaux's 'extreme theophanism' (53), and of course astrology at various points throughout the novel. Such equivocation is the sign, symptom, and source of a restless ambivalence about the feasibility of the philosophical and contemplative life. But the novel's main critique

---

5   Ackerley, *Demented Particulars*, p. 32; Roshen Dalal, *Hinduism: An Alphabetical Guide* (London: Penguin, 2011), p. 429.

of this way of life is less about dilettantism and more about the incommensurability of quietism's 'inner emigration', as J.M. Coetzee calls it,[6] with the need to maintain functioning relationships with other people. This was the primary concern of Beckett's letter about the *Imitation*:

> I isolated myself more & more, undertook less & less & lent myself to a crescendo of disparagement of others & myself. [...] The misery & solitude & apathy & the sneers were the elements of an index of superiority & guaranteed the feeling of arrogant "otherness" (SB to TM, 10/3/35; *LSB1*, 258)

Murphy, begun around about the same time as this letter, can be seen as a dramatization of its worries. The narrator of *The Unnamable* says that Murphy is one of the 'sufferers of my pains' (*U*, 14), and based on the close similarity between the themes of the *Imitation* letter and Murphy's story, it would seem that Beckett would have said the same. Like Beckett, Murphy appears to have internalised much of Thomas à Kempis's advice about the inner life and shorn it of its Christian framework. Thomas advises his reader to flee 'men's fellowship', and 'vain business', in order to 'enter into thy closet, exclude all worldly noise as it is written "Be ye sorry in your chambers"' (*IC*, I.xx, 37). 'Thou shalt,' he adds, 'find there what outside thou shalt ofttimes lose.' On the first page of Beckett's novel, we learn that Murphy has shut himself in his room in West Brompton 'for what might have been six months' and longs to be rid of the various 'sights and sounds' that have 'detained him in the world', particularly the cry of *'Quid pro quo!'* heard in the business of the marketplace below him (3). When Murphy gets to the Magdalen Mental Mercyseat, he is delighted by its padded cells: they are perfect versions of the *Imitation*'s hidden closets, and 'surpassed by far all he had even been able to imagine in the way of indoor bowers of bliss' (113). At several points, Thomas says that the devotee should 'be still' and not 'exceed in words' for in 'silence and quiet the devout soul profiteth' (*IC*, I.xx, 38). Murphy is 'addicted [...] to remaining still for long periods' (*Mu*, 20), as Celia well knows, and

---

6   J. M. Coetzee, *Diary of a Bad Year* (London: Vintage, 2008), p. 12.

he is delighted to discover from his horoscope that silence is one of his 'highest attributes' (22–3). Thomas warns that all 'desires of sensuality' and 'fleshly joy' are snares to be avoided (*IC*, I.xx, 38), and so Murphy, while he loves Celia, still deplores and hates the 'part of him' that 'craved' for her (7). Her voice 'lamented faintly against his flesh' (7). In the *Dream* notebook (86) and in the letter to MacGreevy, Beckett had recorded Thomas à Kempis's 'country of everlasting clearness' (*IC*, III.lxiv, 228), and Murphy seeks to explore a similar inner geography: fed up with his job hunt, he longs to sit quietly and enter 'the first landscape of freedom' which 'lay just beyond the frontiers of suffering' (*Mu*, 51). Thomas counsels against expecting comfort from 'books of doctors' (*IC*, III.lxiv, 228) and tells his reader to cease 'from over-great desire of knowledge' (*IC*, II.ii, 3) and so Murphy, who once slept with a theological tract under his pillow (47), is now a 'strict non-reader' (103). Time and again in the *Imitation*, Thomas à Kempis praises 'innerness' and advises his reader to 'go within' and 'attend to inward things': 'The inward man soon gathereth himself together for he never poureth himself out wholly over outward things' (*IC*, II.i, 61, III.i, 93), 'Ask for thyself a secret place, love to dwell alone with thyself' (III.lviii, 210). Such advice is duly attended to by Murphy when he sits in his rocking chair and lets '[m]ost things under the moon' get 'slower and slower' until they stop altogether. He is 'renouncing all that lay outside the intellectual love in which alone he could love himself' (*Mu*, 8, 112). This sounds a lot like the 'isolationism' that Beckett had adopted, and which turned out to be not a liberation, but rather a 'negation of living'.

In thinking about the antagonism between quietism and sociability, I want to examine the novel in the light of two references that Beckett made while discussing *Murphy* in yet another revealing letter to MacGreevy in July 1936. Here Beckett explains his decision to have the novel 'go on as coolly and finish as briefly as possible' after Murphy's death:

> I chose this because it seemed to me to consist better with the treatment of Murphy throughout, with the mixture of compassion, patience, mockery and "tat twam asi" that I seemed

to have directed on him throughout, with the sympathy going so far and no further (then losing patience) as in the short statement of his mind's fantasy of itself. There seemed to me always the risk of taking him too seriously and separating him too sharply from the others. As it is I do not think the mistake (Aliosha mistake) has been altogether avoided. (SB to TM, 7 July 1936; *LSB1*, 350)

The Sanskrit expression *'tat tvam asi'* means 'thou art that' and was used frequently by Schopenhauer in *The World as Will and Representation* when discussing ethics, metaphysics, and salvation. The 'Aliosha mistake' is a reference to the youngest of Dostoevsky's three *Brothers Karamazov*. Both allusions are important. First, they again suggest the relevance of quietism to the novel. As I mentioned in the last chapter, Schopenhauer was Beckett's main source of quietist thought, while Dostoevsky was, according to Gide, the paradigmatic quietist novelist. But, as I will argue, both references also point towards a version of quietism that is concerned with the lives of others, and with relationship to others, and therefore provide a useful foil to Beckett's 'abject self-referring quietism'. Finally, both references are tacit admissions that Murphy's plight is rooted in Beckett's own experience.

Tat tvam asi

> You do not see *being* here, but it *is* here. This subtle part is what all this has as self. It is truth: it is the self. *You* are that, Svetaketu.
>
> —The Upanishads, Chāndogya 13:2–3[7]

Tat tvam asi (तत् त्वम् असि) is, as Schopenhauer notes, one of the *Mahāvākyas*, or Grand Pronouncements, of Hinduism. It appeared first in the *Chāndogya Upanishad*[8] and has been interpreted by non-dual

---

7   *Upanishads*, trans. by Valerie Roebuck (London: Penguin Classics, 2004), p. 179.
8   David E. Cartwright, *Schopenhauer: A Biography* (Cambridge: Cambridge University Press, 2010), p. 329.

(*advaita*) schools of Hindu Vedanta as referring to the identity of the self—'you', the *ātman*—with the supreme being, ultimate reality, or God—'that', *Brahman*. One corollary of this is that all beings, and perhaps all things, are really one reality. Certainly that seems to be Schopenhauer's reading of the phrase: in *The Two Fundamental Problems of Ethics*, he quotes the formula as an expression of the belief that '[m]y true, inner essence exists in every living thing as immediately as it reveals itself in my self-consciousness to myself alone' and that 'we are all one and the same being'.[9] Schopenhauer believed that this insight into the monistic nature of reality would naturally lead to an eruption of compassion, the same virtue named by Beckett when speaking of Murphy. According to Schopenhauer, the person who is able to say to himself 'you are that' while looking at each and every being that he meets is 'certain of all virtue and bliss, and is on the direct path to redemption' (*WWR*, I.4.66, 401).[10] Schopenhauer quotes the phrase another four times in *The World as Will and Representation* and twice in *On the Basis of Morality* to make much the same point. Gerard Mannion suggests that Schopenhauer admired the phrase because it summarised his ethics and his metaphysics,[11] precisely the two aspects of his philosophy that he said were 'identical' to the matter of quietism (*WWR*, II.4.48, 630). The phrase would serve to counter what Schopenhauer calls 'theoretical egoism', the belief that I am the only real being in the world, and that everyone else is a phantom (*WWR*, I.2.19, 139). As a 'seedy solipsist' Murphy would be particularly prone to this delusion (53), and therefore in need of the sentiments of *tat tvam asi* more than most.

---

9   Arthur Schopenhauer, *The Two Fundamental Problems of Ethics*, trans. by Christopher Janaway (Cambridge: Cambridge University Press, 2009), p. 254.
10 On Schopenhauer's use of this phrase, see Margit Ruffing, 'The Overcoming of the Individual in Schopenhauer's Ethics of Compassion, Illustrated by the Sanskrit Formula of the "Tat Tvam Asi"', in *Understanding Schopenhauer Through the Prism of Indian Culture*, ed. by Arati Barua, Michael Gerhard, and Matthias Koßler (Berlin: Walter de Gruyter, 2013), pp. 97–108.
11 Gerard Mannion, *Schopenhauer, Religion and Morality: The Humble Path to Ethics* (Aldershot: Ashgate Publishing, Ltd., 2003), pp. 199–200.

Like Schopenhauer, Beckett seems to have taken an interest in the Sanskrit formula. He referenced the 'sense of *tat tvam asi*' in his notes on Heinrich Zimmer's *Maya: der Indische Mythos* which he compiled at James Joyce's request in 1937–8.[12] The passage in Zimmer's book that he refers to paraphrases the *Chāndogya Upanishad*:

> In the secret teachings of the Vedas, Aruni told his son Svetaketu to throw a piece of salt into some water, and realize that just as the salt, dissolved in the water, is present throughout, so the finest energy of life pervades in an intangible way all tangible forms, and it is from this finest essence of the universe that the universe is made: "You are that, *tat tvam asi*"— that is, you are not what you appear to yourself to be nor what you seize upon, nor what people usually take their reality and their essence to be. You are not your body, nor the forces of your senses of your spirit with which you reach into the world, nor your soul—in you is something, finer than the finest thing, impalpable as the salt in water, omnipresent, it forms the world: that's what you are.[13]

Beckett also marked up a quotation from the philosopher Jürgen Bona Meyer in the introduction to Frauenstädt's edition of Schopenhauer's complete works, in which *tat tvam asi* is connected to *Mitleid* [compassion or pity], although Meyer argues that the monistic insight would probably foster narcissistic self-pity rather than true altruism.[14] Beckett's copy of Plümacher's *Der Pessimismus* is annotated heavily around her discussion of *Mitleid* in Buddhism,[15] where the following passage appears:

> [The Buddha's] compassion for his household was a driving force behind his moral actions, such as love, friendship and gratitude. All of which can be found in an earlier realisation:

---

12 Thomas E. Connolly, *The Personal Library of James Joyce: A Descriptive Bibliography* (Buffalo, NY: University of Buffalo Studies, 1955), p. 340.
13 Heinrich Zimmer, *Maya der indische Mythos* (Berlin: Deutsche Verlags-Anstalt, 1936), p. 340. My thanks to Jan Wilm for his help with the translation of this German passage and the following one.
14 Nixon and Van Hulle, p. 146.
15 Nixon and Van Hulle, p. 154.

the Brahminical explanation for such feelings was *'tat tvam asi'* (the expression of the essential unity of what appeared to be manifold), which is lacking in Buddhism.[16]

Although Beckett's letter to MacGreevy and indeed the writing of *Murphy* predate his reading of Zimmer, Frauenstädt, and Plümacher, these marginalia demonstrate that, far from being a casual allusion, the invocation of the *'tat tvam asi'* phrase was at the heart of something that Beckett deeply cared about. In Chapter 4, I will argue that he returns to the ethics and metaphysics of *tat tvam asi* with a particularly Buddhist twist in *How It Is*.

Beckett does not simply say that the 'treatment of Murphy throughout the novel' has a been 'a mixture of compassion, patience, mockery and "tat twam asi"' but also adds that this is what 'I seemed to have directed on him throughout' (*LSB1*, 350). In other words, Beckett was able to look at the character of Murphy and say to himself 'you are that'. The letter is, then, an explicit, if somewhat opaque, admission of the autobiographical origins of Murphy's story. Like Murphy, Beckett was an Irishman with solitary, inward tendencies, who had come to London in search of solace for his irrational heart. In the letter to MacGreevy, Beckett claims to find all of his characters 'hateful', including Celia and Murphy, but is nevertheless delighted that MacGreevy thinks them 'lovable' (*LSB1*, 349). Beckett had, of course, found plenty to dislike about himself at the time when he was writing *Murphy* and I suspect that his claimed hatred of the main protagonist stems from this. As the narrator of Paul Valéry's *Monsieur Teste* puts it, 'I have rarely lost sight of myself, I have hated myself, I have adored myself, and so, we have grown old together.'[17] Indeed, even decades later, Murphy still had a presence in Beckett's life. Duncan Scott, a lighting engineer at the Royal Court Theatre, recalls how, in the 1970s, he used to walk through Hyde Park with Beckett, who would point out the locations mentioned in *Murphy*, as if the protagonist 'had been

---

16 Plümacher, p. 25.
17 Paul Valéry, *Monsieur Teste* (Paris: Gallimard, 1946), p. 14.

of flesh and blood' rather than fictional. 'It's Murphy's old haunt,' Beckett would say, 'He used to walk about here a lot. They used to fly kites, but I was here the other day and they don't anymore.'[18]

Murphy's entrance into the Magdalen Mental Mercyseat (MMM) was based on Beckett's own experience walking around the wards of the Bethlem Royal Hospital in south London, the original 'Bedlam' no less. Beckett's friend and former heart doctor Geoffrey Thompson worked as an orderly at Bethlem Royal while he was re-training to be a psychoanalyst and allowed Beckett to accompany him on rounds in September 1935 (SB to TM, [22/9/35]; *LSB1*, 277, 280). It is possible that Beckett was prompted to go to the hospital by the example of Schopenhauer, who, according to the 1929 *Encyclopaedia Britannica*, used 'to visit the Hospital La Charité', a hospital in Berlin with a 'melancholy ward', 'and study the evidence it afforded of the interdependence of the moral and the physical in man', particularly when he was feeling 'lonely and unhappy'.[19] Thompson's wife Ursula recalls that Beckett had a similar reaction to the patients as Murphy: 'Sam was curious, interested in the patients,' she said. 'He regarded himself as a bit of a "loony" and wanted to see the other "loonies"!'[20] These comments suggest that the *tat tvam asi* of *Murphy* cuts two ways: it points not just to the autobiographical origins of Murphy's experience, but also to what both creator and character felt they had in common with the patients they observed. Certainly, in the finished novel, it is Murphy's sense of unity and communality with the patients that proves a pivotal turning point in the story, and in the novel's treatment of quietism.

---

18 Knowlson and Knowlson, p. 70.
19 William Wallace, 'Schopenhauer', ed. by J.L. Garvin, *The Encyclopædia Britannica: A new survey of universal knowledge* (London: The Encyclopædia Britannica Company, Ltd., 1929), 102–4 (p. 102); see also Cartwright, *Schopenhauer: A Biography*, pp. 177–8.
20 Knowlson and Knowlson, p. 72.

The Alyosha Mistake

> even one novel may, perhaps, be unwarranted for such a humble and indefinite hero
>
> —The 'author' in *The Brothers Karamazov*, by Fyodor Dostoevsky[21]

In his preface to the most recent Faber edition of *Murphy*, J.C.C. Mays discusses Beckett's reference to the 'Aliosha mistake' and points out how the novel's projected title—'Sasha Murphy'—is another indication of Murphy's connection to the youngest Karamazov brother: Sasha and Alyosha are both diminutives of Alexei or Alexander. Mays interprets the 'Aliosha mistake' to mean that Beckett felt he had failed 'to bring discordant emotions into line' in the novel.[22] But if Beckett was reading Dostoevsky at Gide's prompting, such a mess of discordant feelings would hardly have constituted a mistake. As I discuss in the next chapter, the capacity to accommodate discord and contradiction was integral to the 'quietist' aesthetic that Gide drew from Dostoevsky, and which Beckett tried to adopt, first in *Dream of Fair to Middling Women* and later, more thoroughly, in *Molloy*. It is more likely that the 'Aliosha mistake' refers to Beckett's worry that Murphy was treated too differently to the other characters. 'There seemed to me always the risk of taking him too seriously and separating him too sharply from the others,' Beckett told MacGreevy (*LSB1*, 350). It is clear to any reader of *The Brothers Karamazov* that Alyosha is a somewhat different being to the people around him. Gide says that Alyosha and his saintly teacher Elder Zosima are 'angelic beings' who, together with Prince Myshkin of *The Idiot*, are the characters who 'best embody Dostoevsky's thinking, or rather, his ethic' (*Dost*, 227). Similarly, Murphy is, according to the narrator, the only character in the book 'who is not a puppet' (*Mu*, 78).

Valentina Vetlovskaya's essay on the 'hagiographic' treatment of Alyosha Karamazov is helpful here. She points out that whereas

---

21 Fyodor Dostoevsky, *The Brothers Karamazov*, trans. by Richard Pevear and Larissa Volokhonsky (London: Vintage, 2004), p. 4.
22 Mays, 'Preface', p. xv.

Dmitri and Ivan Karamazov are introduced to the reader as secondary events in the life of Fyodor Pavlovich in chapters entitled 'He Gets Rid of His Eldest Son' and 'The Second Marriage and the Second Family', Alyosha's chapter title 'The Third Son, Alyosha' clearly demonstrates the preferential treatment he is receiving from the narrator, if not from his father. Vetlovskaya likens the narration of Alyosha's life to the hagiographies of the Eastern Church, in particular the stories of the Orthodox saint Aleksey, Man of God, to whom Alyosha is often compared. Like books in that genre, Alyosha's story is one of youthful piety, idiosyncratic virtue, and a struggle between light and dark, between heaven and earth. Vetlovskaya explains that the hero of a hagiographic *vita* is deemed eccentric by those around him, and so Dostoevsky gives Alyosha a number of unique qualities to make him stand out from the other characters. In many scenes he is completely passive, listening patiently to the paranoid and deluded ravings of Dmitri, or his father, or Madame Khokhlakov. He is frequently described as humble, kind, pensive, charmingly naïve, prone to seclusion, indifferent to money, and remarkably chaste.[23] Such strangeness marks him out as a kind of 'holy fool', an important character trope which, as Harriet Murav has shown, recurs across Dostoevsky's work.[24] His spiritual director, Elder Zosima, dubs him 'my quiet one', while others refer to him an 'ascetic' or a 'mystic'.[25]

Dostoevsky's hagiography is not, however, a simple whitewashing of his protagonist's life story. If Beckett felt he was making the 'Aliosha mistake' with Murphy, there might have been ways in which he also learnt from Dostoevsky's treatment of his hero. Richard Pevear thinks that Dostoevsky was aware that Alyosha was a rather 'slight' and 'unrealized' character, and that he even wanted the reader

---

[23] Valentina Vetlovskaya, 'Alyosha Karamazov and the Hagiographic Hero', in *Dostoevsky: New Perspectives*, ed. by Robert Louis Jackson, trans. by Nancy Pollack and Susanne Fusso (Englewood Cliffs, NJ: Prentice-Hall, 1984), pp. 206–26 (p. 209).

[24] Harriet Murav, *Holy Foolishness: Dostoevsky's Novels & the Poetics of Cultural Critique* (Stanford, CA: Stanford University Press, 1992).

[25] Dostoevsky, pp. 284, 355, 553.

of *The Brothers Karamazov* to laugh at its saintly hero.[26] Even though the narrator is warmly disposed towards Alyosha, he feels the need to fend off criticism about his interest in the character on the very first page of the novel:

> I myself know that he is by no means a great man, so that I can foresee the inevitable questions, such as: What is notable about your Alexei Fyodorovich that you should choose him for your hero? What has he really done? To whom is he known, and for what? Why should I, the reader, spend my time studying the facts of his life?[27]

The novelist is aware of the absurdity of making such an 'indefinite, indeterminate sort' of man into the 'hero' of the book in which he does very little. Celia's grandfather, Mr Kelly, asks similar questions about why we should care about Murphy:

> Who is this Murphy [...] for whom you have been neglecting your work, as I presume? What is he? Where does he come from? What is his family? What does he do? Has he any money? Has he any prospects? He has any retrospects? Is he, has he, anything at all? (*Mu*, 13)

Vetlovskaya also notes that Dostoevsky's hagiographic form permits certain doubts about Alyosha's piety to rise to the surface as part of that struggle between the light and the dark. In particular, his love for Elder Zosima is subjected to criticism:

> there stood before him the person, and only the person—the person of his beloved elder, the person of that righteous man whom he revered to the point of adoration. That was just it,

---

26 Richard Pevear, 'Introduction', in *The Brothers Karamazov*, by Fyodor Dostoevsky, trans. by Richard Pevear and Larissa Volokhonsky (London: Vintage, 2004), pp. xi–xviii (p. xiii).
27 Dostoevsky, p. 3.

that the entirety of the love for "all and all" that lay hidden in his young and pure heart, then and during the whole previous year, was at times as if wholly concentrated, perhaps even incorrectly, mainly on just one being, at least in the strongest impulses of his heart—on his beloved elder, now deceased. True, this being had stood before him as an indisputable ideal for so long that all his youthful powers and all their yearning could not but turn to this ideal exclusively, in some moments even to the forgetting of "all and all".[28]

Vetlovskaya says that the narrator is 'both justifying and condemning Alyosha'.[29] Similarly, Beckett hoped that he treated Murphy with both 'sympathy' and 'mockery'. In *Murphy*, the narrator is responsible for meting out both sentiments, in a role which, as John Bolin argues, has been largely overlooked by readers of the novel. While many critics have taken *Murphy* to be an early flirtation with realism on Beckett's part, Bolin demonstrates that any pretensions to realism are undercut by the meta-fictional role played by the narrator. 'Beckett's speaker,' Bolin writes, 'frequently interferes with the diegesis, using a mixture of deliberate clichés, ironic reflections on literary texts and devices, and references to censors, the reader, or other novels to emphasize *Murphy*'s status as a textual construct'.[30]

While Bolin proposes that the narrators of André Gide's novels provide the most likely template for what Beckett does in *Murphy*, particularly the narrator of *Les Caves du Vatican*, it is possible, given his comment about Murphy and Alyosha, that Beckett also had in mind Dostoevsky's narrators, many of whom interfere in their novels in similar ways. As Gene M. Moore has argued, the narrator of *Demons*, which Beckett read in that 'foul translation' as *Les Possédés*, aspires to be an impartial chronicler, but really is anything but.[31] Like the narrator of *Murphy*, he allows himself several asides and humorous quips at

---

28 Dostoevsky, p. 338.
29 Vetlovskaya, p. 223.
30 Bolin, p. 46.
31 Gene M. Moore, 'The Voices of Legion: The Narrator of *The Possessed*', *Dostoevsky Studies*, 6 (1985), 51–65.

the expense of the characters.[32] In *The Brothers Karamazov* the narrator also occupies a prominent role, and repeatedly points out that he is writing a novel, while also maintaining that its events happened in 'our town'. He often uses asides to the reader to contradict or undercut the wishful thinking of his characters, such as when Dmitri rides to Volovya hoping to secure a loan that will end his troubles: 'So Mitya dreamed, with a sinking soul, but, alas, his dreams were not at all destined to come true according to his "plan".'[33] The narrator of *Murphy* does a similar thing, albeit often less kindly than his equivalent in *The Brothers Karamazov*. When Miss Carridge imaginatively reconstructs the death of the old boy upstairs in her conversation with Celia, the narrator interjects with 'A lie' after each of her forensic fantasies (*Mu*, 91). This escalates quickly into 'Lies' and then 'Pronounced on the analogy of manure'. Another interjection comes when Murphy informs Ticklepenny that he is indifferent as to whether or not he stays at the MMM: the narrator adds 'He was mistaken' (*Mu*, 104).

Beckett's narrator is particularly keen to subject Murphy's quietist aspirations to comic scrutiny, just as Alyosha's spiritual excesses prompted doubts from the narrator of *The Brothers Karamazov*. After telling the reader of the 'disharmony' between Murphy's mind and the starry heaven above (the only 'canons' in which he has the least confidence), the narrator adds, 'So much the worse for him, no doubt' (50). In Chapter 6, the narrator wryly notes that his description of Murphy's mind is not concerned with 'this apparatus as it really was [...] but solely with what it felt and pictured itself to be' (*Mu*, 69). The deluded picture, the narrator explains, was one of 'a large hollow sphere, hermetically closed to the universe without' (69). The picture, taken as truth, becomes another 'force to be obeyed', and Murphy seeks out solitude because he sees this as his natural condition. Beckett's own experiments with quietism led to similarly dangerous self-fulfilling assumptions: inwardness all too easily 'guaranteed' aloofness.

---

32 Richard Pevear, 'Foreword', in *Demons*, by Fyodor Dostoevsky, trans. by Richard Pevear and Larissa Volokhonsky (London: Vintage, 1994), pp. vii–xxiii.

33 Dostoevsky, p. 374.

The narrator voices Beckett's newfound scepticism of that earlier attitude, caricatured in Murphy. But at other times, the mockery softens and that sense of compassion and sympathy that Beckett mentioned is allowed to come through. Take this description of Murphy's rare glimpses of salvation:

> The freedom of indifference, the indifference of freedom, the will dust in the dust of its object, the act a handful of sand let fall—these were some of the shapes he had sighted, sunset landfall after many days. (67)

The phrase 'sunset landfall after many days' is both beautiful and moving, with its implication that Murphy has endured a long and largely fruitless voyage in search of what matters most to him. There is no mockery from the narrator here. Rather, it is a respectful recognition of the small success he has had in his spiritual quest. The metaphor calls to mind Thomas à Kempis's equally beautiful description of 'the coasts of peace and quiet' (*IC*, III.xxv, 147). It anticipates Molloy's unadventurous Geulingian Odyssey and the psycho-spiritual geography imagined and celebrated in Beckett's 1947 poem 'bon bon il est un pays'.[34] In *Dream of Fair to Middling Women*, Beckett had hidden his admiration for such sentiments, dismissing the *Imitation*'s '*Per viam pacis ad patrium perpetuæ claritatis*' as 'horrid Latin', and making fun of its lofty ideal: 'Can you beat it?' (178). But in the letter to MacGreevy, he praised the same phrase as 'lovely', and cited it as one of the many that 'seemed to be made for me' (*LSB1*, 257). This change in attitude is just one of the signs that Murphy, unlike Belacqua, is to be treated with a compassion and sympathy, even as the narrator sustains his criticism of Murphy's inwardness. If *The Brothers Karamazov* was, as I have proposed, one of the sources of this critical and sympathetic attitude, then the 'Aliosha mistake' was also a lesson well-heeded.

---

34 Ackerley, 'The Roots of Quietism', p. 89.

Luciferian Concentration

> Neither shall they say, Lo here! or, lo there! for, behold, the kingdom of God is within you.
>
> —Luke 17:21, King James Version

In the *Imitation* letter, Beckett tells MacGreevy that his solipsistic reading of Thomas à Kempis's book 'could be made [to] subserve the "Sin" of Luciferian concentration' (10/3/35; *LSB1*, 257). Beckett does not explain what he means by the curious expression 'Luciferian concentration', but he provides a clue later in the letter when he mentions that he has been reading Goethe's autobiography, *Dichtung und Wahrheit*. He tells MacGreevy that he has 'got to the Strassberg [i.e. Strasburg] period & contact with Herder' (*LSB1*, 260). Goethe relates his move to Strasburg in the Ninth Book, just after a theological interlude in the Eighth Book which mentions Lucifer in some detail. Goethe explains how the Christian Trinity of three persons is a necessary corollary of the Godhead's self-producing activity, and how Lucifer, a lesser 'bounded' being, subsequently emerged from these three persons. Lucifer then created the angels, fashioned in his own likeness, and '[s]urrounded by such a glory he forgot his higher origin, and believed that he could find himself in himself'.[35] Goethe says that Lucifer 'concentrated himself within himself', and the pain of this isolation led to his rebellion against God and the fall of the angels. This same situation was then replicated in human beings who, like Lucifer, are both perfect and imperfect, both unlimited and bounded by God. The original German text has Goethe's own coinages of 'uns zu verselbsten' for concentrate and 'uns zu entselbstigen' for its opposite, 'to expand'—literally 'to self' and 'to unself'.[36] The classic English translation of *Dichtung und Wahrheit* by John Oxenford, with an introduction by Thomas Carlyle, plumps for 'concentrate', as Beckett seems to have done (and perhaps he was reading the German text side by side with

---

35 Goethe, I, p. 291.
36 Ronald D. Gray, *Goethe: A Critical Introduction* (Cambridge: Cambridge University Press, 1967), p. 103.

the English). The reference to Goethe further indicates how Beckett's 'abject self-referring quietism' was a perversion of quietism's true aims. 'Unselfing' is central to the process of abandonment and surrender in all quietist schools, and in Schopenhauer's version it is of the utmost importance for bringing about compassion towards others.

Murphy's retreat into his mind makes him guilty of the same sin of Luciferian concentration. Chapter 6 begins with the epigraph *'Amor intellectualis quo murphy se ipsum amat'* [the intellectual love with which Murphy loves himself] (69). As Ackerley notes, this is a subversion of Spinoza's description of God's self-love, taken from Windelband's *History of Philosophy*.[37] In *Spinoza et ses contemporains*, which Beckett later borrowed from Brian Coffey,[38] Léon Brunschvicg glosses the *amor intellectualis* phrase and explains that 'the intellectual love of the mind towards God is part of the infinite love with which God loves himself'.[39] Like Goethe's Lucifer, however, Murphy chooses to short-circuit his intellectual love and direct it not towards God, but rather towards himself. He follows Thomas à Kempis's instructions to enter into himself with 'all things being voided and left' (*IC*, II.viii, 76), by shutting out the sights and sounds of the world, but instead of Thomas's goal of being united with God, Murphy finds 'only Murphy himself' (67). One model for Murphy's inwardness is Valéry's Monsieur Teste, as J.D. O'Hara has argued.[40] Like Murphy, Teste lives inside his mind, spurns reading, and spends much of his time sitting in a chair. But his wife Émilie worries about what he will encounter in his inner explorations. 'Will it be God,' she wonders, 'or some dreadful sense of meeting, in the very depths of thought, nothing but the pale rays of his own miserable matter?'[41] Beckett's twisting of the *Imitation* caused him to meet his own 'feathers or entrails', and likewise, Murphy meets only the 'beatific idols of his cave' (*Mu*, 112), Francis Bacon's

---

37 Ackerley, *Demented Particulars*, p. 116.
38 Nixon and Van Hulle, pp. 132–3.
39 Quoted and translated in Ackerley, *Demented Particulars*, p. 116.
40 J.D. O'Hara, 'Beckett Backs Down: From Home to *Murphy* via Valéry', *Journal of Beckett Studies*, 3 (1994), 37–55.
41 Valéry, p. 41.

term for any delusion that is born of a person's character and personality.⁴² To adopt the language of Beckett's letter, Murphy has replaced 'a principle of faith, absolute & infinite, by one personal & finite of fact' (*LSB1*, 258). And it was this, according to Beckett, that led to a 'very baroque solipsism'. Thomas à Kempis actually warns his reader of such dangers: 'If thou seek Jesu in all things, thou shalt find Jesu; and if thou seek thyself, thou shalt find thyself but—to thine own harm' (*IC*, II.vi, 74). In *Dream*, Belacqua is described as 'the lover of the Belacqua Jesus and a very inward man' (63). This is a perversion of Thomas's saintly ideal (*IC*, II.i., 61), in which the self has once again usurped the place of divinity.

Chapter 6 (of thirteen), where the *amor intellectualis* quotation appears, deals with Murphy's mind and is anomalous enough for the narrator to apologise for it: it is an 'unfortunate', even 'painful' exercise (69, 72). Given Murphy's connection to Alyosha, it is worth noting that Book 6 (out of twelve plus an epilogue) of *The Brothers Karamazov* is also a departure from the novel form: the narrative is suspended in order to insert Alyosha's transcriptions of Elder Zosima's life story, and some of the homilies that the saintly man gave at the monastery. Dostoevsky's narrator is also rather apologetic for this section of the novel and says that he will limit himself 'to the elder's story according to the manuscript' of Alyosha, rather than recounting all the details of how he gleaned the facts from conversations with the elder himself. Like Beckett's narrator describing Murphy's mind as it pictured itself to be, he chooses to reproduce a representation rather than pursue the facts. Dostoevsky's narrator hopes that it will be 'shorter and not so tedious' this way.⁴³

The parallel between Beckett's Chapter 6 and Dostoevsky's Book 6 becomes more compelling when we consider that Murphy's mind has a Dostoevskian provenance. According to Gide, Dostoevsky created characters whose minds were divided into three regions. There is the realm of the intellect, the realm of the passions, and then 'a

---

42 Ackerley, *Demented Particulars*, p. 157.
43 Dostoevsky, p. 286.

deeper region, undisturbed by passion'. This third realm can only be reached by mystical means: we must undergo a 'second birth' to get there (*Dost*, 192). 'This region is not at all the soul's hell,' Gide adds, 'but rather its heaven' (216). Murphy similarly has three 'zones of his private world', 'light, half light, dark, each with its speciality' (*Mu*, 71–2). John Bolin points out this parallel[44] and says that while the first two of Murphy's zones do not map on to Gide's, the third zone—the dark—would seem to correspond to the deepest region in *Dostoïevsky*, which Gide describes as 'beyond hate and love', a region

> which is not the region of love, which passion does not reach, and which is at the same time a region so easy and so simple to reach, the very same one, it seems to me, that Schopenhauer spoke of, where all feelings of human solidarity meet, the region where the limits of being fade away, where the sense of the individual and the sense of time are lost, the plane where Dostoevsky sought—and found—the secret of happiness. (*Dost*, 212–3)

The fading of individual consciousness and the movement beyond love and hate are also present in Murphy's third region:

> The third, the dark, was a flux of forms […] nothing but forms becoming and crumbling into the fragments of a new becoming, without love or hate or any intelligible principle of change. Here there was nothing but commotion and the pure forms of commotion. Here he was not free, but a mote in the dark of absolute freedom. (*Mu*, 72)

The Schopenhauerian connection is made further down the page when Murphy's dark is described as 'the will-lessness', a common expression of the quietist attitude found in *The World as Will and Representation*.

---

44 Bolin, p. 44.

Despite being influenced by Gide's *Dostoïevsky*, Murphy's third zone in Chapter 6 would come under attack by the vision of Christian brotherly love put forth in Book 6 of *The Brothers Karamazov*. In the second chapter of Alyosha's transcription of Zosima's autobiography, the elder recalls how shortly before entering monastic life he met Mikhail, a man ridden with guilt for a murder he committed fourteen years ago and for which he has never been charged. Mikhail turned to philanthropy to assuage his soul but remained haunted by the memory of his crime and his need to make amends. He speaks passionately about his belief that the Kingdom of Heaven promised by the gospels is discoverable in this life—"'Paradise,' he said, 'is hidden in each one of us, it is concealed within me, too, right now'"— but rather than going inward, as Murphy does, Mikhail discovers this immanent paradise through communion with others:

> This is a matter of the soul, a psychological matter. In order to make the world over anew, people themselves must turn onto a different path psychically. Until one has indeed become the brother of all, there will be no brotherhood. [...] For everyone now strives most of all to separate his person, wishing to experience the fullness of life within himself, and yet what comes of all his efforts is not the fullness of life but full suicide, for instead of the fullness of self-definition, they fall into complete isolation. For all men in our age are separated into units, each seeks seclusion in his own hole, each withdraws from the others, hides himself, and hides what he has, and ends by pushing himself away from people and pushing people away from himself.[45]

This paragraph could easily stand as a critique of Murphy's seedy solipsism, and indeed that abject self-referring quietism that Beckett told MacGreevy he had drawn from *The Imitation of Christ* in the early 1930s, and then later rejected once he realised the deleterious effects it was having on his ability to connect with other people. Mikhail goes on to

---

45   Dostoevsky, p. 303.

discuss the isolation that arises from the pursuit of material wealth, but Dostoevsky momentarily allows the criticism to sting whatever form of self-absorption that the reader can bring to mind. Murphy, despite his distaste for earning money, would be certainly guilty of the mistake of trying to live 'in his own hole', withdrawn from others. He has not inherited the 'human solidarity' aspect of Gide's third region of mind, which, despite being somehow 'beyond' love and hate, is not amoral. Rather, as Gide later explains, it brings about the knowledge of the essential unity between all human beings. This point is illustrated by a long quotation from *The World as Will and Representation*, in which Schopenhauer describes how, given that all that really exists is the monistic Will, a torturer and tortured are in truth one flesh. We should, therefore, refrain from harming others: to do so would merely be harming ourselves. This motivation for ethical behaviour appears just before Schopenhauer's discussion of *tat tvam asi*. Gide also points out that once Alyosha and Prince Myshkin have tasted the third region of mind, 'this superior state' (227), they are obliged to turn outwards and care for others. Harriet Murav has argued that both characters are examples of the 'holy fool' and that Dostoevsky uses them to negotiate between 'two epochs: the present age of isolation and the future community of brotherly love'.[46] The holy fool's self-abnegation, she says, is the seed of a 'self-sacrificing love of others'. But again, this is what Murphy seems to lack in Chapter 6. His love is, as David Tucker comments, entirely 'self-regarding', even masturbatory.[47] Whereas Gide talked about the fading of the edges of individuality, Murphy instead becomes a 'mote'—that is, a tiny speck. He has concentrated himself, in the Luciferian fashion, rather than expanding his being outward, dissolving, and unselfing in the way that Schopenhauer, Goethe, Gide, and Dostoevsky advocate.

---

46 Murav, p. 160.
47 Tucker, p. 54.

The Need for Brotherhood

Beckett was explicit about the centrality of the tension between sociability and solitude in *Murphy*. In another letter to MacGreevy, he said that the novel was a 'break down' between two positions: the *ubi nihil vales ibi nihil velis* of Geulincx, and the phrase from André Malraux's *La Condition humaine* quoted just before Murphy enters the MMM in Chapter 9: 'Il est difficile à celui qui vit hors du monde de ne pas rechercher les siens' [It is difficult for he who lives outside the world not to seek his own kind]. The Geulincx was the 'position' while the Malraux was the 'negation', according to Beckett (SB to TM, 16/1/36; *LSB1*, 299). As I mentioned in Chapter 1, Beckett would soon come to see that Geulincx's formula was not quite as inward as he had thought from his initial discovery of it in Windelband's *History of Philosophy*. But at this point, before his Geulincx research had properly begun, the formula served as a rallying cry for Murphy's retreat into the little world:

> His vote was cast. 'I am not of the big world, I am of the little world' was an old refrain with Murphy, and a conviction, two convictions, the negative first. How should he tolerate, let alone cultivate, the occasions of fiasco, having once beheld the beatific idols of his cave? In the beautiful Belgo-Latin of Arnold Geulincx: *Ubi nihil vales, ibi nihil velis*. (*Mu*, 112)

This allegiance was struck in the *Whoroscope* notebook, where Beckett had written: 'Murphy: "I am not of the big world, I am of the little world: ubi nihil vales, ibi nihil velis (I quote from memory) & inversely' (UoR MS3000, 8r). The negation is the quotation from Malraux, albeit completely amputated, as Nixon notes,[48] from its context in the novel, where it refers to how Tchen, an activist, finds it difficult to remain on his own, as he must do in order to avoid detection, while planning a suicide attack. For Murphy, the difficulty is in resisting the company of other people, 'les siens', who, like him, seem to relish the life inside

---

48 Nixon, p. 56.

the mind. The Malraux quotation appears in the novel just as Murphy enters the MMM, where he will discover a new sense of *'tat tvam asi'* and a much-needed corrective to his solipsistic quietism.

Neary had trained in Hindu asceticism and Murphy collects his horoscope from another Hindu, Ramaswami Krishnaswami Narayanaswami Suk, a 'swami', 'jossy', and 'Genethliac' (16, 19, 22). But the novel's sense of *tat tvam asi* exists quite separately from the teachings of these two rather dubious gurus. The spirit of the Sanskrit expression is most noticeable in the way that Murphy reacts to the patients at the MMM. After being introduced to various melancholics, paranoids, hebephrenics, and schizoids, Murphy finds that they are 'not at all the terrifying monsters that might have been imagined from Ticklepenny's account' (105–6). Rather, he discovers that the 'most easily identifiable of his immediate feelings were respect and unworthiness' (*Mu*, 106). This is because he believes that the patients are holy fools, idiot savants, even unknowing quietists:

> the impression he received was of that self-immersed indifference to the contingencies of the contingent world which he had chosen for himself as the only felicity and achieved so seldom. (*Mu*, 106)

The word 'indifference' here points to the 'holy indifference'—*sancta adiaphora*—of the Christian Quietists, as well as Schopenhauer's remarks about the ascetic's 'perfect indifference towards all worldly things' (*WWR*, I.4.68, 413). In his philosophy notes, Beckett records how the Epicureans took up Aristotle's belief that the world was contingent, so that they could set the 'sage's self-determination' against it, just as Murphy believes the patients are doing (TCD MS10967, 125r). Adam Potkay compares Murphy's view of the patients to Jonathan Swift's description of Epicurean happiness in *A Tale of a Tub*: 'This is the sublime and refined point of felicity called *the possession of being well deceived*; the serene peaceful state of being a fool among knaves.'⁴⁹ Beckett had borrowed Swift's words in his story 'Echo's Bones'.⁵⁰ Swift thinks that Epicurus has his 'present undoubted successors in the *academy* of *modern Bedlam*',⁵¹ and as we shall see, Murphy is indeed 'well deceived' about his new friends in that very hospital. Murphy's assessment of the patients also recalls Thomas à Kempis's advice not to be 'busy caring of things that are contingently to come' (*IC*, III.xxxv, 160).

The patients are inured to the vicissitudes of the 'big world' in a way that Murphy can only dream of. Unsurprisingly, the only patient that he cannot get on with is the 'manic' because he seemed 'like an epitome of all the self-made plutolaters' (*Mu*, 106): a worshipper of Mammon, and therefore no friend to Murphy who had long refused Celia's attempts to cast him into the 'mercantile gehenna' (*Mu*, 27). Leaving the manic aside, however, Murphy seems happy to say *tat tvam asi* to himself as he regards the patients: he believes 'that they felt in him what they had been and he in them what he would be' (115) and experiences a 'vicarious autology' when contemplating them (118). Where the medical staff only see a 'private dungheap' (111) in the patients' self-immersion, Murphy sees 'his own little dungeon in Spain' (113). Ackerley suspects Beckett was reworking the proverbial 'castles in Spain', meaning an unattainable goal because Spain (it was said) has no castles.⁵² Spain does, however, have dungeons, and they housed several Quietist mystics persecuted by the church, as William Inge recounts:⁵³

---

49 Jonathan Swift, *A Tale of a Tub and Other Works*, ed. by Angus Ross and David Woolley (Oxford: Oxford University Press, 2008), p. 84; Adam Potkay, *The Story of Joy: From the Bible to Late Romanticism* (Cambridge: Cambridge University Press, 2007), p. 24.
50 Samuel Beckett, *Echo's Bones*, ed. by Mark Nixon (London: Faber and Faber, 2014), p. 9.
51 Swift, p. 80.
52 Ackerley, *Demented Particulars*, p. 159.
53 Feldman, 'Agnostic Quietism', p. 189.

> Louis de Leon, who had the courage to say that the Song of Solomon is only a pastoral idyll, was sent to a dungeon for five years. Even St. Teresa narrowly escaped imprisonment at Seville; and St. Juan of the Cross passed nine months in a black hole at Toledo. [...] Molinos ended his days in a dungeon. (*CM*, 217, 234)

For St John at least, the dungeon was a place of intense spiritual revelation, a 'little world' that opened up something far greater than what lay outside the cell. The narrator of *Murphy* insists that he chooses to describe the MMM in 'the terms and orientation of church architecture' out of 'purely descriptive convenience', but the parallel sticks, especially since the single rooms are dubbed 'cells' and then, in a biblically and heavenly fashion, 'mansions' (*Mu*, 105). Such vocabulary suggests the narrator's irrepressible sympathy for Murphy: choosing to follow him, at least part of the way, into his fantasy of the MMM as a community of contemplatives and holy fools.

Sympathy is also noticeable when the narrator says that Murphy was happy to start his work at the MMM straight away, because he 'was only too anxious to test his striking impression that here was the race of people he had long since despaired of finding' (*Mu*, 106). The narrator does not attempt to undercut Murphy's anxiety, despair, or impatience with a snide remark. The phrase that follows next—'Also he wanted Ticklepenny to be free to rig up his fire'—is funny, but it is not a joke at Murphy's expense. Rather, it softens the edges of his zeal for the inner life, by reminding us of his lingering and understandable need for earthly comforts. Similarly, when Murphy is 'silently commended' by Bom Clinch 'for his skill in handling the patients themselves, whose names and more flagrant peculiarities he had fully co-ordinated by the end of the six hours, what he might expect from them and what never hope' (*Mu*, 108), the narrator leaves it at that and the paragraph ends. The recognition of Murphy's achievement with the patients—itself born of a sympathetic attitude—is allowed to stand unimpeded. A significant moment in the novel's negotiation between narratorial mockery and narratorial compassion comes in the following passage:

> He would not have admitted that he needed a brotherhood. He did. In the presence of this issue (psychiatric-psychotic) between the life from which he had turned away and the life of which he had no experience, except as he hoped inchoately in himself, he could not fail to side with the latter. His first impressions (always the best), hope of better things, feeling of kindred, etc., had been in that sense. Nothing remained but to substantiate these, distorting all that threatened to belie them. It was strenuous work, but very pleasant. (*Mu*, 111)

The two-word sentence 'He did' recalls the narrator's dismissive contradiction 'A lie', which was meted out to Miss Carridge (91) and Ticklepenny (109), but here the tone is kinder: there is a concern for Murphy's needs. This need for 'brotherhood'—for 'les siens' of Malraux—is precisely what Beckett ignored in his own personal experiments with quietism, when the words of the *Imitation* 'conduced' to that not-so-splendid 'isolationism'. Treating Murphy with *tat tvam asi* allows Beckett to be sympathetic to his mistakes. The narrator remains outspokenly critical of the wilful error, through the sarcastic 'always the best' and the explicit warning that Murphy is 'distorting' the facts to see what he wants to see, but Murphy's motivations—'the hope of better things, feeling of kindred'—are written sincerely enough that the error seems almost understandable. The narrator's Dostoevskian disagreements continue throughout the chapter, as he expressly states that Murphy has 'lovingly simplified and perverted' the issues at hand, and 'disregarded or muted' anything that threatened his fantasy (112–3). And yet, this chapter also describes Murphy's aspirations in the fullest detail and gives him credit for his 'scandalous' success in working with the patients, who see him as one of their own and are more biddable under his watch than with any other member of staff. Even if Murphy has wilfully perverted and distorted the true nature of the patients' mental life, his willingness to treat them with respect has allowed him to 'bridge the gulf' in a meaningful and beneficial way.

Murphy's greatest admiration is saved for Mr Endon, whose name, as many critics have pointed out, derives from the Greek word for 'within' or 'inside' and which therefore makes him a man of the 'little world' as Murphy aspires to be. He is a 'very inward man' in Thomas à Kempis's sense. In keeping with the sentiments of Schopenhauer's *tat tvam asi*, Murphy feels 'most profoundly one in spirit' with this new friend (115). The narrator tells us that Mr Endon's psychosis was 'so limpid and imperturbable that Murphy felt drawn to it as Narcissus to his fountain' (116). Again, the quietist vocabulary is noticeable here: 'imperturbability' was Windelband's favoured way of rendering the Hellenistic philosophers' *ataraxia* in English.[54] In his philosophy notes Beckett duly records of the Epicureans: 'Joy spiritual not physical. Imperturbability' (TCD MS10967, 119r). Later on he writes:

> Epicureans, Stoics & Sceptics are at one in praising <u>imperturbability, ataraxy, independence of the world</u>, as most prominent characteristics of the wise man. (TCD MS10967, 120r)

The comparison of Murphy with Narcissus does little to cast him as wise, but it does suggest that he identifies—in the sense of *tat tvam asi*—with Mr Endon, as if he were his own reflection.

Schopenhauer had used the Sanskrit phrase amid his discussion of Hinduism and Buddhism, and appropriately enough, Mr Endon appears to Murphy as the third and most revered Asian holy man of the novel:

> Mr. Endon, an impeccable and brilliant figurine in his scarlet gown, his crest a gush of vivid white against the black shag, squatted tailor-fashion on the head of his bed, holding his left foot in his right hand and in his left hand his right foot. (*Mu*, 150)

---

54 Windelband, pp. 116, 165, 167.

Endon sits—apparently radiant and without sin—in the lotus position of a Buddhist monk. The allusion is made clear when we turn to the *Whoroscope* notebook where Beckett had recorded:

> squatting lotus-fashion
>
> ---
>
> "hik!" followed by "phat" ritual ejaculations whereby the spirit of the dying leaves the body by hole in skull (very important) pronounced by lamas, or by dying man himself if he has the science
> suicide by hik! phat! (UoR MS3000, 77v)

These notes correspond to passages in Alexandra David-Neel's travel memoir *With Mystics and Magicians in Tibet*, which Beckett seems to have read in the English translation of 1931.[55] The first quotation is based on the following passage from David-Neel's book:

> As for Dawasandup, who was often present, he squatted tailor fashion (in the East they say "like a lotus") at our feet and his bowl, placed upon the rug, had neither cover nor saucer.[56]

Mr Endon's scarlet gown may derive from the red robes of Tibetan monks or the 'garnet-coloured toga' of the prince who appears in the same scene with Dawasandup. David-Neel describes how one of the lamas advises her to 'blot out the mirage of the imaginary world' in order to 'liberate one's mind from fanciful beliefs' and attain enlightenment.[57] Seeing that Mr Endon has done the blotting out, Murphy assumes, quite wrongly, that the rest has followed.

---

55 Alexandra David-Neel, *With Mystics and Magicians in Tibet* (London: Penguin, 1931), pp. 20–21.
56 David-Neel, p. 28.
57 David-Neel, p. 152.

Into the Big World

> Nor will they say, 'Look, here it is!' or 'There it is!' For, in fact, the kingdom of God is among you.
>
> —Luke 17:21, New Revised Standard Version

'Cana of Galilee' is one of the most remarkable chapters of *The Brothers Karamazov*. Alyosha is exhausted by all his efforts on behalf of his family, which have left him with little time to grieve over the recently deceased Zosima. According to folk tradition, Zosima's corpse should have remained uncorrupted if he were truly holy; its unexpected decay causes Alyosha further anguish, as does the elder's final instruction to him to leave the monastery and return to the world. Alyosha returns from his errands late at night and enters the elder's cell to hear Father Paissy reading the Gospel of John over the corpse. He has reached the story of the miracle at the wedding in Cana (John 2:1–11). This chapter is another departure from form as Dostoevsky introduces a moment by moment account of the '[f]ragments of thought' that move unbidden through Alyosha's mind like a 'whirlwind' as he tries to listen and pray.[58] Alyosha slips into a dream or vision, where he sees Zosima at the Cana wedding banquet in heaven and hears his elder's voice bidding him to 'do your work'.[59] When he wakes, he immediately gets up from where he has been kneeling and goes outside:

> Filled with rapture, his soul yearned for freedom, space, vastness. Over him the heavenly dome, full of quiet, shining stars, hung boundlessly. From the zenith to the horizon the still-dim Milky Way stretched its double strand. Night, fresh and quiet, almost unstirring, enveloped the earth.[60]

---

58 Dostoevsky, pp. 359–60.
59 Dostoevsky, p. 361.
60 Dostoevsky, p. 362.

Alyosha suddenly begins to kiss the earth, weeping tears of joy, and wanting 'to forgive everyone and for everything, and to ask forgiveness, oh, not for himself! but for all and for everything, "as others are asking for me"'. He is now filled with a steadfast desire to obey his master's order and leave the monastery to 'sojourn in the world'.

Murphy's exit from the MMM can be read as a variation on Alyosha's psychological trajectory. While Murphy's progression moves through almost the opposite affective stages to Alyosha's, the conclusion for both indefinite heroes is the same: they must get up and leave to live a life with others. After much agonizing over the 'unintelligible gulf' that remains, despite his successes, between him and the patients, Murphy finally experiences something of the quiet mind that he has been longing for. Towards the end of the chess game with Mr Endon, Murphy 'surrenders' by 'laying his Shah on his side' in an 'act of submission' (152–3). Schopenhauer says that the quietist who has resigned the will to live 'gazes back calmly and smiles back at the phantasm of this world that was once able to move and torment his mind as well, but now stands before him as indifferently as chess pieces after the game is over' (*WWR*, I.4.68, 417). By surrendering before the game is up, Murphy goes one better. He is then admitted into a vision of pure nothingness:

> Murphy began to see nothing, that colourlessness which is such a rare postnatal treat, being the absence (to abuse a nice distinction) not of *percipere* but of *percipi*. His other senses also found themselves at peace, an unexpected pleasure. Not the numb peace of their own suspension, but the positive peace that comes when the somethings give way, or perhaps simply add up, to the Nothing, than which in the guffaw of the Abderite naught is more real. [...] Murphy with his head among the armies continued to suck in, through all the posterns of his withered soul, the accidentless One-and-Only, conveniently called Nothing. (*Mu*, 154)

Although Democritus the guffawing Abderite is the explicit reference here, Schopenhauer's presence can be felt too. Schopenhauer, as a monist, certainly believed in an 'accidentless One-and-Only'—the Thing-in-Itself—but also acknowledged that seeing this might seem like nothing from the perspective of an ordinary consciousness:

> for everyone who is still filled with the will, what remains after it is completely abolished is certainly nothing. But conversely, for those in whom the will has turned and negated itself, this world of ours which is so very real with all its suns and galaxies is—nothing. (*WWR*, I.4.71, 439)

Eventually, however, Murphy's experience of Nothing 'vanished, or perhaps simply came asunder', and Murphy realises that Mr Endon has wandered off. This suggests that Murphy's quietist experience was rather more interpersonal than he originally thought. It was perhaps his feeling of *tat tvam asi* with Mr Endon was what brought about the resignation, and with it, the pleasure of abiding in nothingness. When his companion leaves, that experience is no longer possible. Once he has returned Mr Endon to his cell and tucked him up in bed, he kneels beside him, as Alyosha does beside the corpse of Zosima, and, like Dostoevsky's hero, begins to hear voices. He hears 'words demanding so strongly to be spoken that he spoke them, right into Mr. Endon's face':

> 'the last at last seen of him
> himself unseen by him
> and of himself'

A rest.

'The last Mr. Murphy saw of Mr. Endon was Mr. Murphy unseen by Mr. Endon. This was also the last Murphy saw of Murphy.'

A rest.

'The relation between Mr. Murphy and Mr. Endon could not have been better summed up than by the former's sorrow at seeing himself in the latter's immunity from seeing anything but himself.'

A long rest.

'Mr. Murphy is a speck in Mr. Endon's unseen.' (*Mu*, 156)

Whereas Alyosha moves from frustration to beatitude, Murphy moves in the opposite direction. Alyosha's dream reassures him that his elder, although dead and rotting, is in the company of the saints in heaven, and still watching over him. Murphy's experience tells him that although his beloved Endon is very much alive he is utterly oblivious to Murphy and his spiritual fantasies. Murphy cannot find the 'brotherhood' and 'kindred' he wants with Mr Endon because he will always remain 'unseen' by him. Alyosha's love was 'wholly concentrated, perhaps even incorrectly' on his spiritual master, which is what sent him astray.[61] Murphy feels bound to Mr Endon 'by a love of the purest possible kind' (115), and this is what perpetuates his deluded belief in Mr Endon's sagacity. The words that Murphy hears also confirm that this is the 'last' he will see of Endon and so he resolves to leave. Murphy 'rose from his knees, left the cell, and the building' just as Alyosha does (*Mu*, 156). The 'pitch black' sky is, unlike Alyosha's, 'starless' and he feels 'incandescent' rather than ecstatic. Incandescence could suggest some degree of spiritual or philosophical illumination—Inge uses the word in this way (*CM*, 264)—or alternatively something rather more hot-headed: the *OED* gives 'ardent', 'heated' and 'fiery'. Either way, Murphy is no longer in his third zone of passionless dark. Ackerley points to the following passage from Proust's *Du côté de chez Swann* as the most likely source of Murphy's feeling:[62]

---

61 Dostoevsky, p. 338.
62 Ackerley, *Demented Particulars*, p. 202.

> When I saw an exterior object, my awareness that I was seeing it would remain between me and it, edging it with a thin spiritual border that prevented me from ever directly touching its substance; it would dissipate somehow before I could make contact with it, just as an incandescent body [*un corps incandescent*[63]] brought near a damp object never touches its wetness because it is always preceded by a zone of evaporation.[64]

According to Rachel Burrows, Beckett mentioned this passage in his lectures at Trinity College Dublin: 'Between the incandescent body and the damp body, says Proust. No real tangency between subject and the object.'[65] This implies that Murphy is once again stuck on the other side of that 'unintelligible gulf', perhaps permanently, unable to penetrate the veil of Maya which separates subject and object. It also suggests that, rather than seeking the dissolution of all boundaries between self and other, as in Schopenhauer's understanding of salvation, what Murphy really wants is that sense of touch, that 'tangency' that Proust's narrator desires. Previously, Murphy had tried to escape the passions, trying to conquer his 'deplorable susceptibility to Celia, ginger, and so on' (112). He had also wanted to escape the body: his mind was felt to be 'bodytight' (70) and the body something to be 'appeased' (3). His preferred 'mental experience' was one 'cut off from the physical experience' (69). But this experience of incandenscence suggests that he now thinks differently. As Shira Wolosky says, 'Murphy does not fail to achieve a state of total inwardness; he rejects it.'[66]

---

63 Marcel Proust, *À la recherche du temps perdu*, 3 vols. (Paris: Gallimard, 1954), vol. I, p. 84.
64 Marcel Proust, *In Search of Lost Time, Vol. 1: The Way by Swann's*, trans. by Lydia Davis (London: Penguin, 2003), p. 86.
65 S.E. Gontarski, Martha Dow Fehsenfeld and Dougald McMillan, 'Interview with Rachel Burrows (1982)', *Journal of Beckett Studies*, 11–12 (1989), 6–15 (p. 15).
66 Shira Wolosky, Language Mysticism: The Negative Way of Language in Eliot, Beckett, and Celan (Stanford, CA: Stanford University Press, 1995), p. 95.

It is telling that after realising that he is 'unseen' by Endon, Murphy immediately tries to conjur other faces, beginning with Celia's, in his mind. He is upset to find that he cannot do so, and resolves to calm himself in his chair and then leave the MMM to 'face the music, MUSIC, MUSIC, back to Brewery Road, to Celia, serenade, nocturne, albada' (*Mu*, 157). Like Alyosha resolving to 'sojourn in the world' and marry Liza, Murphy chooses to leave his place of quiet isolation in favour of a life with Celia. Alyosha does not abandon his faith, but aims to live as a monk in the world. Similarly, Murphy's intended return to Celia is perhaps a softening of his quietism rather than a wholescale rejection of it. For Celia is the only person who tolerates his strange habits: she has tried Murphy's rocking chair for herself, making 'an amnion about her own disquiet' (44), just as Murphy looks forward to the 'embryonal repose' of Belacqua's position in Purgatory (51). Celia soon becomes attracted by that 'exquisite depravity', favoured by Murphy himself of being 'naked and bound', and then swooning into a 'trance' (44, 46). She has, 'in spite of herself', begun to understand Murphy's obsessions 'as soon as he gave up trying to explain' (44). Celia is his 'music', his 'serenade, nocturne, albada': two love songs, the evening serenade and the dawn *albada* [aubade], surrounding the nocturne, a composition with a 'quiet, meditative character' (*OED*). Murphy has already made the connection between Celia and heaven (*caelum*) (110), and now that the Kingdom within of Mr Endon is barred to him, she is the obvious person to turn to. Beckett will quickly demolish any trace of sentimentality with Murphy's unfortunate accident and his grim post-mortem state of being scattered across the floor of a pub, but for this brief moment there is an inkling of a happy ending and an anticipation of the antagonistic but affectionate pairings that will take centre stage in much of Beckett's later writing.

Conclusion

In his analysis of Beckett's quietism of the 1930s, David Tucker notes that in 1935 Beckett had come to see both psychotherapy and his idiosyncratic and inward reading of Thomas à Kempis's *Imitation of Christ* as 'avenues of enquiry [...] embroiled in too many concomitant compromises.'⁶⁷ But since Beckett had signed off his letter to Arland Ussher with Thomas's 'Humiliter, Simpliciter, Fideliter' after consulting Arnold Geulincx's *Ethica* at Trinity College Dublin in the spring of 1936, Tucker concludes that Beckett had, no doubt to his surprise, 'rekindled' his interest in inner contemplation, and turned back to several of the ideas and attitudes that he had rejected the previous year. It is very likely that Geulincx himself, who, in Beckett's eyes, lacked the extremes of quietist fanaticism and yet still set forth a philosophy based on humility and self-inspection, played an important role in Beckett's *volte face*. But equally the process of writing *Murphy* must have helped to rehabilitate the quietist project in Beckett's eyes. I have argued that Beckett's references to *tat tvam asi* and Alyosha Karamazov were tacit admissions that Murphy, like Belacqua before him, was another 'vice-exister' for the author himself, another sufferer of his pains.

Beckett invests Murphy with an extremely solipsistic quietist ideal, one which exceeds the human solidarity of Gide's *Dostoïevsky* and the compassionate regard of Schopenhauer, but which matched his own 'twisted' reading of the *Imitation*. By allowing his character to stumble into the realisation that a 'brotherhood' of likeminded and quiet-minded souls who can stand as 'friends and exemplars' (117) was perhaps more important to him than the inner solitude he had previously cultivated, Beckett was exploring viable alternatives. In the *Imitation* letter, Beckett had hoped to find 'some way of devoting pain & monstrosity & incapacitation to the service of a deserving cause' (SB to TM, 10/3/35; *LSB1*, 259), and perhaps found that 'way' through writing *Murphy*, germinating at that very time in the *Whoroscope* notebook. By 25 March 1936, when Beckett wrote his letter to Ussher, the novel was nearly finished.⁶⁸ While *Dream of Fair to Middling Women* and *More Pricks than Kicks* had sneered at Beckett's inward-looking alter-ego Belacqua, *Murphy* treats its protagonist more compassionately

---

67 Tucker, p. 45.
68 Tucker, p. 48.

through the narrator's occasional recourse to sympathetic descriptions of Murphy's goals, and by allowing him his brief moment of insight before his sorry end. As with Dostoevsky's treatment of Alyosha, the narrator's criticism can be seen as indicative of a concern for Murphy and his delusions. In this respect, *Murphy* left its mark on what James Knowlson identifies as the most significant personal consequence of Beckett's tussle with the 'quietistic impulse', namely the transformation of the 'arrogant, disturbed, narcissistic, young man of the 1930s' into the writer known by his friends for his 'extraordinary kindness, courtesy, concern, generosity, and almost saintly "good works"'.[69]

---

69 Knowlson, pp. 353, 179.

Chapter 3
Remnants of a Pensum:
Decay and quietist aesthetics from *Dream of Fair to Middling Women* to *Molloy*

> Paradox is the poisonous flower of quietism, the iridescent surface of the rotting mind, the greatest depravity of all.
>
> —Thomas Mann, The Magic Mountain[1]

'You invent nothing,' says Molloy, 'you think you are inventing, you think you are escaping, and all you did is stammer out your lesson, the remnants of a pensum one day got by heart and long forgotten, life without tears, as it is wept' (*Mo*, 29). In the previous two chapters, I described the various preoccupations that made up Beckett's pensum in the 1930s: his efforts to rid himself of anxiety attacks, his ambivalent relationship to solitude, solipsism, quietism, and melancholy, and his search for a way 'to turn this dereliction, profoundly felt, into literature' (GD, 2/2/37).[2] Molloy's words imply that such concerns are not easily set aside. In this chapter, I propose that quietism—as a theme and an aesthetic—was not confined to Beckett's writing of the 1930s, but lingers, like Molloy's lesson, in the book that bears his name, begun in 1947.

Molloy's maxim actually proves its own point. 'Pensum' is a Latin word which made its way into English, French, and German during the seventeenth century; it means task, duty, or charge. The Latin literally means 'weighed out' and once referred to the wool weighed out and given to a slave to spin each day.[3] This is where the sense of a charge or task comes from, and can carry the notion of

---

1   Thomas Mann, *The Magic Mountain*, trans. by S. Fisher Verlag (London: Vintage, 1996), p. 219.
2   Quoted in Nixon, p. 58.
3   Charles T. Lewis and Charles Short, *A Latin Dictionary Founded on Andrews' Edition of Freund's Latin Dictionary* (Oxford: Oxford University Press, 1879).

punishment, particularly in schools: in *Ulysses*, Joyce describes '*the youthful scholars grappling with their pensums*'[4] and this would fit with Molloy's idea of a 'lesson'. But because a pensum is weighed out, like precious metals might be, it is also something valuable. For Beckett, both these senses of pensum matter—as a penitential task and an 'ancient care' as Molloy would put it. Beckett took the term from Schopenhauer's *Parerga und Paralipomena*—'Das Leben ist ein Pensum zum Abarbeiten: in diesem Sinne ist *defunctus* ein schöner Ausdruck' [Life is a task to be worked off: in that sense *defunctus* is a fine expression (*PP*, II.300)]—and paraphrased it first in a letter to MacGreevy (n.d. [before 5/7/30; *LSB1*, 36) and then in *Proust* (93). If Beckett's conversation with Schopenhauer continued from *Proust* and *Murphy* to *Molloy*, then that would itself constitute a lingering and unfinished pensum. In the English version of *Molloy*, there is an additional reminder of the 1930s in the phrase 'got by heart', replacing the French 'appris'.[5] Beckett's pensum was quite literally 'got by heart' through his anxiety attacks, and not merely learnt by rote. Memorisation did, of course, have its place back then: Belacqua, in *Dream of Fair to Middling Women*, is able to recite Leopardi's 'A se stesso' (62). Molloy, at least in the English text, also seems to know this poem: in place of the French 'je n'avais plus envie d'en tirer quelque chose' [I no longer wanted to get anything out of them] (*MF*, 47), Molloy quotes Leopardi's poem—'non che la speme il desiderio' (35) [not only hope but desire]—and relies on the reader to complete the line with 'è spento' [is spent]. Heartache, Leopardi, and Schopenhauer: all very much part of Beckett's pensum from his younger days, and all tied up with his interest in quietism.[6]

---

4   James Joyce, *Ulysses*, ed. by Declan Kiberd (London: Penguin, 2008), p. 588.

5   Samuel Beckett, *Molloy* (Paris: Éditions de Minuit, 1982), p. 41. Hereafter, *MF*.

6   Material based on this chapter has been previously published in Andy Wimbush, 'The Pretty Quietist Pater: Samuel Beckett's *Molloy* and the Aesthetics of Quietism', *Literature and Theology* 30: 4 (2016), 439–455 and Andy Wimbush, '"Omniscience and Omnipotence": *Molloy* and the end of "Joyceology"', in *Beckett and Modernism*, ed. by Olga Beloborodova, Dirk Van Hulle and Pim Verhulst (London: Palgrave, 2018), pp. 95–109.

Moran's Prayer

One of the most important 'remnants' in *Molloy* is Moran's prayer—his 'pretty quietist Pater' (*Mo*, 175)—'joli Pater quiétiste' (*MF*, 229)—which is recited towards the end of the novel. Moran is the only Beckett character to reference quietism explicitly, and, outside of reviews, *Molloy* is alone among Beckett's published texts to mention it. As Moran returns home after 'great inward metamorphoses' (*Mo*, 171), he says his prayer:

> Our Father who art no more in heaven than on earth or in hell, I neither want nor desire that thy name be hallowed, thou knowest best what suits thee. Etc. The middle and the end are very pretty. (*Mo*, 175)

> Dieu qui n'êtes pas plus au ciel que sur la terre et dans les enfers, je ne veux ni ne désire que votre nom soit sanctifié, vous savez ce qui vous convient. Etc. Le milieu et la fin sont très jolis. (*MF*, 229)

Despite the recent scholarly interest in Beckett's relationship to quietism, Moran's prayer has received markedly little attention. It is nowhere to be seen in the obvious places, such as Mary Bryden's otherwise exhaustive *Samuel Beckett and the Idea of God*, the special edition of *Samuel Beckett Today / Aujourd'hui* devoted to Beckett and religion, or Iain Bailey's *Samuel Beckett and the Bible*.[7] Rubin Rabinowitz sees the prayer as a pessimistic attack on hope, and sets it among the many burlesqued Bible verses in Beckett's work, including another pastiche of the Lord's Prayer from the 1932 poem 'Serena I': 'ah father ah father that art in heaven'.[8] Mark Nixon, in a similar vein, points to Beckett's early parodic prayers in the German Diaries: 'God's whim be

---

7   Iain Bailey, *Samuel Beckett and The Bible* (London: Bloomsbury, 2014).
8   Beckett, *Collected Poems*, p. 16; Rubin Rabinowitz, 'Samuel Beckett's Revised Aphorisms', *Contemporary Literature*, 36 (1995), 203–25.

done' and 'God's velleities be done' (GD, 8 & 9 November 1936).[9] Martha Nussbaum suggests that the prayer demonstrates 'Moran's new distance from religious emotions' and the novel's trajectory whereby there is a 'radical breaking down of religious significances and religious desire'.[10] John Bolin, on the other hand, believes Beckett is actually staying close to a particular kind of religious or quasi-religious narrative, with Moran reaching something akin to the final abjection of the Pastor in André Gide's *La Symphonie pastorale*, while simultaneously parodying the final penitence of Raskolnikov in *Crime and Punishment*, by Gide's own master, Dostoevsky.[11]

What these readers of *Molloy* assume is that the quietist Pater is Beckett's own satirical creation. This would mean that Moran's 'Etc.' and his reference to the 'middle and the end' of the prayer refer to precisely nothing, except whatever the reader can imaginatively extrapolate from Moran's starting point. But there *is* something after that 'Etc.' since Beckett lifted the prayer, word for word, from a satirical text from the seventeenth century, written at the height of the Christian Quietist controversy:

> Dieu qui n'êtes pas plus au Ciel que sur la terre & dans les Enfers, qui êtes présent partout : je ne veux ni ne desire [*sic*] que vôtre [*sic*] Nom soit sanctifié, vous sçavez [*sic*] ce qui nous convient ; si vous voulez qu'il le soit, il le sera, sans que je le veüille & le desire [*sic*]. Que vôtre Roïaume [*sic*] arrive ou n'arrive pas, cela m'est indifferent [*sic*]. Je ne vous demande pas aussi que vôtre volonté soit faite sur la terre comme au Ciel : elle le sera malgré que j'en aïe ; c'est à moi à m'y resigner [*sic*] : Donnez-nous à tous nôtre pain de tous les jours, qui est vôtre grâce, ou ne nous la donnez pas : je ne souhaite de l'avoir ni d'en être privé : De même si vous me pardonnez mes crimes, comme je pardonne à ceux qui m'ont offensé tant mieux ; Si

---

9 Nixon, p. 57.
10 Martha C. Nussbaum, *Love's Knowledge: Essays on Philosophy and Literature* (Oxford: Oxford University Press, 1992), p. 302.
11 Bolin, pp. 151–2.

vous m'en punissez au contraire par la damnation, tant mieux encore, puisque c'est vôtre bon plaisir. Enfin, mon Dieu, je suis trop abandonnée à vôtre volonté pour vous prier de me délivrer des tentations & du peché [*sic*].¹²

[Our Father, who art no more in heaven than on earth or in hell, who art everywhere, I neither want nor desire that thy name be hallowed, thou knowest best what suits thee; if thou wilt, it shall be, unless I want or desire it. That thy kingdom come or not come, it is all the same to me. I do not ask thee that thy will be done on the earth as it is heaven: it will be so no matter what I do, I can only resign myself to it. Give us this day our daily bread, which is thy grace, or give it not to us: I wish neither to have it nor to be without it. Likewise, if thou forgivest my trespasses as I forgive those who trespass against me, that is all well and good. But if thou wouldst rather punish me by damnation, then so much the better, since it is thy pleasure. Finally, Father, I am too abandoned to thy will to ask thee to deliver me from temptation and from evil.]

This is from *Dialogues sur le quiétisme*, by the essayist Jean de La Bruyère (1645–1696). La Bruyère is best known today for his *Caractères*, a set of polemical essays on various aspects of seventeenth-century French life. The *Dialogues*, which follow the style of Pascal's satirical attack on the Jesuits, *Lettres provinciales*,¹³ were compiled and published posthumously in 1699 by the historian and theologian Louis-Elles Du Pin, who most likely wrote the final three chapters.¹⁴ The book consists of ten conversations, most of which are interviews between a penitent and her spiritual director, a card-carrying Quietist. In the fifth dialogue, the penitent tells the director, 'I made myself a version of the Lord's Prayer in our style. I would like to say it, adjusting it to our

---

12 Jean de La Bruyère, *Dialogues posthumes sur le quiétisme*, ed. by Richard Parish (Grenoble: Éditions Jérôme Millon, 2005), pp. 152–3.
13 Phillip Wolfe, 'La Bruyère Critique de Quiétisme', *Papers on French Seventeenth Century Literature*, 15 (1981), 255–66 (p. 265 ff.).
14 Parish, *Catholic Particularity*, p. 180; Parish, 'Introduction', pp. 5–10.

principles and our doctrine.' The director encourages her to recite the prayer and is pleased with what he hears. 'The *Pater noster* thus reformed, would,' he tells her, 'no doubt edify all the souls in perfect abandon. I would like to send it to all our churches'.[15] La Bruyère was a close friend of Bishop Bossuet,[16] the inquisitor of Madame Guyon, and so it is no surprise that the *Dialogues* attempt to make the Quietists look like confused and immoral heretics. La Bruyère allows the director to get caught up in the contradictions of his own doctrine, while he doggedly footnotes each contentious idea with a reference to almost every Quietist text worth mentioning, including those of Guyon and Molinos.

While getting hold of the *Dialogues* would not have been beyond Beckett's means—he possessed a peculiar knack for finding obscure theological and philosophical texts and the *Dialogues* is included in editions of La Bruyère's complete works alongside the better-known *Caractères*—it is more likely that he used a secondary source. Among the books left in Beckett's apartment in Paris after his death was *Curiosités théologiques*, a compendium of religious oddities compiled by Pierre Gustav Brunet. Under Brunet's entry for Quietism, La Bruyère's prayer is quoted in full.[17] Mark Nixon and Dirk Van Hulle have shown how Beckett used Brunet's text a few years earlier when he was composing another satirical passage at the expense of a Catholic character in *Watt*.[18] Mr Spiro, the editor of the Catholic magazine *Crux*, whom Watt meets on the train, says he recently held an essay competition for his readers on the subject of the excommunication of animals. The animals mentioned—including the 'eels of Como' and the 'rats of Lyon' and the 'caterpillars of Valence'[19]—are all taken from Brunet. In the drafts for *Watt*, Beckett also borrows from Brunet's

---

15 La Bruyère, p. 153.
16 Parish, 'Introduction', p. 8, n. 9.
17 Pierre Gustav Brunet, *Curiosités théologiques par un bibliophile* (Paris: Adolphe Delahays, 1861), p. 171.
18 Nixon and Van Hulle, pp. 187–8.
19 Samuel Beckett, *Watt*, ed. by C.J. Ackerley (London: Faber and Faber, 2009), p. 21. Hereafter, *W*.

account of the medieval theological dilemma about what to do with a rat who has eaten a crumb from the consecrated host.[20] The relevant passages are not marked in Beckett's copy of Brunet's book, but this is certainly the source. Likewise, the quotation of the prayer from La Bruyère is accompanied by no marginalia,[21] but the surrounding context in *Molloy* points to Brunet's book, rather than La Bruyère's original, as the source. Moran wonders about the 'algebraic theology of Craig', the self-crucifixion of 'the Italian cobbler Lovat,' and the suckling habits of the infant Saint Roch, all of which can be found in *Curiosités théologiques*.[22]

Even if this makes it unlikely that Beckett ever got to read *Dialogues sur le quiétisme* in full, it is still significant that he chose to quote from the Quietist text rather than from Brunet's accounts of the other heresies. Moran himself implies that there is more to be read, pushing the reader towards the source text with his 'Etc.' and praise of 'the middle and the end' of the prayer, suggesting that unlike the other theological curiosities that Beckett takes from Brunet, it is this one, Quietism, which has particular significance. Giorgio Agamben, writing about the Abbey of Thelema, Rabelais's travesty of western monasticism in *Gargantua*, remarks how the 'perfect comprehension of a phenomenon is its parody':[23] likewise, Beckett no doubt appreciated how La Bruyère's prayer operates as a thumbnail sketch of the quietist attitude, and a very funny one at that. La Bruyère neatly summarises quietism's affinities with pantheism—and even with anti-theism or atheism—and demonstrates its bent towards indifference, resignation of the will, ignorance, and amorality. By taking the prayer that Jesus

---

20 Nixon and Van Hulle, pp. 189–190; C.J. Ackerley, *Obscure Locks, Simple Keys: The Annotated Watt* (Edinburgh: Edinburgh University Press, 2010), pp. 45–6.
21 My thanks to Mark Nixon and Dirk Van Hulle for confirming this (personal communication).
22 Brunet, pp. 143, 124, 33.
23 Giorgio Agamben, *The Highest Poverty: Monastic Rules and Form-of-Life*, trans. by Adam Kotso (Stanford, CA: Stanford University Press, 2013), p. 5.

taught and turning it on its head, La Bruyère lampoons the presumptuousness with which Quietism subverted Christian orthodoxy and appropriated scripture for its own ends. And as with Beckett's own writing, La Bruyère's prayer gets much of its humour by shuttling quickly from religious fervour to disillusionment and accidie: think of Hamm's abrupt move from earnest prayer to Promethean curse in *Endgame*. In La Bruyère's prayer, the hopeful language of the traditional paternoster sits awkwardly, and comically, beside the gloomy acquiescence of the deflated Quietist devotee.

In this chapter, I will argue that quietism has, in *Molloy*, a reach beyond the confines of the prayer. Molloy and Moran both have moments where they lapse into the quietist attitude, as Beckett knew it from Inge, Schopenhauer, and Plümacher. But I also want to argue that *Molloy* shows Beckett experimenting with how quietism could further inform his literary practice: the novel marks a rejection of two very different writers, Balzac and Joyce, in favour of the quietist resignation that Beckett found in the work of André Gide and Fyodor Dostoevsky. There are, in other words, more than a few remnants of this particular pensum.

Molloy and the Contemplative Life

Moran presents himself as concerned with the external deportment of his Catholic faith, but Molloy, like Belacqua, Murphy, and Watt before him, is a man of the inner world:

> there seem to be two ways of behaving in the presence of wishes, the active and the contemplative, and though they both give the same result it was the latter I preferred, matter of temperament I presume. (*Mo*, 51)

A contemplative approach to wishes might resemble the 'ablation of desire' that Beckett mentions in *Proust* (18). Molloy says that he finds himself 'perishing' in 'want of need' (32). 'The truth is I haven't much will left,' he says (*Mo*, 3). Beckett may have remembered Gide's definition of 'a contemplative life' as one in which 'all intelligence and all will' has been 'resigned' (*Dost*, 227). Elsewhere, Molloy reflects:

> My life, my life, now I speak of it as of something over, now as a joke which still goes on, and it is neither, for at the same time it is over and it goes on, and is there any tense for that? (*Mo*, 34)

Perhaps there is no tense for what Molloy experiences, but there is at least an analogy to be found in seventeenth-century Quietism. In her autobiography, Madame Guyon writes: 'Everything is indifferent to me: I *cannot* will anything any longer: I often do not know whether or not I exist'. Schopenhauer quotes theses lines in *The World as Will and Representation*, and adds that 'after the will dies out, there can be nothing bitter about the death of the body', before quoting Guyon again: 'whoever has suffered the first death will no longer feel the second death' (*WWR*, I.4.68, 418). The ascetic, sage, or quietist is one whose 'essence has already died here long ago through voluntary self-negation, with the exception of the feeble remnant that appeared as the vitality of this body' (*WWR*, I.4.68, 409). This is the same liminal state that Molloy seems to experience, and which recalls how Belacqua's mind in *Dream of Fair to Middling Women* is likened to a 'sick room', and a 'chapelle ardente', a place where the body lies in state before cremation or burial (*Dream*, 44).

Molloy makes another allusion to the contemplative life when he describes the burial of Lousse's dog. The dead animal is placed in the grave 'as he was, no box or wrapping of any kind, like a Carthusian monk' (*Mo*, 34; 'comme un chartreux', *MF*, 48). The Carthusians are the most cloistered and austere of Christian monastic orders: the majority of their monks and nuns live an eremitical life, almost entirely devoted to solitary, silent prayer. Molloy identifies with these contemplatives through the proxy of the dog: 'I contributed my presence,' says Molloy as he watches Lousse fill in the hole, 'As if it had been my burial. And it was' (34). Later, Molloy says that the 'dog's grave [...]

was mine too in a way' (59). He also imagines Lousse burying her parrot in a similarly Carthusian manner—'In his cage probably'—and yet again refers to himself: 'Me too, if I had stayed, she would have buried' (36). The Carthusians are encouraged to maintain a gloomy outlook on life: 'As the duty of a good monk is rather to lament than to sing,' their rule proclaims, 'we must so sing that lamentation, not the joy of singing, be in our hearts'.[24] Molloy also lives his life in this minor key: 'The glorious, truly glorious weather would have gladdened any other heart than mine. But I have no reason to be gladdened by the sun and I take good care not to be' (*Mo*, 27).

While a contemplative life is not the same as a quietist life, Christianity has often seen quietism as the enduring temptation of its most advanced contemplatives.[25] Just before quoting La Bruyère's prayer, Brunet describes how 'certain devout souls, by dint of their desire to raise themselves to the loftiest heights of contemplation, imagined that the soul could gather itself into the divine essence'.[26] In *Christian Mysticism*, Inge explains the distinction between the active and contemplative life in his discussion of the Quietist François Fénelon. Inge describes how 'unitive or contemplative life' takes one to the very edge of union with God, and that this is 'the ideal limit of religion', for the attainment of true union would be 'at once its consummation and annihilation' (*CM*, 12). Heretical Quietism would be to exceed this ideal limit, annihilate the self and merge wholly with God, perhaps even dispensing with God himself along the way. Inge tries to exonerate a number of the mystics usually labelled as Quietists—including Guyon and Fénelon—and therefore has to disassociate them from the goal of total self-annihilation. But a glance at their writings proves the futility of his efforts. In a passage from *Spiritual Torrents*, which is quoted in the footnotes of La Bruyère's *Dialogues*, Madame Guyon writes:

---

24 Douglas Raymund Webster, 'The Carthusian Order', *The Catholic Encyclopedia* (New York, NY: Robert Appleton Company, 1908) <http://www.newadvent.org/cathen/03388a.htm> [accessed 15 September 2019].
25 See Parish, *Catholic Particularity*, p. 182.
26 Brunet, pp. 171–2.

the state of annihilation [*anéantissement*[27]] through which [a soul] has passed has placed it below all humiliation; for in order to be humbled, we must *be something*, and nothingness [*le néant*] cannot be brought lower; its present state has placed it above all humility and all virtue by its transformation into God.[28]

Inge has problems even when faced with a mystic not usually accused of quietism. He quotes John of Ruysbroeck as follows:

"In this highest stage the soul is united to God without means; it sinks into the vast darkness of the Godhead." In this abyss, [Ruysbroeck] says, [...] "the Persons of the Trinity transcend themselves"; "*there* is only the eternal essence, which is the substance of the Divine Persons, where we are all one and uncreated, according to our prototypes." Here, "so far as distinction of persons goes, there is no more God nor creature"; "we have lost ourselves and been melted away into the unknown darkness". (*CM*, 170)

Inge then adds his own caveat that the creature is never completely absorbed into God. Even in union, he says, there remains a distinction between the soul and the divine. In his treatment of both Ruysbroeck and Fénelon, Inge resists their pull towards darkness and annihilation, in favour of a neatly bounded religion and a distinct and differentiated God.

Beckett used Inge's book while writing *Dream of Fair to Middling Women* in 1932, where these same unitive tendencies of the contemplative life can be found. When the narrator encourages Belacqua to think beyond categories, he invokes St Bonaventure's understanding of God as having 'a centre everywhere and a circumference nowhere' and also the transcendental Christ:

---

27 La Bruyère, p. 150.
28 Jeanne Marie Bouvier de La Mothe Guyon, *A Short Method of Prayer and Spiritual Torrents*, trans. by A.W. Marston (London: Sampson Low, Marston, Low & Searle, 1875), p. 215.

> As all mystics, independent of creed and colour and sex, are transelemented into the creedless, colourless, sexless Christ, so all categories of beauty must be transelemented into yours. (*Dream*, 35).

Similarly, in *Molloy*, both quietist themes—self-annihilation and the loss of Christianity's usual elements—are present in one of Molloy's accounts of his loss of bodily identity:

> the confines of my room, of my bed, of my body, are as remote from me as were those of my region, in the days of my splendour.[29] And the cycle continues, joltingly, of flight and bivouac, in an Egypt without bounds, without infant, without mother. And when I see my hands, on the sheet, which they love to floccillate already, they are not mine, less than ever mine. (*Mo*, 66)

The biblical story of Joseph and Mary's rest on their flight to Egypt with the infant Jesus has been a popular subject for painters and Beckett saw several different versions on his trips to galleries in Germany, Britain, and Ireland. But there are two in particular that are important here: Rembrandt's version, which Beckett saw in the National Gallery of Ireland,[30] and another by Adam Elsheimer—whose pictures Beckett thought 'exquisite' (SB to TM, 20/2/35; *LSB1*, 253)—which he saw in Munich's Alte Pinakothek in 1937.[31]

---

29 Madame Guyon believed that 'proprieté'—that is, a sense of wilful ownership of one's actions—was the highest sin. She advises the Quietist to be moved by God's will alone, even if that were to lead the soul into behaviour usually deemed sinful by the Church. See *The Complete Madame Guyon*, trans. by Nancy C. James (Brewster, MA: Paraclete Press, 2011), p. 89. La Bruyère mocks this tendency of her thought mercilessly in the *Dialogues*. See for example, pp. 177–179.
30 Knowlson, p. 58.
31 John Haynes and James Knowlson, *Images of Beckett* (Cambridge: Cambridge University Press, 2003), pp. 79–80.

Figure 1: Rembrandt van Rijn. *Landscape with Rest on the Flight into Egypt.* (1647) Oil on wood panel. 34 x 48 cm. National Gallery of Ireland.

Figure 2: Adam Elsheimer, *The Flight into Egypt.* (c. 1609) Oil on copper. 31 cm × 41 cm. Alte Pinakothek, Munich.

Take away the travellers and their camps from these pictures—as Molloy's 'without infant, without mother' suggests—and all that remains is a dark mass of blurred brushstrokes, pierced by a glimmer of light from the moon and stars. Beckett was first introduced to Elsheimer's work by R.H. Wilenski's *Dutch Painting*, recommended to him by MacGreevy in the early 1930s, and on which he took copious notes.[32] Wilenski describes Elsheimer's sky as 'no longer a backcloth but a symbol for boundless space',[33] which Beckett echoes in the 'Egypt without bounds' in *Molloy*. Remove the 'bounds' of the painting, and this darkness becomes all-consuming, swallowing and dissolving the viewer, just as Molloy's identity is dissolved and scattered, no longer able to reside wholly within his body. By erasing Jesus and falling into a boundless darkness, Molloy takes his contemplative life to extremes and repeats the quietist heresy.

The Thing in Ruins

Molloy's tendencies towards will-lessness, contemplation, self-annihilation, ecstasis and marginalisation of Christian doctrine all suggest his affinity with quietism. But one aspect of Molloy's story is particularly important in drawing together Beckett's now long-running interest in quietism as a theme with his concerns about aesthetics and form: the novel's treatment of decay. Molloy himself is a piece of 'jetsam', something from a 'wreck, washed up by the storm' (*Mo*, 75). His testicles are described as 'decaying circus clowns' (34) and his greatest wish is to be left 'rotting in peace' (76). 'To decompose is to live,' says Molloy defiantly, as if to justify his ebbing away as a valid means of remaining in this world. These passages and others have been variously read as a

---

32 Angela Moorjani, '"Just Looking": Ne(i)ther-World Icons, Elsheimer Nocturnes, and Other Simultaneities in Beckett's *Play*', in *Beckett at 100: Revolving it All*, ed. by Angela Moorjani and Linda Ben-Zvi (Oxford: Oxford University Press, 2008), pp. 123–38.

33 R.H. Wilenski, *Dutch Painting*, Revised edition. First published 1929. (New York, NY: Beechhurst, 1955), p. 68.

Kristevan 'disintegrating voyage toward the mother',[34] a loss of confidence in the Cartesian *cogito*[35] and a 'Jungian quest for an integrated self'.[36] I want to suggest that it also has something to do with quietism.

The claim that decay might have anything to do with spirituality might at first seem strange, not least because Christianity has so often shied away from it. Standing in the pulpit of St Paul's Cathedral, theatrically dressed in the shroud that would inspire Beckett's *What Where*,[37] John Donne spoke about the 'inglorious and contemptible vilification' that takes place after death, whereby the dust of a person's body must be dispersed and 'mingled with the dust of every highway and of every dunghill'.[38] Donne presents God's action on the Last Day as a kind of anti-decay, gathering up the particles that had been subject to putrefaction and breathing new life into them. Dostoevsky, who was transfixed and terrified by Holbein's *Dead Christ*,[39] depicts, in *The Brothers Karamazov*, the horror of Alyosha and other pious souls when they witness the decomposition of the body of Elder Zosima. But this traditional aversion towards putrefaction is turned on its head in the writings of Madame Guyon, who chose metaphors of decay to describe the soul's purification. La Bruyère picked up on this in *Dialogues sur le quiétisme*: the spiritual director explains that the 'annihilation' that he teaches entails 'the burial of the soul, a rot, a stink, a corruption that is an abomination to all men and to God himself'.[40] This is La Bruyère's paraphrase of a passage from Guyon's *Spiritual Torrents*, which he quotes in the footnotes, alongside another line from that

---

34 Beatrice Marie, 'Beckett's Fathers', *Comparative Literature*, 100 (1985), 1103–9 (p. 1105).
35 Hugh Kenner, *Samuel Beckett: A Critical Study* (Berkeley, CA: University of California Press, 1968), p. 131.
36 Phil Baker, *Beckett and the Mythology of Psychoanalysis* (London: Palgrave Macmillan, 1997), p. 381.
37 Knowlson, p. 827.
38 John Donne, *Selected Prose*, ed. by Neil Rhodes (Harmondsworth: Penguin, 1987), p. 318.
39 Joseph Frank, *Dostoevsky: A Writer in His Time*, ed. by Mary Petrusewicz (Oxford: Princeton University Press, 2010), pp. 549–550.
40 La Bruyère, p. 182.

book describing how the soul 'becomes gradually corrupted'. Despite the language of abomination, neither Guyon nor the director is talking about something bad here: the rot which leads to the soul's destruction is also its way to perfection. What really decays, Guyon explains, is the 'old Adam': the wilful agent who fills the soul's actions with sinful propriety and activity, and who blocks the way to assimilation into God. The director also explains that the soul that has lost its will is 'abîmée',[41] a word which means 'sunk'—as into the depths of God—but also spoiled, decayed, and rotten.

While we cannot assume that Beckett was aware of Guyon's vocabulary of rot, it is worth noting that he frequently made his own links between decay and something like quietism in his writing before *Molloy*, and associated both with his own literary output.[42] In his Clare Street notebook, Beckett wrote a version of a Schopenhauerian soteriology replacing Schopenhauer's veil of Maya with what he calls the 'veil of hope'. This, according to Beckett, is humanity's obstacle to self-awareness and liberation. Beckett writes: 'Die Hoffnung ist des Geistes Star; der nicht zu stechen ist, ehe er ganz faulreif wird.' (UoR MS5003, 17r–18r) [Hope is the cataract of the spirit, which cannot be pierced until it is completely ripe for decay[43]]. Despite being a great admirer of Madame Guyon, Schopenhauer did not adopt her vocabulary of putrescence and decay in describing his own brand of quietism: the addition of 'faulreif' is therefore Beckett's invention. Later on Beckett imagines how the self might be 'zersetzt' [decomposed] into its constituent parts. Nixon proposes that the German passage in the Clare Street notebook is 'highly revealing as to [Beckett's] aesthetic concerns at the time', building on his previous thoughts on the relationship between subject and object, artist and world.[44]

---

41 La Bruyère, p. 178.
42 For more on this subject, and its connection to psychoanalysis, see Nixon, chap. 3.
43 Translation from Nixon, p. 170.
44 Nixon, p. 170.

The 'Great Dereliction' of St Teresa of Ávila provided another locus around which quietism, decay, and literature could coalesce in Beckett's mind. As I mentioned at the end of Chapter 1, Beckett recorded 'Great dereliction' in his *Dream* notebook (100) and worked it into his aspiration to turn 'this dereliction profoundly felt, into literature' in the German Diaries (2/2/37).[45] In *Dream of Fair to Middling Women*, Belacqua feels that such dereliction is the 'silver lining' to the 'affliction of being a son of Adam and cursed with an insubordinate mind' (5–6). Beckett took the phrase from Inge, who argues that Teresa, despite her unshakable position in the ranks of the saints, should really be numbered among the Quietists. According to Inge, her 'teaching about passivity and "the prayer of quiet" is identical with that which the Pope afterwards condemned in Molinos' (*CM*, 222). He adds that Teresa's confessor, St Pedro of Alcántara, should be seen as the real founder of Quietism, and says that the 'quietists of the next century might find much support for their controverted doctrines' in Teresa's writings (*CM*, 218, 230). The Great Dereliction, then, has a quietist pedigree. Molloy continues in the direction set by Belacqua, expecting that his 'ruined works will one day speak of God, to the worms' (*Mo*, 34). Whereas St Teresa had seen dereliction as a temporary stage of purgation, and Guyon had made the putrefaction of the soul a condition of divine union, Molloy makes God the interim stage, and decay the ultimate destination: the sentence moves from decay to God, and then back to decay again via the worms. Likewise, Belacqua's beatitude arrives when his mind is 'entombed', or slowly decaying in that 'chapelle ardente', once the 'glare of living' has been 'consumed away' (*Dream*, 44–5). Spiritual burial, like dereliction, is also seen by Beckett to be something that might help foster artistic creation. In his 1948 essay 'Peintres de l'Empêchement', Beckett describes how the painters Bram and Geer van Velde turn their art into 'l'analyse d'un état de privation' [an analysis of a state of privation]; this already suggests a kind of ascetic or monastic self-denial, confirmed in Beckett's

---

45 Quoted in Nixon, p. 58.

discussion of the artist's 'cellule' [cell] later on, but Beckett also describes this state as a kind of 'ensevelissement' [burial] (*Dis*, 136). For Beckett, the rigours and trials of the contemplative and the artist are not just comparable, but comparable through their relationship to entombment, and hence decay.

In his letters to MacGreevy, Beckett uses the language of waste to describe both himself in relation to quietism, and his literary output. In the letter debating the value of *The Imitation of Christ*, Beckett writes:

> I cannot see that [my situation] allows of any philosophical or ethical or Christlike imitative pentimenti, or in what way they could redeem a composition that was invalid from the word "go" & has to be broken up altogether. If the heart still bubbles it is because the puddle has not been drained, and the fact of its bubbling more fiercely than ever is perhaps open to receive consolation from the waste that splutters most when the bath is nearly empty. (SB to TM, 10/3/35; *LSB1*, 259)

Beckett is describing his anxiety attacks and heart problems, which he says are merely a 'bubble on the puddle' of his 'pre-history': a delayed sign of an event long past, much like the light of that distant star in Mann's *Buddenbrooks*. It is telling that Beckett sees himself as a kind of text in this letter: his life is a 'composition' which begins with a 'word'. In *Molloy*, 'decomposition' becomes important not just thematically but structurally as well: as I will argue, the rot that afflicts Molloy also starts to seep into the text. Beckett's talk of the 'waste that splutters most' is perhaps a further reference to that Great Dereliction that he wants to turn into literature: the word 'waste' also anticipates a letter to MacGreevy in which he describes, after a mention of a heart attack, how 'the only plane on which I feel my defeat not proven is the literary waste' (SB to TM, 16/1/[36]).[46] As Nixon points out, Beckett fre-

---

46 I am following the transcription in Nixon, p. 59. The editors of the letters end the sentence after 'literary', and read the next word as 'Warte nur...' [just wait]. *LSB1*, 302.

quently used the language of human waste to describe his writing, referring to 'my Proust turd' and comparing a poem to diarrhoea (SB to SP, [9/31]; SB to GR, 8/10/32; *LSB1*, 86 & 124). And just as burial and entombment describe both artist and quietist, Beckett brings the language of bowels to bear on souls:

> [Belacqua] scaffolded a theory of the mystical experience as being geared, that was his participle, to the vision of an hypostatical clysterpipe, the apex of ecstasy being furnished by the peroration of administration and of course the Dark Night of the Soul (and here we were scandalised by slight consonantal adjustments) and the Great Dereliction coinciding with the period of post-evacuative depression. (*Dream*, 185)

A clysterpipe is an instrument for injecting into the rectum a medicine that cleans out the bowels. Hypostasis refers to the union of the persons of the Trinity, or to the union of divine and human natures in Jesus Christ. It also refers to the extremes of contemplation whereby a mystic becomes united with God. Again, Beckett took the term from Inge, who uses it several times including in a quotation from *The Lives of the Saints* by Fénelon: 'It is false to say that transformation is a deification of the real and natural soul, or a hypostatic union, or an unalterable conformity with God' (*CM*, 13, 239). As with Molloy's dark and boundless Egypt, Beckett resists Inge's tendency to stand back from contemplative heresies, choosing instead to try to beat a suspected Quietist heretic like Fénelon at his own game. Belacqua's scandalous 'consonantal adjustments' are made explicit in the *Dream* notebook, where Beckett records 'The Dark Shite of the Hole' (*DN*, 101), lampooning the purgative stage on the spiritual path described by St John of Cross. Earlier in the novel, Belacqua finds himself in a state of bliss where he is 'casting out his innermost parts, his soul at stool, per faecula faeculorum' (*Dream*, 45). Beckett deliberately misreads the long or medial 's' (ſ) of pre-nineteenth century texts as an 'f', thereby distorting the Vulgate Bible's description of eternity—'per saecula saeculorum' [the century of centuries] (Ephesians 3:21)—and slipping from eschatology to scatology.

Beckett had, then, long juxtaposed the language of waste and decay with notions of spiritual purgation that he borrowed from writers associated with quietism: Schopenhauer, St Teresa, St John of the Cross, and Thomas à Kempis. Not only that, but both decay and quietism were related to his own personal affliction and his literary ambitions. The presence of decay in *Molloy* therefore constitutes another lingering remnant of that 1930s pensum. Decay becomes most clearly linked to something resembling quietism when Molloy begins his lengthy assessment of what he calls 'my ruins,' (38; 'mes décombres', 52):

> Oh I've tried everything. In the end it was magic that had the honour of my ruins, and still today, when I walk there, I find its vestiges. But mostly they are a place with neither plan nor bounds and of which I understand nothing, not even of what it is made, still less into what. And the thing in ruins, I don't know what it is, what it was, nor whether it is not less a question of ruins than the indestructible chaos of timeless things, if that is the right expression. It is in any case a place devoid of mystery, deserted by magic, because devoid of mystery. And if I do not go there gladly, I go perhaps more gladly there than anywhere else, astonished and at peace, I nearly said as in a dream, but no, no. But it is not the kind of place where you go, but where you find yourself, sometimes, not knowing how, and which you cannot leave at will, and where you find yourself without any pleasure, but with more perhaps than in those places you can escape from, by making an effort, places full of mystery, full of the familiar mysteries. I listen and the voice is of a world collapsing endlessly, a frozen world, under a faint untroubled sky, enough to see by, yes, and frozen too. And I hear it murmur that all wilts and yields, as if loaded down, but here there are no loads, and the ground too, unfit for loads, and the light too, down towards an end it seems can never come. For what possible end to these wastes where true light never was, nor any upright thing, nor any true foundation, but only these leaning things, forever lapsing and crumbling away,

beneath a sky without memory of morning or hope of night. These things, what things, come from where, made of what? And it says that here nothing stirs, has never stirred, will never stir, except myself, who do not stir either, when I am there, but see and am seen. Yes, a world at an end, in spite of appearances, its end brought it forth, ending it began, is it clear enough? And I too am at an end, when I am there, my eyes close, my sufferings cease and I end, I wither as the living cannot. (38)

Molloy's ruins are the descendent of Murphy's third zone and Belacqua's wombtomb, a state of mind where distinctions and identity seem to cease and crumble. This passage is also one of many instances in which, as Joshua Landy puts it, 'the trilogy's forward line is continually being interrupted' by 'backtracking (the retraction of a hypothesis) or by horizontal shifts (the proposal of a new hypothesis)'.[47] Molloy posits and then retracts magic, ruins, mysteries, dreams, end, light, and even things. Landy sees this process in terms of the *logoi* and *antilogoi* of ancient Greek Pyrrhonism, defined by Sextus Empiricus as the ability to 'set out oppositions among things' so as to 'come first to suspension of judgement and afterwards to tranquillity'.[48] But Beckett may have also been thinking of the tendencies of Christian Quietism here, since Molloy prefaces this passage with a statement of his admiration for the techniques of negative theology. 'What I liked in anthropology,' says Molloy, 'was its inexhaustible faculty of negation, its relentless definition of man, as though he were no better than God, in terms of what he is not' (37–8). As Inge explains, negative or apophatic theology is the 'doctrine that God can be described only by negatives':

---

47 Joshua Landy, *How to Do Things with Fictions* (Oxford: Oxford University Press, 2012), p. 129.
48 Quoted in Landy, *How to Do Things with Fictions*, p. 127.

> Since God is the Infinite, and the Infinite is the antithesis of the finite, every attribute which can be affirmed of a finite being may be safely denied of God. Hence God can only be *described* by negatives; He can only be *discovered* by stripping off all the qualities and attributes which veil Him; He can only be *reached* by divesting ourselves of all the distinctions of personality, and sinking or rising into our "uncreated nothingness"; and He can only be *imitated* by aiming at an abstract spirituality, the passionless "apathy" of an universal which is nothing in particular. (*CM*, 111)

Several critics have explored the affinities between Beckett's writing and the practices of negative theology.[49] For my purposes here, it will be enough to note how the discipline of apophatic negation might lead someone, at least in Inge's view, to the dispositions and attitudes of quietism, including apathy, indifference, and sinking into self-annihilation, and also, as Inge suggests, to see negative theology as a process of de-creation and subtraction, perhaps even decay. As Beckett said to Charles Juliet, the negative theologians such as Eckhart and Ruysbroeck were useful to his literary efforts because of 'their burning illogicality [...] which consumes the filth [*saloperie*] of logic'.[50] Molloy admires anthropology as a discipline which can negate the human being just as apophatic theology negates God.

Molloy's negative anthropology turns him into a ruin, but as it does so language and thought are ruined as well. Beckett even pushes the questioning into the noun 'ruins' itself. In its plural form, the noun denotes something that remains after the destruction of a thing; the same is true of the French word 'décombres'. Ruins, therefore, point

---

[49] See for example: Mary Bryden, *Samuel Beckett and the Idea of God* (Basingstoke: Macmillan, 1998), pp. 186–7; Wolosky; Marius Buning, 'The "*Via Negativa*" and Its First Stirrings in *Eleutheria*', *Samuel Beckett Today / Aujourd'hui*, 9 (2000), 43–54; Buning, 'Samuel Beckett's Negative Way: Intimations of the *Via Negativa* in His Late Plays.'
[50] Charles Juliet, *Rencontres avec Samuel Beckett* (Paris: Éditions Fata Morgana, 1986), p. 51.

to something outside of themselves, to the thing that this pile of rubble once was. But Molloy has no idea what exactly has been ruined. 'I understand nothing, not even of what it is made, still less into what [...] the thing in ruins. I don't know what it is, what it was'. In this mess of uncertainties, what remains is not a collection of remnants (ruins), but simply the process of 'a world collapsing endlessly' (ruin). Molloy finds himself caught up in this entropic process—'I wither as the living cannot'—and true to quietist form, it brings him some relief from self, however temporary: 'I am too at an end, when I am there, my eyes close, my sufferings cease and I end' (38).

The Fundamental Unheroic

With Molloy's ruins, Beckett matches the form and structure of the novel to its thematic content. In this section, I want to consider how quietism informs Beckett's aesthetics, particularly in relation to decay. From the start of his writing career, Beckett wanted to bring disintegration into his texts, and seems to have connected this aspiration with quietism. In *Dream of Fair to Middling Women*, written fifteen years before *Molloy*, the narrator apologises to the reader for the way the 'refractory constituents' of the novel refuse to 'bind together'. Not only do these constituents 'shrink from all that is not they', but they also 'strain away from themselves': 'Their centres are wasting' (*Dream*, 119). Lucien is said to be 'disintegrating', 'his whole person a stew of disruption and flux' (*Dream*, 116–7). The narrator gives artistic reasons for this disintegration, distinguishing *Dream* from the work of classical novelists like Honoré de Balzac and Jane Austen. Both Balzac and Austen are said to pay most attention to 'odd periods of recueillement [recollection]' in the lives of their characters. If there is anything that threatens to shake the novel's world or form, there is an immediate 'nervous recoil into composure', a 'centripetal backwash that checks the rot' (*Dream*, 119). The elements of the classical novel are 'artificially immobilised'.

As John Bolin has pointed out, this passage in *Dream* is indebted to André Gide's *Dostoïevsky*, and Beckett's lectures on Gide at

Trinity College Dublin.[51] The narrator's comment about the resemblance of Balzac's characters to 'clockwork cabbages' (119) resembles Beckett's snipe in his lecture: 'B[alzac] considers humanity as so much vegetable inertia' (TCD MIC60, 58). As we have already seen, Dostoevsky is repeatedly described as a quietist by Gide, and Beckett quotes and agrees with this assessment in his lecture.

The book that Beckett relied on, *Dostoïevsky: articles et causeries*, grew out of a set of six talks that Gide gave in February and March 1922. Dostoevsky's novels were not well-known in France at that time and Gide spends much of his discussion explaining what makes them so distinctive and worthy of a wider audience. He acknowledges that the importance of humility and abnegation in Dostoevsky's writing are challenging to the 'Western mind', but says that this is precisely why they need to be read, and particularly in France. To illustrate this, Gide approvingly quotes the critic Jacques Rivière's description of the process of writing a novel:

> Once the idea of a character has arisen in his mind, the novelist has two different ways of putting it to work. Either he can insist on the character's complexity, or he can emphasise their coherence. (quoted in *Dost*, 166–7)

According to Rivière, the French have always chosen the latter:

> We, on the other hand, faced with a soul's complexity, however much we try to represent it, we instinctively seek to organize it. […] If need be, we give it a helping hand; we suppress a few little discrepancies and interpret certain obscure details in whatever sense is most advantageous to the creation of a psychological unity. (quoted in *Dost*, 167–8)

---

51 Bolin, chap. 1.

Gide then applies Rivière's description to Balzac, who is cast as the French foil to Dostoevsky. Although there are odd moments of incoherence and contradiction in Balzac's novels, Gide says that these are of no interest to the author himself, who ploughs on with his narrative regardless of the slip, or, as Beckett puts it, makes a 'nervous recoil into composure' (*Dream*, 119). These moments are 'failles'—faults—from Balzac's perspective. According to Gide, the French—or Western European—attachment to the illusion of psychological unity in literature is an expression of will and *amour propre*. Gide complains that too many of Balzac's most strong-willed characters ('volontaires'; *Dost*, 145) are also the most virtuous and respectable. Following Rivière, Gide suggests that all Westerners, but particularly the French, try to live their lives according to this Balzacian ideal, believing strongly in 'their unity, [...] their continuity' and ignoring all the moments of contradiction, negation, instability and disorganisation (169). Most of us, Gide says, have only a 'disquieting premonition of [our] inconstancy', which we try and suppress (178). 'We have an unfortunate tendency in France,' he adds, 'to stick to the formula—which quickly becomes a method—and to rely on it, without seeking to override it' (181). This is surely what Beckett's narrator calls the 'procédé that seems all falsity, that of Balzac' (*Dream*, 119).

Dostoevsky could not be less like Balzac. According to Gide, the Russian novelist is a quietist, who believes in salvation via the renunciation of the will, the abnegation of self and a deep sense of humility:

> Balzac's *Human Comedy* arose from the contact between the Gospel and the Latin mind; the Russian comedy of Dostoevsky emerged from the contact between the Gospel and Buddhism, the Asian mind. (*Dost*, 148–9)
>
> Dostoevsky leads us, if not to anarchy, then to a sort of Buddhism, or at least quietism (226–7)

And it is precisely this quietism, humility, and renunciation that allows Dostoevsky to see the self as it really is: a collection of 'most contrary sentiments' and an 'extraordinary wealth of antagonisms' (117). Forty years before Mikhail Bakhtin put forward his celebrated reading of Dostoevsky's 'polyphonic' novels and the 'unfinalizability' and 'unclosedness' of their characters,[52] Gide made a remarkably similar argument that stressed Dostoevsky's radical embrace of inconsistency, instability, and contradiction. The classical realist novel, Gide claimed, tries to ignore or supress these contrary tendencies of the human mind. On this count, at least, Dostoevsky's novels are more 'realist' than those of a classical realist like Balzac. In a letter to his friend Apollon Maikov, Dostoevsky described his aesthetic as 'fantastic realism':

> I have a totally different conception of reality and realism than our novelists and critics. My idealism—is more real than their realism. God! Just to narrate sensibly what we Russians have lived through in the last ten years of our spiritual development—yes, would not the realists shout that this is fantasy! And yet this is genuine, existing realism. This is realism, only deeper; while they swim in shallow waters ... Their realism— cannot illuminate a hundredth part of the facts that are real and actually occurring.[53]

Joseph Frank adds that Dostoevsky's realism becomes fantastic because it 'delves beneath the quotidian surface into the moral-spiritual depths of the human personality'.[54] Like Dostoevsky, Beckett aspired to plumb the depths of the inner world through his art. In the *Whoroscope* notebook, he imagined a 'geology of conscience' (UoR MS3000, 6v), a phrase that embraces not just the moral life of a human being but also the psychological: the *OED* notes an archaic sense of 'con-

---

52 Mikhail Bakhtin, *Problems of Dostoevsky's Politics*, trans. by Caryl Emerson (London: University of Minnesota Press, 1984), pp. 53, 63.
53 Quoted in Frank, p. 575.
54 Frank, p. 575.

science' as 'inward knowledge', and John Pilling points out that Beckett's bilingualism may have left its mark here, since the French *conscience* means something more like sensibility or consciousness than moral perspicacity.[55] In the manuscript of *Watt*, this excavation of consciousness is suggested in the expression 'auto-speliology' [*sic*]:[56] perhaps a practice of delving deep into the caverns of the self, and searching out whatever is '[b]uried in who knows what profounds of mind', as *Ohio Impromptu* has it (*CDW*, 448). In *Dream*, Belacqua is described simultaneously as a cave explorer—wanting to 'troglodyse' himself and be 'drawn down to the blessedly sunless depths' into the 'bearings of the earth' (122–3)—and as a kind of contemplative recluse: the narrator compares him to 'La Fontaine's catawampus' (122), an allusion to the fable of the rat who retires from the world to live in a cheese, isolated like a hermit, a monk, or a dervish.[57] Beckett, then, wanted to base his writing on an inner archaeology resembling the introspective practices of religious contemplatives.[58] This suggests that he would have appreciated why Gide chose to align Dostoevsky with the Buddhists and the quietists.

Beckett's writing on Marcel Proust shows more evidence of how he was continuing to draw on Gide's aesthetic judgements in *Dostoïevsky*. Beckett commended Proust's 'fertile research' in *À la recherche du temps perdu* for being 'excavatory, immersive, a contraction of the spirit, a descent' (*PTD*, 65). According to Beckett, Proust's 'insane inward necessity' results in 'a fine Dostoievskian contempt for the vulgarity of a plausible concatenation'; that is, his novel refuses any straightforward causality (*PTD*, 81–2). Beckett connects Proust to something quietistic when he links Proust's project to the 'wisdom of all the sages' (*PTD*, 18). Four years later, reviewing Albert Feuillerat's

---

55   John Pilling, 'Dates and Difficulties in Beckett's *Whoroscope* Notebook', *Journal of Beckett Studies*, 13 (2004), 39–48 (p. 46).
56   Ackerley, *Obscure Locks*, p. 24.
57   Jean de La Fontaine, *Fables* (Tours: Alfred Mame et fils, 1870), pp. 234–5.
58   For more on Beckett's inner archaeologies, see Andy Wimbush, 'Palaeozoic Profounds: Samuel Beckett and Ecological Time' in *Time and Temporality*, ed. by MDRN (Leuven: Peeters Publishing, 2016), pp. 3–14.

Comment Proust a composé son roman in 1934, Beckett made a similar point. I briefly mentioned in Chapter 1 that Beckett saw the 'conflict between intervention and quietism' as constituting 'the essence of Proust's originality' (*Dis*, 65). Quietism here refers to the occasions when Proust allowed his work to stand without too much commentary and explanation, thereby imbuing the novel with 'perturbations and dislocations' (*Dis*, 64). Beckett says that this was the Proust that Gide admired, the one who 'abominated' such things as '[u]niformity, homogeneity, cohesion, selection scavenging for verisimilitude' and 'naturalism' (*Dis*, 64). Feuillerat, however, thinks that Proust had wanted to 'remove all discord and dissension' and his book explains how the novel's incongruities might have been be smoothed over had Proust lived long enough. This review is clearly indebted to Gide's quietist aesthetic in *Dostoïevsky*: Beckett says that what Feuillerat wants is 'the sweet reasonableness of plane psychology à la Balzac'.

Beckett felt Gide had imbibed the lesson of Dostoevsky: Burrows records Beckett mentioning that *La Porte étroite* and *Les Faux-Monnayeurs* have a 'quality of inconclusiveness' and 'integrity of incoherence', both of which were earned through Gide's own 'humility' and 'Renunciation' (TCD MIC60, 43, 37, 25, 14). In *Dream*, the narrator's discussion of the refractory elements of the novel make it clear that Beckett aims to follow Gide and his Dostoevskian aesthetic of humility and quietism, and the language of waste, decay, and rot is introduced in support of this Gidean quest for incoherence. The narrator then highlights the relevance of quietism and introspection for this project by promptly turning to Belacqua's quietist tendencies as soon as Balzac has been dismissed:

> [Belacqua's] third being was the dark gulf, when the glare of the will and the hammer-strokes of the brain doomed outside to take flight from its quarry were expunged, the Limbo and the wombtomb alive with the unanxious spirits of quiet cerebration, where there was no conflict of flight and flow. (*Dream*, 121)

As we saw in the last chapter, this 'third being', like Murphy's third zone of dark will-lessness, is indebted to Gide's description of Dostoevsky's characters. Belacqua's habits, then, are themselves a statement of Beckett's aesthetic and philosophical allegiance: against Balzac, but with Gide, Dostoevsky, Schopenhauer, and quietism.

Nevertheless, *Dream of Fair to Middling Women* remains an unquiet, wilful, even arrogant novel, bursting with obscure allusions and foreign languages. As Anthony Cronin says, the tone can be 'ingratiating, cocky and would-be Olympian'.[59] Much of this was because Beckett had not yet been able to extricate himself from the feeling that he should try to write like his literary mentor, James Joyce, whose 'notesnatching' tendencies he had adopted while researching the novel (SB to TM, n.d. [c. 8/31]).[60] 'I wouldn't touch this with a barge-pole,' wrote Edward Garnett after reading *Dream* for the publisher Jonathan Cape, 'Beckett is probably a very clever fellow, but here he has elaborated a slavish and rather incoherent imitation of Joyce'.[61] Thomas MacGreevy was of the same opinion: he read 'Sedendo et Quiescendo', a story extracted from *Dream* (64–73), and told Charles Prentice at Chatto & Windus that Beckett 'went Joyce in it, though he denies that it is Joyce'.[62] Beckett was eventually forced to admit the same: 'Of course it stinks of Joyce,' he wrote to Prentice, 'in spite of my most earnest endeavours to endow it with my own odours' (15/8/31, *LSB1*, 81). The text seems to be rotting, but somehow it was not yet a decomposition that he could call his own. Beckett had perhaps spent too much of his energy setting himself up against Balzac's classicism, and not nearly enough trying to break away from the influence of Joyce.

In *Dream*, Beckett had called Balzac the 'absolute master of his material' (119), and blamed Balzac's overweening control of his novels for their inability to accommodate Dostoevskian incoherence. In *Proust*, he wrote that, unlike the author of *À la recherche du temps perdu*,

---

59 Anthony Cronin, *Samuel Beckett: The Last Modernist* (London: HarperCollins, 1996), p. 170.
60 Quoted and related to Joyce in Nixon and Van Hulle, p. 11.
61 Quoted in Knowlson, p. 163.
62 Quoted in Pilling, *Beckett before Godot*, p. 56.

the 'classical artist'—like Balzac, for example—'assumes omniscience and omnipotence' so that he can raise 'himself artificially out of Time in order to give relief to his chronology and causality to his development' (*PTD*, 81). But much later in life, Beckett used precisely the same words to distinguish himself from Joyce. He told Israel Shenker in 1956:

> Joyce is a *superb manipulator of material*—perhaps the greatest. He was making words do the absolute maximum of work. There isn't a syllable that's superfluous. The kind of work I do is one in which I'm not master of my material. The more Joyce knew the more he could. He's tending toward *omniscience and omnipotence* as an artist. I'm working with impotence, ignorance.[63]

Thirty-three years later, just months before his death, Beckett repeated this point to James Knowlson, describing Joyce as going 'as far as one could go' in 'the direction of knowing more' and of being 'in control of one's material'.[64]

It seems such an unlikely choice on Beckett's part to describe Joyce in exactly the same terms as he used for Balzac. Not just because of the obvious and striking differences in their approach to novel writing, but also because Beckett was a great admirer of Joyce, while, like Gide, he scorned Balzac. It suggests that Beckett believed that Joyce and Balzac were both opposed to the quietist aesthetic position that he adopted after reading Gide's *Dostoïevsky*, albeit in different ways. 'I realised,' Beckett told Knowlson, 'that my own way was in impoverishment, in lack of knowledge and in taking away, in subtracting rather than adding'.[65] The qualities that Beckett adopts to differentiate himself from Joyce—impotence, impoverishment, ignorance, loss of control—suggest that *Dream of Fair to Middling Women* had not been nearly

---

63 Israel Shenker, 'Interview with Beckett', in *Samuel Beckett: The Critical Heritage*, ed. by Lawrence Graver and Raymond Federman (London: Routledge, 2005), pp. 160–64 (p. 162).
64 Beckett, quoted in Knowlson, p. 352.
65 Beckett, quoted in Knowlson, p. 352.

quietist enough. As Ackerley and Feldman have shown, this recognition that a humble quietism had to be integrated further into his writing was a crucial part of Beckett's aesthetic development over the course of the 1930s.[66] Ackerley points to an entry in Beckett's German diaries, in which he discusses Walter Bauer's novel *Die Notwendige Reise* [The Necessary Journey] and the 'heroic, the nosce te ipsum [know thyself], that these Germans see as a journey':

> Das notwendige Bleiben [the necessary staying-put] is more like it. That is also in the figure of Murphy in the chair, surrender to the thongs of self, a simple materialisation of self-bondage, acceptance of which is the fundamental unheroic.[67] (GD, 18/1/37)

Like Gide's Dostoevsky, Beckett finds self-knowledge not through heroic journeying, but through surrender, inwardness, and acceptance. And once again this stands in contrast to Beckett's assessment of Joyce's work, which he dubbed a 'heroic achievement'.[68] Ackerley adds:

> The "fundamental unheroic" offered Beckett a way of accommodating the ethic of [Thomas] à Kempis and Geulincx to the exigencies of the contingent world. The aesthetic is one with the ethic. Beckett's reaction to Joyce reflects the desire to escape the heroic consciousness of language exemplified in "Work in Progress" (an endless echo-chamber of resonance, metaphor and connotation), to attempt to write "without style". [...] His way, taking its point of departure from the quietism of Thomas à Kempis and the *humilitas* of Arnold Geulincx, would be fundamentally unheroic.[69]

---

66   Ackerley, 'The Roots of Quietism'; Feldman, 'Agnostic Quietism'.
67   Quoted in Nixon, p. 73.
68   Beckett, quoted in Knowlson, p. 352.
69   Ackerley, 'The Roots of Quietism', p. 89.

Even the 'heroic' epithet that Beckett applies to Joyce may have stemmed from Gide's criticism of Balzac. According to Gide, Balzac's characters are heroes and examples of the 'grand homme'. In Dostoevsky, however, greatness is exemplified by Elder Zosima, who according to Gide is 'a saint, not a hero' (146).

Beckett's desire to shake off Joyce's influence seems to have been part of that lifelong pensum that Molloy alludes to. 'I vow I will get over J.J. ere I die', Beckett wrote to Samuel Putnam in June 1932 (28/6/32; *LSB1*, 108). After the war, he reached a turning point in this struggle. In December 1950, Beckett told the critic and writer Niall Montgomery that he felt 'Joyceology' had become 'impossible' for him, adding: 'Hope to have a book to send you soon, illustrative of this process' (29/12/50).[70] This book was *Molloy*, which would finally reach publication through Éditions de Minuit in March 1951. 'Only then did I begin to write the things I feel', he later said.[71] In *Molloy*, the task of dispensing with Joyce is reiterated allusively. As a number of critics have pointed out,[72] *Molloy* makes many references to Homer's *Odyssey*, the story that Joyce appropriated to create *Ulysses*. Molloy is, however, no Odysseus:

> I who had loved the image of old Geulincx, dead young, who left me free, on the black boat of Ulysses, to crawl towards the East, along the deck. That is a great measure of freedom, for him who has not the pioneering spirit. And from the poop, poring upon the wave, a sadly rejoicing slave, I follow with my eyes the proud and futile wake. Which as it bears me from no fatherland away, bears me on to no shipwreck. (*Mo*, 50)

---

70 Samuel Beckett, *The Letters of Samuel Beckett: Volume 2, 1941–1956*, ed. by George Craig and others (Cambridge: Cambridge University Press, 2011), p. 209. Hereafter, *LSB2*.
71 Gabriel d' Aubarède, 'Interview with Beckett', in *Samuel Beckett: The Critical Heritage*, ed. by Lawrence Graver and Raymond Federman (London: Routledge, 2005), pp. 238–40 (p. 240).
72 See for example Rubin Rabinowitz, 'Molloy and the Archetypal Traveller', *Journal of Beckett Studies*, 5 (1979), 25–44; K.J. Phillips, 'Beckett's *Molloy* and *The Odyssey*', *The International Fiction Review*, 11 (1984), 19–24.

As Beckett explained in a letter to Erich Franzen, the German translator of *Molloy*, the allusion is to a passage in Geulincx's *Ethica*. Geulincx uses the image of a man walking from the bow to the stern of a moving boat as a metaphor for free will in this universe governed by divine decree:

> Just as a ship carrying a passenger with all speed towards the west in no way prevents the passenger from walking towards the east, so the will of God, carrying all things, impelling all things with inexorable force, in no way prevents us from resisting his will (as much as is in our power) with complete freedom.[73]

Beckett adds the reference to *The Odyssey*, which, he told Franzen, comes via Dante's *Inferno*. In Canto 26, Ulysses tells Virgil and the pilgrim how he encouraged his crew to risk the dangerous passage beyond the Pillars of Hercules in search of adventures in the western seas. As Tucker points out, Dante's Ulysses resorts to 'flattery of their inner lives as well as their heritage and heroism in the "big" physical world'.[74] Such heroism is, of course, an anathema to Molloy. 'I imagine,' wrote Beckett to Franzen, 'a member of the crew who does not share the adventurous spirit of Ulysses and is at least at liberty to crawl homewards (nach Osten) along the brief deck' (SB to EF, 17/2/54; *LSB2*, 458). In his analysis of the passage in *Molloy*, Tucker does not, however, choose to say anything about Joyce, whose name would have been inextricably linked to the Latinate 'Ulysses' in Beckett's mind. Beckett was indeed a member of Joyce's crew in the 1930s—aboard the *Work in Progress*—and perhaps felt that he was that unadventurous sailor watching his mentor's proud *Wake* emerge. If, as Tucker says, Molloy's rejection of Dante's Ulysses via Geulincx is a rejection of heroism, then it must also stand in for Beckett's own rejection of Joyce's 'heroic achievement' in favour of his own 'fundamental unheroic'.

---

73 Arnold Geulincx, *Arnold Geulincx' Ethics: With Samuel Beckett's Notes*, ed. by Han Van Ruler and Anthony Uhlmann, trans. by Martin Wilson (Leiden: Brill, 2006), p. 134.
74 Tucker, p. 120.

Dante followed Horace's lead in ascribing to Ulysses an overweening desire for knowledge, paraphrasing the *Ars Poetica* in Ulysses's admission of his 'long desire, burning to understand how this world works, and know of human vices, worth and valour' (XXVI.98).[75] As Robin Kirkpatrick explains, Dante saw Ulysses as both 'a possible model for intellectual heroism' and 'a problematical figure', whose example can be embraced 'only with extreme qualification':

> By inventing the figure of Ulysses as an imaginative *alter ego*, Dante now holds up a critical mirror to many of the principles which underlie not only his fictive journey through the other world, but also the intellectual, narrative and linguistic procedures on which his poem is founded.[76]

Beckett's relationship to Joyce could be expressed in similar terms, and as his words to Montgomery suggest, *Molloy* was a pivotal moment in the development of his own literary practice away from 'Joyceology'. Dante's admiration for Ulysses is eventually reined in by Catholic orthodoxy and Virgil's calm, detached presence. For Beckett, Geulincx plays this role, countering the heroic example of Ulysses with the exemplar of the man who knows the limits of his freedom. As I mentioned in Chapter 1, Geulincx played a fundamental role in rehabilitating quietism within Beckett's life, and complemented the aesthetics and ethics of humility that he derived from Gide.

The Tranquillity of Decomposition

Molloy, then, is a continuation of the aesthetic project begun with *Dream*, but now with Joyce's high modernism as well as Balzac's classical realism as its foil and antagonist. As we have seen, the narrator of *Dream* justifies an aesthetics of decomposition and incoherence just

---

75 Dante Alighieri, *Inferno*, trans. by Robin Kirkpatrick (London: Penguin, 2006), p. 231 On Horace, see Kirkpatrick's note on p. 418.
76 Robin Kirkpatrick, 'Commentaries and Notes', in Dante Alighieri, pp. 412–413.

before describing Belacqua's will-less, quiet mind. Similarly, in *Molloy*, where quietism and decomposition are noticeable thematic concerns, the narration also hints at their aesthetic relevance. Molloy says:

> It is in the tranquillity of decomposition that I remember the long confused emotion which was my life, and that I judge it, as it is said that God will judge me, and with no less impertinence. (*Mo*, 22)

As Dirk Van Hulle has pointed out, this is an inversion of a passage from Wordsworth's own statement of aesthetics in his preface to *Lyrical Ballads*, in which poetic composition is defined as 'the spontaneous overflow of powerful feelings' arising 'from emotion recollected in tranquillity'.[77] Beckett alludes to Wordsworth's definition elsewhere: in 'The Expelled'—'Recollecting these emotions, with the celebrated advantage of tranquillity' (*CSP*, 58)—in *Texts for Nothing*—'what tranquillity, and know there are no more emotions in store' (*CSP*, 125), and, most significantly for my purposes, immediately before Belacqua's theory of the hypostatical clysterpipe in *Dream of Fair to Middling Women*: 'On this emotion recollected in tranquillity' (185). Wordsworth sees tranquillity in composition: composure in composure perhaps. But Molloy, holding true to the principles of Guyon, and also those of Gide and Dostoevsky, believes that it is decomposition where we find true tranquillity. While this 'attitude of disintegration'[78] would fail to fit with what Beckett called, in his lectures on Gide, the 'artificial Romantic fabricated model' of wilful self-creation (TCD MIC60, 21), it accords perfectly with the quietist impulse towards annihilation, and with Gide's belief that Dostoevsky's work itself can bring about some kind of quietude in the reader. Gide says that *The Eternal Husband*, for example, can transport us to that third region of mind, the one so

---

77 Dirk Van Hulle, 'Accursed Creator: Beckett, Romanticism, and the Modern Prometheus', *Samuel Beckett Today / Aujourd'hui*, 18 (2007), 15–29 (p. 19).
78 Beckett, quoted in Shenker, p. 162.

cherished by Murphy and Belacqua. Just as Belacqua found 'emancipation, in a slough of indifference and negligence and disinterest, from identity' (*Dream*, 121), so Gide describes this region as one 'where the limits of being vanish, where the sense of self and sense of time are lost' (212–3). Molloy too seems to reach a similar state every now and again:

> Yes, there were times when I forgot not only who I was, but that I was, forgot to be. Then I was no longer that sealed jar to which I owed my being so well preserved, but a wall gave way. (*Mo*, 48)

The preservation in the 'sealed jar' suggests Balzac's 'chloroformed world' (*Dream*, 119). Beckett imagined that Feuillerat's classical Balzacian Proust would have 'embalmed the whole' of *À la recherche du temps perdu* by obliterating its quietism and papering over its contradictions. To be out of that embalmed and chloroformed world is to be free to rot, to allow the constituents of the self and text to waste away and be annihilated. No longer 'sealed' inside a self, Molloy fulfils Gide's Dostoevskian imperative to avoid unity, Guyon's teachings on decay, St Teresa's Great Dereliction, and also Schopenhauer's instruction to reject the illusion of separation from the rest of the world: the *principium individuationis*.

If Balzac and Jane Austen recoil from fragmentation, then *Molloy* recoils from composition. Part I of the novel decomposes itself when Molloy starts to admit the fictitiousness of it all. He, or perhaps a more fundamental narratorial voice, or possibly even Beckett himself, announces:

> when I say I said, etc., all I mean is that I knew confusedly things were so, without knowing exactly what it was all about. And every time I say, I said this, or I said that, or speak of a voice saying, far away inside me, Molloy, and then a fine phrase more or less clear and simple, or find myself compelled to attribute to others intelligible words, or hear my own voice

uttering to others more or less articulate sounds, I am merely complying with the convention that demands you either lie or hold your peace. (*Mo*, 89)

This is the 'convention' of fiction: to invent, to lie, to tell stories, rather than holding one's peace and remaining silent. At this point in *Molloy*, the fictional curtain starts to slip and the reader gets a glimpse of the novel's inner workings. The novel 'decomposes' by quoting itself and calling attention to the process of composition: 'I might doubtless have expressed otherwise and better,' Molloy says, 'if I had gone to the trouble' (*Mo*, 90). This is not emotion recalled in composition, but composition recalled in composition. Molloy has tried to leave the forest by walking in a circle: he reasons that if walking in a straight line usually results in you walking in a circle, then the best way to walk in a straight line would be to try as hard as possible to walk in a circle. Getting out of the forest becomes tantamount to finishing the narration, and so circling back on itself and recalling its own composition might actually cause the whole thing to come to an end.

Moran Checks the Rot

Moran's 'order' is 'to see about Molloy' (*Mo*, 95; 'm'occuper de Molloy', *MF*, 127), but neither he nor the reader is ever quite clear what exactly this would entail: 'I could not determine [...] how I was to deal with Molloy, once I had found him' (143). Moran's love of 'decorum' (106), however, suggests that he would find himself at home in the world of 'composure' that Beckett finds in the novels of Austen and Balzac. Perhaps his task is simply to tell a story without it disintegrating in the way that Molloy's does: his role is to write the 'centripetal backwash that checks the rot' (*Dream*, 119). A number of critics have pointed out how Beckett's argument with Balzac continues from *Dream* into *Malone Dies*. Ruby Cohn notes that Malone's story of the Lamberts, who are called the Louis in the French text, are indebted to Balzac's 1832 novel, *Louis Lambert*, and John Bolin has shown how Beckett makes a number of ironic allusions to Balzac's story.[79] The Unnamable's story about the

---

79 Bolin, p. 157.

lovers separated by war (*U*, 125–6) is a parody of Balzac's *Le Colonel Chabert* (1832), according to Bolin.[80] It's not surprising then that Balzac's presence can be found in *Molloy* as well.

Moran has, at first sight, all the 'assurance' that Gide found in Balzac's characters. Molloy was unable to decide whether his account was written—'This should all be re-written in the pluperfect' (13), 'Oh it's only a diary' (61)—or spoken—'I speak in the present tense' (23), 'truly it little matters what I say' (29). He also begins his narrative uncertain of his name and how he has arrived at his present situation. Moran, by contrast, introduces himself in the first paragraph, says that he is writing a report, establishes his location, and explains how he received the order from Youdi to start his hunt for Molloy. Moran's first name Jacques suggests that he might be French. If this is the case, then—according to his compatriots Rivière and Gide—he would be a believer in psychological continuity, living his life according to a Balzacian ideal. True to form, he enjoys 'thinking in monologue' (98) and abhors 'Vagueness' (103) and 'light-mindedness' (99). Whereas Dostoevsky's characters have 'abîmes' [gulfs] according to Gide and Rivière, and Molloy enjoys the 'spurious deeps' (*Mo*, 18), Moran describes himself as 'a sensible man, cold as crystal and free from spurious depth' (117). In Balzac's novels, Beckett said, 'characters can't change their minds or artistic order crashes—must be consistent' (TCD MIC60, 41). 'I […] never changed my mind before my son,' says Moran, suggesting that he sees it as shameful or weak to do so (107). In *Dream*, the narrator attacks Balzac for being able to plan his novels in advance:

> He is absolute master of his material, he can do what he likes with it, he can foresee and calculate its least vicissitude, he can write the end of the book before he has finished the first paragraph, because he has turned all his creatures into clockwork cabbages and can rely on their staying put wherever needed or staying going at whatever speed in whatever direction he chooses. (*Dream*, 119–120)

---

80 Bolin, p. 175.

Moran, who loves 'punctuality' just a little less than decorum (106), is cast from the same mould:

> I had a methodical mind and never set out on a mission without prolonged reflection as to the best way of setting out. It was the first problem to solve, at the outset of each enquiry, and I never moved until I had solved it, to my satisfaction. [...] how can you decide on the way of setting out if you do not first know where you are going, or at least with what purpose you are going there? (*Mo*, 101–2)

This is in contrast to Molloy, of course, but also to Beckett who told Charles Juliet: 'When I wrote the first sentence of *Molloy* I did not know where I was going. [...] I had planned nothing. Worked out nothing.'[81]

Phil Baker suggests that Moran's surname goes back to Beckett's earliest encounter with the French language. Beckett named the Elsner sisters in *Molloy* (109) after the two women who ran the kindergarten he attended. It is possible, argues Baker, that Beckett took Moran's surname from another childhood memory, in this case J.A. Moran, the author of the textbook *French Grammar and Composition*, which was widely used in Dublin classrooms in the early twentieth century.[82] Molloy found tranquillity in decomposition, and now Moran is here to impose re-composition and orderly grammar-like rules. Moran's Frenchness may also be indebted to Beckett's reading of Schopenhauer's *World as Will and Representation*. Schopenhauer thought it was remarkable that one of the strictest of Christian monastic orders, the Trappists, should have emerged in France, 'the most cheerful, sensual, frivolous nation in Europe'. While the Trappists, much like Molloy's Carthusians, are busy renouncing worldly pleasures, the French, Schopenhauer says, go about with a great 'lust for life' (*WWR*, I.4.68, 422). He makes a similar point later on:

---

81 Juliet, p. 17.
82 Phil Baker, 'Beckett's Bilingualism and a Possible Source for the Name of Moran in *Molloy*', *Journal of Beckett Studies*, 3 (1994), 81–84.

> The huge difference between the English, or more properly Chinese garden and the traditional French garden […] is ultimately grounded in the fact that the former are laid out in an objective and the latter in a subjective manner. Specifically, in the former, the will of nature, as it objectifies itself in trees, shrubs, mountains, and bodies of water, is allowed the purest possible expression of these Ideas, which is to say of its own being. The French garden on the other hand reflects only the will of the owner, who has subjugated nature so that instead of its own Ideas, nature bears the forms that suit him but have been forced upon it, as tokens of its slavery: clipped hedges, trees cut into all sorts of shapes, straight avenues, archways, etc. (*WWR*, II.3.33, 421–2)

Moran owns a garden, and is, as Schopenhauer suggests, very possessive about it. He speaks of 'my lemon-verbena', 'my daisies', 'my Beauty of Bath' (a kind of dessert apple) (97), 'my hives' (183), 'my hens', 'my birds' and 'My trees, my bushes, my flower-beds, my tiny lawns' (133). As he leaves the garden he asserts his power and will over it: 'I offered my face to the black mass of fragrant vegetation that was mine and with which I could do as I pleased and never be gainsaid' (133). His garden contains nothing that did not, in Schopenhauer's words, 'grow up under the whipping stick of the great egoist' (*WWR*, II.3.33, 421). Molloy, on the other hand, demonstrates his allegiance to the English and Chinese traditions. In one of his ecstatic moments of self-forgetting, Molloy feels his 'life become the life of this garden as it rode the earth of deeps and wilderness' (*Mo*, 48). This is appropriate because Schopenhauer also says that untamed, wild nature, like beautiful works of art, can act as a 'cathartic of the mind'. Rather than owning the garden as Moran does, Molloy allows the garden to take him over: 'I filled with roots and tame stems' (48). Molloy's dissolution into the natural world owes something not just to the English Romantics, but also, as Geoff Hamilton has argued,[83] to their Renaissance precursor Andrew Marvell, whose poem 'The Garden' imagines:

---

83 Geoff Hamilton, 'Annihilating All That's Made: Beckett's *Molloy* and the Pastoral Tradition', *Samuel Beckett Today / Aujourd'hui*, 15 (2005), 325–39.

> Annihilating all that's made
> To a green thought in a green shade.[84]

Molloy has Chinese affinities too: when he weeps, he says that it 'was like being in China' (23), and he seems to admire the 'peaceful' and 'vague oriental' who comes into his room at Lousse's house (42). In Schopenhauer's garden analogy, Molloy corresponds to the resignation of his own will, whereas Moran, unsurprisingly, asserts his will over the natural world.

If rot has been aligned with quietism in the first part of *Molloy*, it is fitting that Moran should at first appear to be a devout practising Catholic who, unlike the Quietists, enjoys the external rituals of his faith. He sneers at the 'free-thinker' who lives nearby (101) and seems to regard proofs of the existence of God as 'superfetatory' (103), that is, superfluous. He has a maid called Martha, which recalls the sister of Mary of Bethany (traditionally identified with Mary Magdalene). In the gospel account, Mary chooses to sit at Jesus's feet when he arrives at their house, while Martha busies herself with serving the guests. Martha asks Jesus to tell Mary to help her, but he replies:

> Martha, Martha, thou art careful and troubled about many things: But one thing is needful: and Mary hath chosen that good part, which shall not be taken away from her. (Luke 10:38–42)

Theologians from Origen and Augustine onwards have seen Martha as a representative of the active part of Christian life, while Mary stands for the contemplative life that Molloy has embraced.[85] Madame

---

84 Andrew Marvell, *The Complete Poems*, ed. by Elizabeth Story Donno (Harmondsworth: Penguin, 1996), p. 101.
85 Charlotte Radler, 'Actio et Contemplatio / Action and Contemplation', in *The Cambridge Companion to Christian Mysticism*, ed. by Amy Hollywood and Patricia Z. Beckman (Cambridge: Cambridge University Press), pp. 211–22 (pp. 212–213).

Guyon identifies with Mary in her book, *A Short and Easy Method of Prayer*, in a passage quoted by La Bruyère:

> Martha did good things, but because she did them under the power of her own spirit, Jesus Christ chided her. [...] Mary, it is said, has chosen the better part, peace, tranquillity, and repose: She had stopped acting in order to let herself be moved by the spirit of Jesus Christ, [...] and this is why it is necessary to renounce our own operations and ourselves so that we can follow Jesus Christ.[86]

Like the Biblical Martha, Moran likes to get on with things: 'I knew my business' (97). He never misses mass (98) and likes to sit in the front row at church, so that his religious habits are visible to both his neighbours and his employers (103). He is a man of 'meticulous piety' (99). He worries about the effect of a pint of beer on his capacity to receive communion, and frets over whether consuming alcohol before taking the sacrament constitutes a sin (100). This is the opposite of the Quietist tendency to neglect the formal trappings of religion. In La Bruyère's *Dialogues*, for instance, the penitent is encouraged to be remain indifferent to vice and virtue, and is told that the 'resigned soul' will eventually become disgusted with Sunday prayers, good works, and the sacraments of confession and communion.[87] And rather than embrace his powerlessness in the manner of Beckett's unheroic aesthetic and the passive resignation of the Quietists, Moran attempts to 'gild [his] impotence' (109). Finally, Moran describes himself as 'patiently turned towards the outer world' (118), and therefore unlike the seedy solipsists found in Beckett's other novels. This matches Beckett's assessment of Arnold Geulincx: 'very patiently turned outward' (SB to TM, 5/3/36; *LSB1*, 319). As I discussed in Chapter 1, this outward turn was what Beckett chose to distinguish Geulincx from the '*Schwärmerei*' of quietism. Geulincx's legacy, then, is split in two in

---

86 La Bruyère, p. 67. Translation modified from *The Complete Madame Guyon*, p. 79.
87 La Bruyère, p. 134.

Molloy: Molloy gets the quietist aspect—the will-lessness of the unadventurous crew member aboard Ulysses's black cruiser—while Moran inherits Geulincx's outward turn, and little, it seems, of his interest in the inner world or humility. But this does not last long.

Moran's Putrefaction

The beginning of Part II sees Moran in Balzacian-Catholic mode, full of assurance and external pieties, ready to hunt out Molloy, the Dostoevskian-Quietist. But there are more than a few hints that the quietist rot he has been sent to correct has set in irrevocably. For one thing, Moran has a number of quietist tendencies himself, which are apparent from the beginning of his story and which become more prominent the closer he gets to his 'quietist Pater'. When Gaber brings him his assignment, he appears in the garden as a 'high mass' (96): a Catholic presence in other words. Moran thinks dismissively of Gaber's 'heavy, sombre Sunday best', saying to himself: 'This gross external observance, while the soul exults in rags, has always appeared to me an abomination' (97). A suspicion of external observances is a Protestant trait, but also a Quietist one as we saw in the reports of Bishop Burnet and the Archbishop of Naples in Chapter 1.

And just as the Quietists seemed to forget about God as their contemplative prayer deepened, Moran, barely set out on his journey, finds that 'God [...] is beginning to disgust me' (109). In the French version of the novel, he refers to his writing task as a 'pensum', that Schopenhauerian task he must work off, like Molloy and like Beckett:

> c'est une des caractéristiques de ce pensum qu'il ne m'est pas permis de brûler les étapes et de dire tout de go de quoi il s'agit. (183)

> it is one of the features of this penance that I may not pass over what is over and straight away come to the heart of the matter (138)

Molloy often speaks of listening to the sounds of nature and even to silence itself. He enjoys a 'night of listening':

> when there is more vigilance, and then something else that is not clear, being neither the air nor what it moves, perhaps the far unchanging noise the earth makes and which other noises cover, but not for long. For they do not account for that noise you hear when you really listen, when all seems hushed. (47–48)

Like the Quietist before God, Molloy aims to surrender to the night, to 'open to it like the flower to the sun' (67). He finds that 'about me all goes really silent, from time to time' (26). Moran, as he seeks Molloy, starts to get a taste for this kind of silent listening. He says:

> Not one person in a hundred knows how to be silent and listen, no, nor even to conceive what such a thing means. Yet only then you detect, beyond the fatuous clamour, the silence of which the universe is made. (126)

The exhortation to listen deeply is commonplace in quietist and contemplative texts. Moran's distinction between the deep silence that sustains the universe and the 'fatuous clamour' of everyday life is remarkably similar to one made by Thomas à Kempis in *The Imitation of Christ*: 'Blessed are the ears which receive the echoes of the soft whisper of God, and turn not aside to the whisperings of this world' (III.I). Even though he does not employ theistic language, Moran's point is the same. Another instruction appears in *Christian Mysticism*, given by pseudo-Hierotheus, a Syrian mystic whom Inge calls a preacher of 'Pan-Nihilism' and whose method of prayer 'is that of the Quietists':

> To me it seems right to speak without words, and understand without knowledge, that which is above words and knowledge; this I apprehend to be nothing but the mysterious silence and mystical quiet which destroys consciousness and dissolves forms. (*CM*, 103)

Finally, Molinos himself, paraphrased by Inge, teaches this practice:

> The best kind of prayer is the prayer of silence; and there are three silences, that of words, that of desires, and that of thought. In the last and highest the mind is a blank, and God alone speaks to the soul. (*CM*, 232)

Moran, however, quickly recoils from such contemplative silent listening, and adopts a proprietary mode of thinking, considering how this quietistic trait might give his son an 'advantage' in life, staying 'aloof' from others, and living well, rather than working out the best way to renounce and be at peace. But later on, when he has sent his son off to buy a bicycle in Hole, Moran learns how to listen:

> I surrendered myself to the beauties of the scene, I gazed at the trees, the fields, the sky, the birds and I listened attentively to the sounds, faint and clear, borne to me on the air. For an instant, I fancied I heard the silence mentioned, if I am not mistaken, above. (152)

Beckett told Charles Juliet that he would often spend entire days in his house in Ussy-sur-Marne just sitting and enjoying the silence. When Juliet asked him what he did when there was nothing happening, he replied: 'There is always listening' [*Il y a toujours à écouter*].[88] The act of listening does not require a God, or even a Schopenhauerian world essence, for it to still be an act of surrender and openness. Beckett's dramatic work, writes Catherine Laws, 'makes us aware of what it is to listen. And in doing so, we experience the performativity of listening: the reflexive awareness of our own acts of listening, our own attempts to find meaning in sound.'[89]

Moran also starts to delight in thoughts of death, just as Molloy did. He describes how he has set up his grave already:

---

88 Juliet, p. 35.
89 Catherine Laws, *Headaches Among the Overtones: Music in Beckett / Beckett in Music* (Amsterdam: Rodopi, 2013), p. 15.

> It was a simple Latin cross, white. I wanted to have my name put on it, with the here lies and the date of my birth. Then all it would have wanted was the date of my death. They would not let me. Sometimes I smiled, as if I were dead already. (141)

For Schopenhauer, the Christian grave, with its cross, 'the symbol of suffering and death', points towards 'the *denial* of the will, to redemption from this world'.[90] Moran calls his grave 'my plot in perpetuity' (141), treating it with the same sense of propriety as he does his garden. Nevertheless, this *memento mori* leads him to a further quietistic thought:

> To be literally incapable of motion at last, that must be something! My mind swoons when I think of it. And mute into the bargain! And perhaps as deaf as a post! And who knows as blind as a bat! And as likely as not your memory a blank! And just enough brain intact to allow you to exult! And to dread death like a regeneration. (146)

Moran's words resemble Inge's descriptions of the 'Great Dereliction' of St Teresa that captured Beckett's imagination in the 1930s. In this state, which is brought about by the 'prayer of quiet', Teresa experienced 'a kind of catalepsy' in which 'all the faculties are quiescent' (*CM*, 221). St John of the Cross taught how 'the soul sinks into a holy inertia and oblivion', a state which Inge compares to the 'torpor of the Indian Yogi or of the hesychasts of Mount Athos' (*CM*, 227). Malone combines St John and St Teresa when he talks about 'Night, storm and sorrow, and the catalepsies of the soul' (*MD*, 24). Thomas à Kempis similarly exhorts his reader to 'esteem thyself as one dead upon the earth' and to pass by worldly things 'with deaf ear' (*IC*, III.xliv). La Bruyère's director describes one particularly adept Quietist he once knew who, after practising the prayer of quiet, became lifeless and mute:

---

90 Arthur Schopenhauer, *Studies in Pessimism*, trans. by T. Bailey Saunders (London: Swann Sonnenschein & Co., 1893), p. 26.

> [Her soul] is a stump, a plank, a dead body. She is so far empty of her own mind, so strongly accustomed to doing absolutely nothing, that you could say that she has lost herself.[91]

In following these examples, Moran has, once again, become more like Molloy: dead to the world before death itself. And as befits a corpse, Moran starts to decay. At first, he thinks he is aging, but quickly corrects himself in the language of rot and quietist annihilation:

> what I saw was more like a crumbling, a frenzied collapsing of all that had always protected me from I was always condemned to be. Or was it like a kind of clawing towards a light and countenance I could not name, that I had once known and long denied. But what words can describe this sensation at first all darkness and bulk, with a noise like the grinding of stones, then suddenly as soft as water flowing. And then I saw a little globe swaying up slowly from the depths, through the quiet water, smooth at first, and scarcely paler than its escorting ripples, then little by little a face, with holes for eyes and a mouth and other wounds, and nothing to show if it was a man's face or a woman's face, a young face or an old face, or if its calm too was not an effect of the water trembling between it and the light. But I confess I attended but absently to these poor figures, in which I suppose my sense of disaster sought to contain itself. And that I did not labour at them more diligently was a further index of the great changes I had suffered and of my growing resignation to being dispossessed of self. (*Mo*, 155–6)

This passage appears as Moran tries to bring the 'missing instructions concerning Molloy' into his mind (*Mo*, 156). But instead of finding them, he becomes infected with Molloy's language. His words here recall Molloy's ruins and his broken jar. Moran is no longer 'protected' or 'contained', just as Molloy was no longer 'preserved' in his jar, no

---

91 La Bruyère, pp. 94–95.

longer in his chloroformed Balzacian world. And like Molloy, Belacqua, Madame Guyon, and St Teresa, Moran finds that decay is accompanied by a deepening sense of spiritual exploration. Moran's 'clawing towards a light and countenance I could not name' resembles the mystic's search for an ineffable God. While the French text has only 'visage' (*MF*, 204), the archaic English 'countenance' alludes to the King James Bible, where the word is often used to describe the face of God or that of Christ after the resurrection (Numbers 6:26, Psalms 44:3, 89:15, Matthew 28:3, and Revelation 1:16). Beckett may also have been thinking of the 'Countenance Divine' in William Blake's preface to *Milton*, best known as Hubert Parry's hymn 'Jerusalem'.[92] The impossibility of naming the face also suggests divinity, as does the fact that Moran has 'long denied' it: the French text has 'renié', a verb which has particular connotations of renouncing one's faith in God. True to quietist form, however, this Godlike face is quickly passed over in favour of 'growing resignation to being dispossessed of self', or, in the French text, 'combien il me devenait indifférent de me posséder' (*MF*, 205). Moran feels his own 'disintegrations' (165) and 'failing flesh' (173) and thinks of himself as a 'turd waiting for the flush' (170). As it did for Molloy, this ruin and rot starts to bring Moran some quietude and peace. 'I grew gradually weaker and weaker and more and more content', Moran says, 'And though suffering a little from wind and cramps in the stomach I felt extraordinarily content, content with myself' (170). He starts to 'savour [his] exhaustion' (170). Just as he repeated Molloy's act of listening, Moran repeats the trope of a ruin without something to ruin: he moves towards 'what I would have called my ruin if I could have conceived what I had left to be ruined' (173).

Alongside this decay of the body, the text itself starts to break down again. Early on, when Moran has one of his 'moments of lucidity', he starts to doubt the existence of the other agents whom he presumes make up the 'vast organization' in which he is employed. He 'came even to doubt the existence of Gaber himself' and just barely

---

[92] William Blake, *The Complete Poetry and Prose*, ed. by David V. Erdman (New York, NY: Anchor Books, 1988), p. 95.

manages to avoid 'conjuring away the chief too and regarding myself as solely responsible for my wretched existence' (112). In other words, Moran turns out to be a seedy solipsist after all, and feels the same pull towards self-annihilation as Molloy: 'And having made away with Gaber and the chief (one Youdi), could I have denied myself the pleasure of—you know' (112). Later on, he wonders whether he had 'invented' Molloy: 'found him ready-made in my head' (116).

The text's entropic decline starts to break up the 'composure' of Moran's narration. He describes how his own 'firm hand is weaving inexorably back and forth and devouring my page with the indifference of a shuttle' (138, 'une main ferme, inexorable navette que mange ma page avec l'indifférence d'un fléau', 182). The words 'shuttle' and 'navette' refer to an instrument used in weaving, while 'fléau' means 'plague'. Even as the story is spun out, it is eaten, consumed, decaying. Moran, the Balzacian character brought into a Dostoevskian world, never really stood much of a chance. His assurance at the beginning and his meticulous plans give way to the aesthetic of unknowing that his author favours:

> If there is one question I dread, to which I have never been able to invent a satisfactory reply, it is the question what am I doing. (181)

The famous final line of his report—'It was not midnight. It was not raining' (184)—negates everything that he has written, 'denarrating' the text in a process that will continue into *Malone Dies* and *The Unnamable*.

Quietism, Violence, and Contradiction

Before closing this chapter, I want to address the violence in *Molloy* and how this relates to the quietism that I have found in the novel. According to Schopenhauer, the quietist or ascetic who has quietened or denied the will to live will act with compassion and care towards other beings. This is patently not the case with Molloy. Despite his efforts to lead a contemplative life, he is prone to 'burst[s] of irritation' (43), and has a disturbing capacity for aggression, as demonstrated by the 'thumps' he regularly applies to his mother's head (15) and the 'good dint on the skull' that he gives to the 'charcoal burner' he meets in the forest (85). Moran, too, is increasingly violent: shortly after meeting a stranger who 'vaguely resembled him', Moran beats his face to 'a pulp' and leaves him 'stretched on the ground' (158). How can either of these characters possibly be quietists if they are so angry and aggressive?

The discrepancy arose, I suspect, from the competing demands of Beckett's use of quietism as a *theme* and quietism as an *aesthetic principle*. Once again, André Gide will provide some help here. According to Gide, Dostoevsky was attentive to the 'irrational, the resolute, and often irresponsible nature of his characters' (*Dost*, 68). This is part of the 'integrity of incoherence' that Beckett was so interested in. Gide adds:

> Do not be mistaken about this seeming ferocity that often appears in Dostoevsky's work. It is an integral part of his quietism, as it is of Blake's. Dostoevsky's quietism led me to conclude that his Christianity had closer affinities with Asia than with Rome. But this acceptance of energy on Dostoevsky's part, which, in Blake's hands, becomes an outright glorification of energy, is rather more western than eastern. (257–8)

Any writer seeking to follow Dostoevsky's quietist aesthetic must, ironically, be prepared to accept 'inquiétante' [disquieting] contradictions within their characters. In his lectures, Beckett pointed out that Alissa's mystical tendencies in Gide's *La Porte étroite* are 'unexplained,' whereas Balzac's 'must be consistent' (TCD MIC60, 39, 41). For Beckett, as for Gide, consistency and purposiveness ran contrary to his chosen aesthetic. Even Franz Kafka, a writer who superficially might seem to have far more in common with Beckett than Balzac, failed to get it right:

> The Kafka hero has a coherence of purpose. He's lost but he's not spiritually precarious, he's not falling to bits. My people are falling to bits. Another difference. You notice how Kafka's form is classic, it goes on like a steamroller.[93]

Balzac is like 'clockwork', Kafka is like a steamroller, and therefore both are classical novelists. Anne Atik recalls Beckett saying that 'Kafka's subject matter called for a more disjointed style.'[94] Atik also describes Beckett becoming 'tense with attention, suddenly sitting bolt upright as though pierced by an electric current' after she read out another manifesto for literary incoherence, Keats's definition of 'Negative Capability': 'when a man is capable of being in uncertainties, mysteries, doubts, without any irritable reaching after fact and reason'.[95] Beckett apparently repeated the words to himself with excitement.

Molloy and Moran are anything but consistent in their quietism, and it is that, ironically, that makes *Molloy* a 'quietist' novel in the lineage of Gide and Dostoevsky. Beckett also said that, for Gide, the 'struggle between [the] artist and [the] idea must be incorporated in [the] novel' (TCD MIC60, 41): in rehearsing his own tussles with quietism from the 1930s, and in opposing Schopenhauerian ethics with Gidean aesthetics, Beckett was staying true to this principle. As Gide says, in a passage from his journal which Beckett quoted in his lecture:

> the most contradictory tendencies have never tormented me. This kind of dialogue which is almost intolerable for so many others, became necessary for me. (Translated from the French in TCD MIC60, 37)

---

93 Beckett, quoted in Shenker, p. 162.
94 Anne Atik, *How It Was: A Memoir of Samuel Beckett* (London: Faber and Faber, 2001), p. 66.
95 Atik, p. 71.

In *Molloy*, Beckett chose to follow the incoherent, even ferocious, literary quietism of Gide and Dostoevsky rather than turning his characters into perfect quietist saints. In the next chapter, I will argue that Beckett stayed much closer to the quietism of Schopenhauer and of Asia in the creation of *How It Is*, a novel preoccupied with ethical matters.

Conclusion

Molloy, it seems, was right: there are a number of important 'remnants' from Beckett's pensum of the 1930s in the novel that bears his name. Moran's prayer is the most overt indication that quietism continues to be an important thematic concern for Beckett, something which can be felt in Molloy's contemplative and Schopenhauerian tendencies, and the way Moran himself eventually adopts such attitudes. But, as I have argued, the most important pensum is Beckett's own aesthetic task, inspired by Gide and Dostoevsky. Their literary quietism offers an aesthetic of incoherence, humility, abnegation, and contradiction that provided Beckett with a way of dispensing with Joycean heroics and the carefully calibrated clockwork of the classical novel epitomized by Balzac's *Comédie humaine*. The connection between quietism and decay—apparent from Beckett's interest in St Teresa's dereliction and other tropes in his early writing—added further impetus to this aesthetic, as Beckett allowed the rot to set into his characters, language, and fictional conceits, so that his novel could 'fall to bits' and refuse to cohere or to recoil into composure and composition.

Chapter 4
The Sage Under the Bo:
How It Is, Ernst Haeckel and
Beckett's (German) Buddhism

> The Oriental Renaissance, slowly prepared in the offices of the doctors of the Rhine [...] Scratch a German and underneath you will see an old follower of the Buddha come back into view.
>
> —Louis-Alexandre Foucher de Careil,
> *Hegel et Schopenhauer*[1]

This chapter is an attempt to make sense of a particularly tantalising reference in Beckett's 1961 novel *Comment c'est* and its 1964 translation *How It Is*.[2] In Part II of the novel, the narrator describes an 'eastern sage', 'squatting in the deep shade of a tomb or bo his fists clenched on his knees'.[3] As Paul Davies and Éduoard Magessa O'Reilly have suggested, this figure could be the Buddha.[4] The word 'bo' is the Sinhalese corruption of the Sanskrit word *bodhi* which means awakening

---

1   Quoted in Roger-Pol Droit, *The Cult of Nothingness: The Philosophers and the Buddha*, trans. by Pamela Vohnson (Chapel Hill, NC: The University of North Carolina Press, 2003), p. 102.
2   Earlier versions of parts of this chapter can be found in Andy Wimbush, 'The Buddha, Biology and the Beasts: The influence of Ernst Haeckel and Arthur Schopenhauer on Samuel Beckett's *How It Is*', in *Encountering Buddhism in Twentieth-Century British and American Literature*, ed. by Lawrence Normand and Alison Winch (London: Bloomsbury, 2013), pp. 123–38.
3   Samuel Beckett, *How It Is*, ed. by Édouard Magessa O'Reilly (London: Faber and Faber, 2009), p. 45. Hereafter, *HII*. Samuel Beckett, *Comment c'est, How It Is And / et L'image: A Critical-Genetic Edition / Une Edition Critic-Genetique*, ed. by Édouard Magessa O'Reilly (London: Routledge, 2001), pt. II.12. Hereafter, *CC*. Quotations from the French cite part number and paragraph number.
4   Paul Davies, *The Ideal Real: Beckett's Fiction and Imagination* (London: Associated University Presses, 1994), p. 235; Édouard Magessa O'Reilly, '*Molloy*, Part II, Where the Shit Hits the Fan: Ballyba's Economy and the

or 'perfect knowledge', and therefore suggests the 'Bodhi Tree' under which the Buddha sat on the night of his awakening. Since Beckett has, occasionally and often carelessly, been associated with Buddhism, and since Buddhism has, occasionally and equally carelessly, been associated with quietism, this reference seems worth exploring. While it is only a brief mention in an entire novel, this should not put us off. Dirk Van Hulle likens the words in Beckett's works to the tip of an iceberg: beneath the surface of the published text there often lies an occluded mass of erudition, allusion and editing, which can be found in manuscripts and source material.[5] In this chapter I will try to reconstruct the iceberg beneath the 'eastern sage', and propose that it can offer a new way of understanding *How It Is* as one of Beckett's most ethically challenging works.

Beckett and Buddhism: A Biographical and Critical History

Around 1931, as he was thinking about Gide's quietist aesthetic and putting together his manuscripts towards *Dream of Fair to Middling Women*, Beckett read *Degeneration* by the social critic Max Nordau.[6] The *Dream* notebook contains many words and phrases lifted from *Degeneration*, but the content of Nordau's book could hardly have been more antithetical to Beckett's own views. Published in Germany as *Entartung* in 1892, *Degeneration* is a polemical diagnosis of what Nordau supposes to be the decline of European society and culture at the end of the nineteenth century. Artists and intellectuals are subjected to particular

---

Worth of the World', *Genetic Joyce Studies*, 6 (2006) <http://www.geneticjoycestudies.org/GJS6/GJS6OReilly.htm> [accessed 6 November 2012].

5 Dirk Van Hulle, 'Writers' Libraries and the Extended Mind' (presented at the Writers and their Libraries, Senate House, University of London, 2013).

6 C.J. Ackerley, 'Samuel Beckett and Max Nordau: Degeneration, Sausage-Poisoning, the Bloody Rafflesia, Coenaesthesia, and the Not-I', in *Beckett after Beckett*, by S.E. Gontarski and Anthony Uhlmann (Gainesville, FL: University Press of Florida, 2006), pp. 167–76 (p. 174).

scorn, as are people who suffer from 'a condition of moral weakness and despondency' that Nordau associates with pessimism, melancholy, and quietism:

> The degenerate who shuns action, and is without will-power, has no suspicion that his incapacity for action is a consequence of his inherited deficiency of brain. He deceives himself into believing that he despises action from free determination, and takes pleasure in inactivity; and, in order to justify himself in his own eyes, he constructs a philosophy of renunciation and of contempt for the world and men, asserts that he has convinced himself of the excellence of Quietism, calls himself with consummate self-consciousness a Buddhist, and praises Nirvana in poetically eloquent phrases as the highest and worthiest ideal of the human mind. The degenerate and insane are the predestined disciples of Schopenhauer and [psychoanalyst Eduard von] Hartmann, and need only to acquire a knowledge of Buddhism to become converts to it.[7]

Nordau would say that Beckett's degenerate nature, evident from his youthful melancholy and irrational attachment to art, inevitably led him to the ideas of Schopenhauer and to other exponents of quietism that I have explored in previous chapters. These should have, in turn, brought him to Buddhism, a religion that has been dubbed 'quietistic' both by rival Asian philosophies, such as Confucianism, and by the Christian missionaries who first encountered it in the seventeenth century.[8] Schopenhauer certainly believed that Buddhism was a form of quietism, though of course, unlike Nordau, he praised it for being so. For Schopenhauer, Buddhism had pre-eminence over all other religions: he felt that his own philosophy was in close agreement with its teachings (*WWR*, II.1.17, 178), and even called himself

---

7   Max Nordau, *Degeneration* (London: William Heinemann, 1895), pp. 20–21.
8   Bernard Faure, 'In the Quiet of the Monastery: Buddhist Controversies over Quietism', *Common Knowledge*, 16 (2010), 424–38.

a Buddhist.[9] If Beckett was such an avid admirer of Schopenhauer, then surely, Nordau would argue, he too was bound to find Buddhism of interest.

Several of Beckett's readers have had similar hunches and have tried to read his work through the lens of Buddhism. Casual asides about the matter are surprisingly common, even in recent studies. John Calder suggests in passing that the 'mythology that Beckett invents to replace the standard expectation of a heaven or hell waiting for us is very simple, and owes something to spiritualism and to Buddhism'.[10] Robert Harvey, in his recent book on *Worstward Ho*, calls Beckett 'the unavowed Zen Buddhist French Irishman'[11], while Joshua Landy, in his 2012 book *How to Do Things with Fictions*, remarks how the 'telos' of Beckett's work 'appears to be a Buddhist nothingness rather than a Heideggerian plenitude, a full absence (so to speak) rather than a full presence.'[12] Other studies have treated the matter in more depth, and have tried to align Beckett with specific Buddhist schools: Paul Foster and John Kundert-Gibbs opt for Japanese Zen,[13] while Paul Davies tries to develop a supposedly 'direct' and 'precise' connection between Beckett's prose fragment 'neither' (1979) and Tibetan Dzogchen.[14] The problem with all of these readings is that they are at a loss to say how Beckett might have encountered these Buddhist teachings in his reading, or through his relationships. The unfortunate result is that, after

---

9   Moira Nicholls, 'The Influences of Eastern Thought on Schopenhauer's Doctrine of the Thing-in-Itself', in *The Cambridge Companion to Schopenhauer*, ed. by Christopher Janaway (Cambridge: Cambridge University Press, 2006), pp. 171–212.
10 John Calder, *The Philosophy of Samuel Beckett* (London: Calder Publications, 2001), p. 35.
11 Robert Harvey, *Witnessness: Beckett, Dante, Levi and the Foundations of Responsibility* (London: Continuum, 2010), p. 81.
12 Landy, *How to Do Things with Fictions*, p. 208.
13 Paul Foster, *Beckett and Zen: A Study of Dilemma in the Novels of Samuel Beckett* (Somerville, MA: Wisdom, 1989); John L. Kundert-Gibbs, *No-Thing Is Left to Tell: Zen / Chaos Theory in the Dramatic Art of Samuel Beckett* (London: Associated University Presses, 1999).
14 Paul Davies, '"Womb of the Great Mother Emptiness": Beckett, the Buddha and the Goddess', *Samuel Beckett Today / Aujourd'hui*, 9 (2000), 119–31 (pp. 119, 123).

many pages of comparison, the two subjects—Beckett and Buddhism—remain just as disconnected as they did at the start: we learn little about what Beckett's work is about, how it was made, or what it does. As Malone might have said, they are well-meaning squirms that get us nowhere (*MD*, 51).

Beckett never got the chance to reply to these critics who would, either casually or expressly, connect his work to Buddhism. But according to the writer Lawrence Shainberg, himself a Zen Buddhist practitioner, Beckett did have his say on the matter during a run of a production of *Endgame* in London in 1981:

> One of the people who hung around rehearsals was a puppeteer who cast his puppets in Beckett plays. At a cast party one night he gave a performance of *Act Without Words* [*I*] which demonstrated, with particular force, the consistency of Beckett's paradox and the relentlessness with which he maintains it. [...] As it happened, the puppeteer's wife was a Buddhist [... and she] was understandably anxious to confirm what she, like many people, took to be his sympathies with her religion. In fact, not a few critical opinions had been mustered over the years concerning his debt to Buddhism, Taoism, Zen and the Noh theatre, all of it received—as it was now received from the puppeteer's wife—with curiosity and appreciation and absolute denial by the man it presumed to explain. "I know nothing about Buddhism," he said. "If it's present in the play, it is unbeknownst to me." Once this had been asserted, however, there remained the possibility of unconscious predilection, innate Buddhism, so to speak. So the woman had another question which had stirred in her mind, she said, since the first time she'd seen the play. "When all is said and done, isn't this man, having given up hope, finally liberated?" Beckett looked at her with a pained expression. He'd had his share of drink that night, but not enough to make him forget his vision or push him beyond his profound distaste for hurting anyone's feelings. "Oh, no," he said quietly. "He's *finished*."[15]

---

15 Lawrence Shainberg, 'Exorcising Beckett', *Paris Review*, 1987, 100–136 (p. 111).

Beckett's denial, so late in his life, of any knowledge of Buddhism, would seem the final word on the matter. But Beckett made similar denials about his interest in philosophy, claiming in 1961 to 'never read' contemporary philosophy, despite his familiarity with the work of Camus and Sartre.[16] Even if Beckett felt obliged to express ignorance about Buddhism in the presence of someone who was an adherent of that religion, he may nevertheless have known some of the basic details. Indeed, he betrays himself when telling Charles Juliet in 1968 that he has never read 'the oriental thinkers' because 'they offer a way out [*proposent une issue*], and I felt that there wasn't one'.[17] This denial of knowledge about Asian philosophy is simultaneously an admission that he knew enough to reject it.

Fortunately, we do not have to speculate about the matter. Looking back over his published work and archives provides enough evidence of Beckett's occasional interest in Buddhist doctrine and imagery. Although some of these instances are hardly more sophisticated than Nordau's diagnosis, when taken together they do amount to a passable account of Buddhism. The first reference comes in *Proust* in the maxim I have already quoted several times before:

> the wisdom of all the sages, from Brahma to Leopardi, the wisdom that consists not in the satisfaction but in the ablation of desire. (*PTD*, 18)

Shainberg suspects that Beckett intended to refer to Buddhism here.[18] Replacing 'Brahma' with 'Buddha' would certainly make more sense. Brahma is not a sage, but a Hindu god, who, as Schopenhauer puts it, is the 'lowest and most sinful god of the Trimurti', associated with 'pleasure of procreation' (*WWR*, I.4.54, 303; 69, 26): hardly the god of

---

16 Matthew Feldman, 'Beckett, Sartre and Phenomenology', *Limit(e) Beckett*, 2010 <http://limitebeckett.paris-sorbonne.fr/zero/feldman.html> [accessed 28 October 2011]; Beckett's comment comes from D'Aubarède, p. 239.
17 Juliet, p. 17.
18 Shainberg, p. 111.

ablating desire, then. The Buddha, on the other hand, most definitely did teach the ablation of desire: the second of the Four Noble Truths attributes suffering to desire, or more literally, unquenchable thirst or craving (Pali: *tanhā*). It seems likely that Beckett got the names confused. In 1930, shortly after writing *Proust*, Beckett makes another reference to Buddhism, this time getting the name right, in 'Le Concentrisme', his spoof lecture to the Trinity College Dublin Modern Language Society about a fictional French poet, Jean du Chas. Beckett purports to find the following passage in the notebooks that du Chas has left behind after his death:

> Vous allez vous appeler les *Concentristes*. C'est moi qui vous le dis, moi, inventeur du Concentrisme, moi, le Bouddha biconvexe. Vous direz à vos contemporains: —Jean du Chas, illustre fondateur de notre ordre, inventeur du Concentrisme, le Bouddha biconvexe, fils unique, illégitime et posthume d'un agent de change belge et d'une salaudine [*sic*] germano-toulousaine, vous invite, tutti quanti, à un festin religio-géologique, où vous pourrez vous farcir, à perte de boutons, de sainte nourriture sous la double forme de lentilles cartesiennes [*sic*] et concierges synthétiques. (*Dis*, 40)

> [You shall call yourself the *Concentrists*. It is I who say this to you. I, the inventor of Concentrism. I, the biconvex Buddha. You shall say to your contemporaries: Jean du Chas, illustrious founder of our order, inventor of Concentrism, the biconvex Buddha, the only son, illegitimate and posthumous, of a Belgian stockbroker and a Germano-Touloussian bastardess, invites you, tutti quanti, to a religio-geological feast, where you can stuff yourself, until your buttons pop off, with holy food in the double form of Cartesian lenses and synthetic concierges.]

The reference to the 'biconvex Buddha' is probably a joke about du Chas's girth, as Beckett makes the common error of mistaking the Chinese folk deity Pu-tai, represented as a fat laughing monk, for the founder of Buddhism.[19] But there may be more to it than this: Beckett is at pains to describe du Chas's unusual relationship to social interaction, which he treats as 'une dimension, ou l'attribut d'une dimension, inévitable, comme la friction, une condition de son adhésion à la surface de la terre' [translated by John Pilling as 'a mere tittle, or the tithe of a tittle, unavoidable, like friction, a condition of his adherence to the surface of the earth'[20]]. Perhaps the Nordauian stereotype of a hermetic, quietist, navel-gazing Buddhist is what he has in mind here. As Pilling has suggested, portions of 'Le Concentrisme' 'obliquely show Beckett struggling with his own demons'.[21] Du Chas, after all, shares Beckett's birthday of 13 April 1906, and his struggles with life's social aspects resemble those that Beckett outlines in the letter to MacGreevy of 10 March 1935 about *The Imitation of Christ*. Du Chas's self-association with the Buddha is therefore perhaps an echo of Beckett's own interest in Schopenhauer and Thomas à Kempis at the time.

We have already seen two other Buddhist references in previous chapters. First, the mention of 'Dost[oevsky]'s quietism' that is 'almost Buddhism' in Burrows's notes on Beckett's 1930 lectures on André Gide and the modern novel, following Gide's analysis in *Dostoïevsky* (TCD MIC60, 24). And second, the reference to Alexandra David-Neel's *With Magicians and Mystics in Tibet* in the *Whoroscope* notebook, which provided Beckett with the squatting lotus position of Mr Endon in *Murphy*. This is another Nordauian move on Beckett's part: since Mr Endon is completely cut-off from all contact with the world, he should look like a Tibetan Buddhist, complete with a red robe. In the 1930s, then, Beckett certainly did not know much about Buddhism, and he appears to have adhered to the view, found in different

---

19 Damien Keown, 'Pu-Tai', *A Dictionary of Buddhism* (Oxford: Oxford University Press, 2004) <http://www.oxfordreference.com/view/10.1093/acref/9780198605607.001.0001/acref-9780198605607-e-1462> [accessed 29 August 2014]. Thanks to Matt Spencer for this suggestion.
20 Samuel Beckett, '"Le Concentrisme" and "Jean Du Chas": Two Extracts', trans. by John Pilling, *Modernism / modernity*, 18 (2011), 883–86.
21 John Pilling, 'Introduction to Samuel Beckett, "Le Concentrisme" and "Jean Du Chas"', *Modernism / modernity*, 18 (2011), 881–881.

forms in Schopenhauer and Nordau, that Buddhism is a form of solipsism or quietism.

Beckett seems to have been content with pre-1900 German sources for his knowledge of Buddhism, even as he ceased using it in quite such a flippant way. Olga Plümacher's *Der Pessimismus*, first read by Beckett in 1939 and which remained in his library until his death,[22] presents Buddhism as thoroughly nihilistic.[23] Plümacher explains that, although Buddhism can be considered a development of the abstract monism of Brahmanism, it posits as its absolute not God, but 'das reine Nichts': pure nothingness. Buddhism is an *Erlösungsreligion*, a soteriological religion, but its salvation, *nirvāna*, is an 'Ort des Verlöschens', a place of extinction. As Plümacher presents it, *nirvāna* is not in any sense a transcendence of this world. She says that because Buddhists believe that there is nothing on the other side of the veil of Maya—the Indian equivalent of Kant's gap between phenomenon and noumenon—there is nothing beyond earthly knowledge. Plümacher writes: 'so all proud knowledge and all joyful cognition falls away, because no one comes any closer to divine knowledge, but only to nothingness'.[24] Beckett's pencil annotations in *Der Pessimismus* show that he was particularly interested in this paradoxical idea of salvation, and also in Buddhist ethics, which Plümacher, like Schopenhauer, explains in terms of *Mitleid*: compassion or pity. *Mitleid*, for Plümacher, is the 'moral principle *par excellence* of pessimism.'

Closer to the time of writing *How It Is*, Beckett makes another reference to Buddhism in a 1952 essay written for a private showing of Henri Hayden's paintings and published in *Cahiers d'art* in November 1955:

> On me demande des mots, à moi que n'en ai plus, plus guère, sur une chose que les récuse. Exécutons-nous, exécutons-la.

---

22 Nixon and Van Hulle, p. 154.
23 On pre-1900 nihilistic interpretations of Buddhism by European philosophers, see Droit.
24 Plümacher, p. 25.

Gautama, avant qu'ils vinssent à lui manquer, disait qu'on se trompe en affirmant que le moi existe, mais qu'en affirmant qu'il n'existe pas on ne se trompe pas moins.

Il s'entend dans les toiles de Hayden, loin derrière leur patient silence, comme l'écho de cette folle sagesse et, tout bas, de son corollaire, à savoir que pour le reste il ne peut qu'en être de même. (*Dis*, 146)

[They ask me for words, me, who no longer has any, hardly any, and on a topic that rejects them. Let's do it, execute it.

Gautama, before words forsook him, said that it is a mistake to say that the self exists, but no less of a mistake to say that it does not.

Something like the echo of this crazy wisdom can be heard in Hayden's paintings, far behind their patient silence, and, in a whisper, of its corollary, namely that everything else can only be the same.]

There is no Nordauian laziness here. Beckett not only refers to the founder of Buddhism by his family name 'Gautama' rather than the honorific 'Buddha' ('awakened one'), he also seems aware of the subtleties of one of the most important elements of the Buddha's teaching. According to the Buddha, people generally adopt one of two 'extreme' ontological views: either they reify and believe in existent things or, taking a more nihilist bent, they deny the existence of things. The Buddha explains that he teaches 'the Dhamma by the middle' that posits neither the existence nor non-existence of all phenomena, including the self.[25] And so while it is not entirely untrue to say that the Buddha denied the existence of the self insofar as he rejected the then-prevalent Brahminical view of an *ātman* or soul that was permanent and unchanging, it is more accurate to say that he claimed that that the self, as well as all other phenomena, is a 'dependent arising': something that only comes into being based on causes and conditions and which

---

25 Samyutta Nikāya 15 in *The Connected Discourses of the Buddha: A Translation of the Samyutta Nikāya*, trans. Bhikkhu Bodhi (Somerville, MA: Wisdom Publications, 2000), p. 544.

therefore lacks the inherent existence that we intuitively ascribe to it.[26] Beckett's words quoted above demonstrate that he was aware of some of the nuances of this teaching, which, incidentally, escaped the notice of Schopenhauer.[27] It is also interesting that, as in 'Le Concentrisme,' Beckett makes an implicit comparison between himself and the Buddha: both are authorities from whom words are slowly taking their leave.

Finally, Beckett may have gleaned some Buddhist insights from the writings of the Romanian philosopher E.M. Cioran. In 1956, Beckett told Richard Roud that he had recently found 'great stuff here and there' in Cioran's essay collection *La Tentation d'exister* and expressed his wish to 'reread his first', *Petit précis de decomposition* (28/11/56; *LSB2*, 678). In 1960, he recommended the same books to Barbara Bray: 'there are very good things in the Petit Traité [*sic*] and Tentation' (13/6/60, *LSB3*; 340). Although it would be several years before the two men would meet face to face, Beckett found an intellectual and spiritual ally in Cioran.[28] Like Beckett, Cioran was an apostate from a Christian childhood (in his case Eastern Orthodoxy) whose writing was composed in the long shadow of that religion. He shared Beckett's agonistic relationship to mysticism and quietism, which simultaneously repelled and attracted him. In the early 1930s, while Beckett was casting Belacqua as the 'dud-mystic' in *Dream of Fair to Middling Women* (186), Cioran was dabbling with the figure of the 'failed mystic' in his early Romanian text *Lacrimi și Sfinți* (*Tears and Saints*), an investigation of Christianity's ascetics and visionaries.[29]

---

26 Mark Siderits, *Buddhism As Philosophy: An Introduction* (Aldershot: Ashgate Publishing, 2007), chap. 3; Andrew Olendzki, *Untangling Self: A Buddhist investigation of who we really are* (Somerville, MA: Wisdom Publications, 2016), pp. 2–7, 40–41, and 109–126; Steven Collins, *Selfless Persons: Imagery and Thought in Theravāda Buddhism* (Cambridge: Cambridge University Press, 1982), pp. 104–105.
27 Nicholls, p. 194.
28 David Wheatley, '"Sweet Thing Theology": Beckett, E.M. Cioran and the Lives of the Saints', in *Samuel Beckett: Debts and Legacies*, ed. by Peter Fifield and David Addyman (London: Bloomsbury, 2013), pp. 39–62.
29 E.M. Cioran, *Tears and Saints*, trans. by Ilinca Zarifopol-Johnston (London: University Of Chicago Press, 1995), p. 67.

When Cioran, like Beckett, abandoned his native tongue to write in French in the 1940s, he broadened his horizons to consider the saints of eastern religions. In both the books that Beckett mentioned to Roud and Bray, Cioran frequently turns to Buddhism. In *La Tentation d'exister*, Cioran contrasts the Christianity of St Paul with the 'different notion of man' found in Taoism and Buddhism:

> Neither Lao-Tse nor Buddha allude to an identifiable Being; scorning the artifices of faith, they invite us to meditation; to engage our minds, they establish its limit: the Tao, Nirvana.[30]

Cioran thought that Quietism was the nearest equivalent that Europe had to Buddhism and Taoism, but for the most part he felt that Buddhism's uncompromising negativity was too much for the average European, who remains haunted by the idea of God:

> When Nothingness [*le rien*[31]] invades me and, according to an Oriental formula, I attain to the "vacuity of the void," it so happens that, crushed by such an extremity, I fall back on God, if only out of a desire to trample my doubts underfoot, to contradict myself and, multiplying my *frissons*, to seek in Him a stimulant. The experience of the Void is the unbeliever's mystic temptation, his possibility for prayer, his moment of plenitude. At our limits, a God appears, or something that serves his turn. (*TE*, 121)

What 'Western thinker', Cioran asks in *Petit précis*, 'would survive a comparison with a Buddhist monk?' For Cioran, the Buddha was 'superior to all the sages'.[32] And although Cioran follows the nihilistic and pessimistic interpretation of Buddhist *nirvāna* and emptiness, he recognises—

---

30 E.M. Cioran, *The Temptation to Exist*, trans. by Richard Howard (New York, NY: Arcade Publishing, 2012), p. 170. Hereafter, *TE*.
31 E.M. Cioran, *La Tentation d'exister* (Paris: Gallimard, 1956), p. 181.
32 E.M. Cioran, *A Short History of Decay*, trans. by Richard Howard (Oxford: Basil Blackwell, 1975), p. 154. Hereafter, *SHD*.

as Schopenhauer did—that Buddhism's talk of 'nothingness' was really a 'positive experience expressed in negative terms'. He calls the 'Void' of the 'Orient' a triumph and a 'conquest of salvation' (*TE*, 63).

This evidence from Beckett's notebooks, articles, and reading gives the lie to his denial of any knowledge about Buddhism. From these fragments we get a picture of a quietistic and pessimistic religion, founded by Gautama Buddha, which teaches a nuanced doctrine of *anattā* ('not-self'), an ethics of compassion, and a soteriology based on the ablation of desire, quasi-suicidal self-annihilation, and dissolution into nothingness. This is by no means a perfect account of Buddhist doctrine, but is at least a reasonable summary of how it was seen by European interpreters in the late nineteenth century.

The Western Religious Epic in *How It Is*

A Buddhist *How It Is* would differ significantly from the way in which the novel has been understood in previous critical studies, and so I want to spend some time rehearsing prevailing views before I propose my own reading. For the most part, *How It Is* has been understood as a parody of the epic narratives of the West, particularly the theodicies and creation myths of Christianity. H. Porter Abbott has argued that the novel should be read as a 'travesty of the epic', which critiques 'the deeply held Western proclivity to see "how it is" as design'.[33] As many readers have noted, the French title *Comment c'est* is a pun on 'commencer', to begin, and perhaps also the imperative 'commencez'.[34] From the title page, then, the novel absorbs two functions of the Western epic: the first (*commencer*) is the creation myth, the story of how life began; the second (*comment c'est*) is the theodicy, a description of the way life is now and why it is justified in the eyes of God. The narrator of *How It Is* remembers a woman telling him, perhaps in the

---

33 Abbott, p. 92.
34 For example, Ruby Cohn, *A Beckett Canon* (Ann Arbor, MI: University of Michigan Press, 2001), p. 255; Simon Critchley, *Very Little … Almost Nothing: Death, Philosophy and Literature* (London: Taylor & Francis, 2004), p. 263.

manner of Julian of Norwich, that 'all is well he is working' (*HII*, 6). Anthony Cordingley points out how the 'natural order', repeatedly cited by the narrator of *How It Is*, evokes the orders of Aristotle, the Christian Middle Ages, Dante and Milton.[35] The suffering of the novel has also been interpreted in Christian terms: Peter Boxall compares Pim, the victim of the story, to a version of Christ being flagellated.[36]

It is certainly true that Beckett draws on the works of Milton and Dante, and sections of the Bible to create his world. The setting of the novel, a landscape of mud and 'familiar slime' (*HII*, 13) filled with violent inhabitants taking it in turns to torture each other, is almost certainly borrowed from Dante's *Inferno*.[37] In Canto 7, Virgil and the pilgrim enter the swamp which borders the river Styx and encounter those being punished for their anger:

> As there I stood, intent and wondering,
> I saw there, plunged within that stagnant fen,
> a peevish people, naked, caked with mud.
>
> Each battered each—and not with fists alone,
> also with head butts, kicks and charging chests.
> Their teeth, too, tore them, bit by bit to shreds. (7.109–114)[38]

Just as the wall of hell 'bags up [*insacca*] all the evil of the universe',[39] the narrator of *How It Is* keeps 'all the suffering of all the ages' in his sack (*HII*, 31). Like the damned in Dante's hell, the denizens of *How*

---

35 Anthony Cordingley, 'Beckett and "L'ordre naturel": The Universal Grammar of *Comment c'est / How It Is*', *Samuel Beckett Today / Aujourd'hui*, 18 (2007), 185–99 (p. 185).
36 Peter Boxall, *Since Beckett: Contemporary Writing in the Wake of Modernism* (London: Continuum, 2009), p. 103.
37 Philip Terry, 'Waiting for God to Go: *How It Is* and *Inferno* VII–VIII', ed. by Marius Buning, *Samuel Beckett Today / Aujourd'hui*, 7 (1998), 349–60; Daniela Caselli, *Beckett's Dantes: Intertextuality in the Fiction and Criticism* (Manchester: Manchester University Press, 2005).
38 Dante Alighieri, pp. 62–63.
39 Dante Alighieri, p. 57.

It Is have 'abandoned here the effect of hope' (*HII*, 39). A hellish setting is also suggested in the narrator's memories of 'a life said to have been mine above in the light' (*HII*, 4), which recalls the fallen Satan's longing for the 'happy Realms of Light' in Milton's *Paradise Lost* (I.85). Beckett also alludes to the Book of Job, no doubt the most overtly theodical book of the Bible, with the narrator's 'muckheap' (*HII*, 29), a version of Job's dunghill.

But whereas authors of conventional theodicies seek to illuminate, Beckett's text is made deliberately muddy. While he borrows images and vocabulary from the works of previous religious epics, he also flouts the rules of the genre. This might be why *How It Is* mentions Friedrich Klopstock (*HII*, 34), a German poet who was inspired by Milton to write his own epic, *Der Messias*. According to George Robertson's *History of German Literature*, which Beckett read and took notes on sometime in 1934,[40] Klopstock fundamentally 'misunderstood [...] the conditions of the religious epic': he did not make enough effort to 'humanise' his religious themes and supernatural characters. Without 'humanly interesting characters,' claims Robertson, 'dramatic action or movement is naturally impossible.'[41]

> [The] "divine inaction" of its personages [...] makes it so difficult to follow the thread of the *Messias*. Klopstock describes "feelings" for us, not actions; he swims in a sea of lyric sentiment, and forgets even the first duty of an epic poet, to describe something that happens.[42]

With *How It Is*, Beckett wilfully breaks Robertson's rules. His characters are barely recognisable as human beings. Their bodies are indistinct, they are unsure of their names, they have no idea how they came to be where they are despite having memories of childhood and adolescence. The reliable guidance of Virgil and the song of the Heavenly

---

40 Nixon, p. 63; Frost and Maxwell, pp. 113–123.
41 Robertson, pp. 262–3.
42 Robertson, p. 263.

Muse are replaced by an indeterminate 'voice once without quaqua on all sides' (*HII*, 3) which sometimes merges with the narrator's own, and at other times seems wholly distinct from him. The narrator is sometimes called Bom, as I will call him throughout this chapter for the sake of ease, but at other times he has no name at all. There is no room in Beckett's epic for Milton's 'adventurous song': this is a tale 'ill-said ill-heard ill-recaptured ill-murmured' (*HII*, 3). As Abbott says, the role of *How It Is* is 'not to enlighten, but to stupefy'.[43] There is no small irony in the fact that one of the clearest allusions in the novel is to 'Heraclitus the Obscure' (*HII*, 28). Archibald Alexander, author of *A Short History of Philosophy*, which Beckett read in the 1930s,[44] describes Heraclitus as 'one of those disdainful prophetic souls who are not anxious to make themselves intelligible to the multitude'.[45] This attitude would fit with what Cordingley identifies as the main characteristics of Beckett's postwar poetics:

> He neutralizes the content of his inevitably learned language by employing references in a private way, such that they no longer affirm their source meaning but are rather the raw material for his own creation.[46]

Darwin and the Natural Order

If Beckett aspires to Heraclitean obfuscation, however, he needs to befuddle not just the Christian epic, but also its main modern rival: Darwin's theory of evolution by natural selection. Friedrich Ueberweg in his *History of Philosophy*, also read by Beckett in the 1930s, calls Heraclitus the 'riddler',[47] but for Darwinians, the riddle has been solved:

---

43 Abbott, p. 101.
44 Frost and Maxwell, pp. 67–68.
45 Archibald Alexander, *A Short History of Philosophy* (London: Macmillan, 1922), p. 29.
46 Anthony Cordingley, 'Beckett's Ignorance: Miracles / Memory, Pascal / Proust', *Journal of Modern Literature*, 33 (2010), 129–52 (p. 130).
47 Friedrich Ueberweg, *A History of Philosophy from Thales to the Present Time: Vol. 1* (New York, NY: Charles Scribner's Sons, 1889).

> The greatest, vastest, and most difficult of all cosmic problems is that of the origin and development of the world—the "question of creation," in a word. Even to the solution of this most difficult world-riddle the nineteenth century has contributed more than all its predecessors; in a certain sense, indeed, it has found the solution. We have at least attained to a clear view of the fact that all the partial questions of creation are indivisibly connected, that they represent one single, comprehensive "cosmic problem," and that the key to this problem is found in the one magic word—evolution.[48]

So writes the German naturalist Ernst Haeckel, who gets a mention in *How It Is* when Bom imagines being 'mad or worse transformed à la Haeckel born in Potsdam' (34). The quotation above is from Haeckel's 1901 book *The Riddle of the Universe*, which provided James Joyce with Buck Mulligan's description of God as a 'gaseous vertebrate' in *Ulysses*[49] and likely informed Beckett's comparison of the development of the human embryo with the larval stages of an insect in *Murphy*.[50] As well as the link through Joyce, Beckett may have encountered Haeckel through his meeting with the Austrian painter and philosopher Karl Ballmer in Hamburg in November 1936:[51] Ballmer had written a book in 1929 comparing Haeckel with the anthroposophist Rudolf Steiner.

Haeckel was a younger contemporary of Darwin and an enthusiastic champion of natural selection in Germany. While Darwin had been famously cautious in expounding his theory, in Haeckel's hands he becomes a thundering prophet of science:

---

48 Ernst Haeckel, *The Riddle Of The Universe*, trans. by Joseph McCabe (London: Watts & Co., 1934), p. 191.
49 Geert Lernout, *Help My Unbelief: James Joyce and Religion* (London: Continuum, 2010), pp. 157–158; Haeckel, *The Riddle Of The Universe*, p. 225; Joyce, p. 253.
50 Ackerley, *Demented Particulars*, p. 85.
51 Nixon, pp. 154–157.

> Darwin's theory of the natural origin of species [...] at once gave us the solution of the mystic "problem of creation", the great "question of all questions" the problem of the true character and origin of man himself. [52]

Beckett would have had little sympathy with Haeckel's enthusiasm. He picked up a copy of *On the Origin of Species* in 1932, but told MacGreevy that he had 'never read such badly written catlap' (4/8/[32]; *LSB1*, 111). For Beckett, evolution is merely another Western just-so story to be lampooned, and so among the prayers and reveries of *How It Is* there are references to 'loss of species' (*HII*, 21), the 'natural order' (3), 'primeval mud' (7), 'scissiparous frenzy' (referring to the splitting of simple organisms via fission) (98) and 'the different orders of the animal kingdom beginning with the sponges' (31). The English version of the novel is Darwinian from the first page since it renders the French words 'un temps énorme puis à partir de là ce moment-là et suivants quelques-uns l'ordre naturel des temps énormes' (*CC*, I.7) as 'vast stretch of time on from there that moment and following not all a *selection natural* order vast tracts of time' (*HII*, 3, my emphasis), and so alludes to Darwin's theory. Remembering encounters with a llama and an albatross, Bom, the narrator, recalls 'the history I knew my God the natural' (28), which suggests natural history. Indeed he seems to be a naturalist engaged in dissection when he 'scissored into slender strips the wings of butterflies' (*HII*, 5). Haeckel describes forming 'a very pretty collection of butterflies and beetles, skins of birds and beasts' in one of his travel memoirs and his penchant for specimen hunting may have inspired the ubiquitous tins of *How It Is*. Haeckel frequently carried 'phials and tin boxes for what we might collect'.[53] The people in *How It Is* are able to absorb nutrients from the mud 'by

---

52 Haeckel, *The Riddle Of The Universe*, p. 64.
53 Ernst Haeckel, *A Visit to Ceylon*, trans. by Clara Bell (New York, NY: Peter Eckler, 1911), pp. 223, 116. Hereafter, *VC*.

osmosis' (*HII*, 56), much like Haeckel's 'organisms which float in water'.[54] The origins of this mud are various—Dante's Stygian bog, Leopardi's 'fango è il mondo' and Beckett's mole-ridden lawn outside his house in Ussy[55]—but the fact that it is 'primeval' may owe a debt to Haeckel. In 1868, the biologist Thomas Henry Huxley claimed to have discovered a 'gelatinous substance' that he believed was undifferentiated and primitive protoplasm, similar to the primordial soup from which all life emerged. He named this substance *Bathybius haeckelii*— 'Haeckel's mud'—after his friend Ernst Haeckel. Huxley retracted his claim after scientists discovered that *B. haeckelii* was actually an inorganic substance, but Haeckel remained attached to the idea for some years to come.[56]

The Eastern Sage

The appearance of the 'eastern sage' in this clash of Western cosmologies, Darwinism and Christianity, complicates matters. It suggests that Beckett believed the tendency to construct world-justifying narratives is not just a 'Western proclivity', as Abbott has suggested, and that similar theodicies might be found in Asian religions.

In addition to being a naturalist, Ernst Haeckel was also a travel writer: the passage about his butterfly collection quoted above comes from his 1882 *Indische Reisebriefe*, translated as *A Visit to Ceylon*. In that book, Haeckel makes a number of extended reflections on the religions he encounters in Ceylon and India, including Buddhism and Hinduism.[57] My contention is that Beckett used this book to create

---

54 Haeckel, *The Riddle Of The Universe*, p. 91.
55 Knowlson, pp. 460–1.
56 Philip F. Rehbock, 'Huxley, Haeckel, and the Oceanographers: The Case of *Bathybius haeckelii*', *Isis*, 66 (1975), 504–33 (p. 504); Charles S. Blinderman, 'Huxley, Pater, and Protoplasm', *Journal of the History of Ideas*, 43 (1982), 477–86 (p. 480).
57 In this chapter I will use the terms 'Hinduism' and 'Brahmanism' interchangeably. Technically 'Brahmanism' should refer to the ancient religion which arose out of the Vedas and which was known to the Buddha.

several of the images and scenarios in *How It Is*, including the 'eastern sage' who is 'squatting in the deep shade of a tomb or bo' (*HII*, 45). The 'bo' or Bodhi Tree is called the 'bo-gaha' or 'Buddha tree' by Haeckel, who also notes its scientific name: the 'sacred fig (*Ficus religiosa*)' (*VC*, 123). In the drafts for *Comment c'est*, Beckett has the sage live under 'un figuier religieux (Bo)'.[58] Bom considers becoming like this 'oriental' and so plans to 'renounce' and 'have no more desires' (48). This again suggests Buddhism since, as mentioned above, the Buddha attributed suffering to desire or craving. The description of a memory disappearing 'like a lamp gone out' (*HII*, 11) recalls the etymology of Buddhist salvation, *nirvāna*,—literally to go out, blow out or be extinguished—as well as the metaphor of the butter lamp being blown out, one of the most common images associated with *nirvāna* in Buddhist texts.[59]

But Beckett also describes the sage's ascetic practice, and it is decidedly not a Buddhist one:

> having clenched his fists from the tenderest age [… until] at last a little before his nails his death [*sic*] having pierced the palms through and through was enabled to see them emerging at last on the other side (*HII*, 45)

The Buddha, having tried self-mortification himself to little effect, rejected such practices.[60] In *The World as Will and Representation*, Schopenhauer explains that Buddhism 'is free from that rigorous and excessive asceticism that plays such a large role in Brahmanism, that is to say intentional self-torture' (II.4.48, 622). Indeed, what Schopenhauer calls 'Brahmanism' is the source of the sage's practice, and Beckett finds it in Haeckel's *A Visit to Ceylon*:

Haeckel, however, uses it when he is talking about what we would now call Hinduism, and so will I.
58 Beckett, *Comment c'est*, p. 405.
59 Steven Collins, *Nirvana: Concept, Imagery, Narrative* (Cambridge: Cambridge University Press, 2010), p. 63.
60 Siderits, p. 16.

> In front of the temple steps and on those of the sacred tank, pious penitents squat or pray with the most extraordinary and various gestures and devotional exercises. [...] The sole virtue of most of these Fakirs consists in the mutilation of some limb. One has held his fist convulsively clenched for a number of years, so that his nails have grown deep into the palm of his hand; [...] few forms of religion, probably, engender such monstrous births of this class as the Brahminical. (*VC*, 60–61)

Beckett's eastern sage is therefore a blend of Buddhism and Hinduism, but certainly of eastern provenance, and therefore not (or at least not only) a reworking of the crucified Christ as Mary Bryden has suggested,[61] nor, as Daniella Caselli proposes, yet another Beckettian reimagining of the Belacqua figure from Dante's *Purgatorio*.[62] In the earliest drafts of the novel, the narrator was a desert ascetic, a 'monstre des solitudes', based on the story of St Anthony.[63] As the genesis of *Comment c'est* progressed, the asceticism remained, but its geography shifted eastward. Where Beckett mentions the 'figuier religieux' in the manuscript, in place of the 'bo' in the final novel, he has 'un temple' in place of 'une tombe', which further helps to pinpoint the reference to Haeckel's temple fakirs.[64]

The presence of this Buddhist-Hindu sage and the influence of Haeckel's memoir on *How It Is* illuminate other aspects of the novel which do not fit with the Christian and Darwinian accounts of life and death. Take the following passage, for example:

> you are there somewhere alive somewhere vast stretch of time then it's over you are there no more alive no more then again you are there again alive again it wasn't an error you begin again all over more or less in the same place or in another as when another image above in the light you come to in hospital in the dark (16)

---

61 Bryden, p. 140.
62 Caselli, *Beckett's Dantes*, p. 151.
63 C.J. Ackerley, '"Primeval Mud Impenetrable Dark": Towards an Annotation of *Comment C'est / How It Is*', *Modernism / modernity*, 18 (2011), 789–800 (p. 795).
64 Beckett, *Comment c'est*, p. 405.

Philip Terry rightly notes that this vignette demands 'an entirely new way of construing the narrative',[65] but his suggestion of a dreamer falling asleep and waking up again falls somewhat short. The passage, despite its demands for a new conceptual framework, is actually quite clear: it describes a process of life, death and rebirth: in other words, reincarnation. The French text describes a 'connaissance' in the hospital (*CC*, I.116), which although means 'coming to' also contains the French word for 'birth'. The doctrine of reincarnation, common to both Buddhism and Hinduism, provides Beckett with an Asian counterpart to the theodicies of Dante, Milton and the Bible, as well as a mechanics of life to rival Darwinian evolution. The hospital passage is the clearest allusion to reincarnation in *How It Is*, but there are suggestions of it elsewhere: Bom seems to accept that certain things are different 'this time' (7) and that what he experiences during the novel is only the 'present formulation' (4). He has, it seems, had other lives. Even where sleep is evoked, it still seems a metaphor for death before rebirth:

> from sleep I come to sleep return between the two there is all the doing suffering failing bungling achieving until the mud yawns again that's how they're trying to tell me this time part one before Pim from one sleep to the next (17)

It seems that Beckett was interested in the idea of reincarnation long before writing *How It Is*. While reading Heinrich Zimmer's *Maya: der indische Mythos* for Joyce in 1938–9, Beckett made a pencil highlight beside the following passage, in which Zimmer recounts the tale of the king turned hermit, Muchukunda, taken from the Sanskrit epic, the *Mahābhārata*.

> He found himself awake, against his will again exposed to the aimless play of the births, to the senseless change of desire and loss, to the illusory joys of the self-conscious I and to its despairs, out of which the Maya of the God, endlessly glistening,

---

65 Terry, p. 355.

> weaves itself. [...] Life's knowing perception of his endless game with joy and agony in aimless alternation uncovered the reason why he wished to sleep while the world plays and time passes, and why he wanted to turn into ashes whoever dared awaken him. He speaks to the god: "For eternities I have been going astray in the circle of this *samsara*, I am overcome by the fire of all sufferings, and nowhere could I find cessation's rest."[66]

As in the last passage I quoted from *How It Is*, sleep is likened to death, and waking up is the equivalent to being thrown back into suffering at birth. Muchukunda complains of being lost in *saṃsāra*, a Sanskrit and Pali term which literally means 'wandering on' and which designates the process of straying helplessly from one life to the next in Indian cosmology. Although Beckett returned the book to Joyce, it seems that some of Zimmer's exposition of Indian mythology lingered in his mind.

Crucially, Schopenhauer also thought highly of what he called the 'myth of the transmigration of the soul' (*WWR*, I.4.63, 382). All religious doctrines, he claimed, are 'mythological cloaks for truths that are inaccessible to the untutored human senses', and in this respect, the doctrine of reincarnation is especially profound. It is, he says, a mythological 'surrogate' for the insight that the essential and true nature of all living things is, as his own philosophy taught, a monistic will. If individuality is only an illusion in appearance, and the reality of the universe is monistic, then there is justice in the world: when a being hurts another being it 'sinks its teeth into its own flesh, not knowing that it is only hurting itself' (*WWR*, I.4.70, 381). In the supplementary material, Schopenhauer returns once again to the Sanskrit formula *tat tvam asi* that Beckett found so fascinating, and connects it to reincarnation:

---

66 Quoted in Connolly, p. 44. Translation by Kurt P. Tauber. The original reference is Zimmer, p. 91.

> Saying that time and space are mere forms of our cognition, not determinations of the things in themselves, is the same as saying that the doctrine of metempsychosis ("one day you will be reborn as the one you are now harming, and you will suffer the same harm") is identical with the frequently cited Brahmanic formula *tat twam asi*, "you are that". (*WWR*, II.4.47, 616)

In Buddhism and Hinduism, salvation consists of liberating oneself from the rounds of rebirth. Schopenhauer felt that his soteriology, based on escaping the clutches of the will through self-denial, ethics, and asceticism, was simply a demythologised version of these Indian doctrines. In fact, Schopenhauer proposes that Buddhism already demythologised the earlier Indian idea of reincarnation since what it teaches is not 'metempsychosis' strictly speaking—whereby an individual's soul moves from one life to the next—but rather 'a distinctive palingenesis' (*WWR*, II.4.41, 520). After all, Buddhism is explicit about the fact that there is no stable soul or essence to anything, including the human subject. Schopenhauer says that when he speaks of reincarnation, what he really means is the continuation of the will-to-live, and not what he calls the ψυχη [*psyche*], that is, the soul or knowing subject.

Haeckel also uses the word 'palingenesis' in *The Riddle of the Universe*, in yet another way. His glossary explains that it literally means 'older birth', which in his Darwinian formulation means 'the development of the species in past time.'[67] It is also significant that Beckett had already allied Darwinian evolution, Schopenhauer, and a cyclical cosmology in another early notebook. These are his notes on Empedocles, drawn from Windelband's *History of Philosophy*:

> Endlessly repeated archetypical world cycle under this double aegis. From unity of love (non-world) through appearance of world in its opposition to hate, to disintegration of world of hate & reintegration into worldless unity of love. Love—Strife—Hate—for ever & ever.

---

67   Haeckel, *The Riddle Of The Universe*, p. 823.

> Living an expiation of the arrogant desire for individual existence. From plant through animal to man, who is finally worthy to return to primal unity. Propagation is evil, because it retards reorganisation of primitive unity.
>
> Precursor of Darwin and Schopenhauer. (TCD MS10967, 28r)

Windelband himself notes the way in which Empedocles describes a 'survival of the fittest' which foreshadows Darwinism,[68] but it is Beckett who brings in Schopenhauer. In *The World as Will and Representation*, the will is described as something *Ursprüngliches* [primordial] (*WWR*, I.4.55, 316), and this may have inspired the connection.

Victims and Tormentors

Beckett's quotations from *On the Origin of Species* in his *Whoroscope* suggest that he was particularly fascinated by the parasitical aspects of the natural world. He notes that the 'American cuckoo makes her own nest', in contrast to her parasitic European cousins. He also writes down details from Darwin's accounts of

> Slave-making ants (FORMICA rufescens—European? & Formica sanguine—British) The slave Formica flava (UoR MS3000, 77r)

The abuse of a fellow creature is a central theme in *How It Is*, as is the idea of an endlessly repeated world cycle. But even if Beckett had Darwin and Empedocles in mind, I am going to suggest that he also draws on two vignettes from Haeckel's Ceylon memoir, both of which are associated with Buddhism, in creating the cyclical suffering of *How It Is*.

First, let me recap what exactly takes place in the novel. Bom comes to see that everyone in his world takes it in turns to be the victim and to be the tormentor. As Schopenhauer might have put it,

---

68 Windelband, p. 53.

he 'recognizes the whole, comprehends its essence, and finds that it is constantly passing away, caught up in vain strivings, inner conflict, and perpetual suffering' (*WWR*, I.4.68, 405–6). Bom spends part two of *How It Is* abusing Pim and realises that eventually he must go to face his own tormentor, a third character with an indeterminate name. Pim, meanwhile, will become the tormentor to another victim. Quite how many players exist in this gruesome game is unclear: Bom imagines as few as four and as many as 'billions' (*HII*, 44). Whatever the number, each person will only ever meet two of the others: his tormentor and his victim, his two 'lifelong acquaintances' (*HII*, 105), over and over again. The tragedy is that by the time a person becomes a tormentor, he has forgotten that he was once tormented himself, and yet still feels himself to be 'a traveller to whom life owes a victim' (*HII*, 124). And so, mercilessly, the process of cruelty continues without any possibility of having compassion for one's victim or one's tormentor. This process resembles Zimmer's description of *saṃsāra* as an 'endless game with joy and agony in aimless alternation' that Beckett highlighted in Joyce's copy of *Maya*.

Although Haeckel's Ceylon memoir is largely cheery in tone he does describe several instances of Darwinian struggle and human cruelty. Two of these, both connected with Buddhism, are relevant to *How It Is*. The first takes us back to the bo tree. In the same chapter of *A Visit to Ceylon* in which Haeckel mentions the self-mortifying fakir, he also describes a murderous tendency of Indian fig trees. As in other passages (*VC*, 123), Haeckel uses the term 'banyan' to describe both *Ficus religiosa* (the Buddha's bo tree) and *Ficus benghalensis* (a true banyan):

> Here, too, are huge primaeval specimens of the banyan, the sacred Indian fig. [...] Out there, see—a stalwart parasite of the fig family is choking the noble palm it holds in the tight embrace of its twining stems, and a few paces farther stands another, its very brother, now mere cylindrical trellis of plaited stems bare of leaves; the throttled palm first died and decayed, and now the same fate has overtaken its murderer. (*VC*, 65)

The banyan is an epiphyte: it grows inside a host, usually a member of its own species, which it then kills. Bom does not kill Pim, for important reasons that I will explain below, but he realises that in the chain of beings in his universe the tormentor will encounter the 'same fate' (*HII*, 123) as his victim. Bom also describes Pim as his 'brother' and pictures the 'imaginary brothers' that he might journey with in the future (*HII*, 64, 99).

The second instance of repetitive cruelty that Beckett may have taken from *A Visit to Ceylon* concerns animals and also the doctrine of reincarnation. During his travels, Haeckel witnessed a great deal of animal suffering, particularly involving beasts of burden such as oxen and horses. Although Haeckel was more than happy to kill animals in search of food and the name of scientific research, he hated seeing animals needlessly made to suffer. Biology, Haeckel argued, demonstrates that animals 'have the same nerves and sense-organs as we, and the same feelings of pleasure and pain'.[69] The theory of evolution should, he believed, make us see that all creatures are in some sense 'our brothers.'[70] On this point, Beckett was likely in agreement with Haeckel: he hated seeing animals in captivity, and once ran up to save a rat from being killed by one of his neighbours.[71] As a child, he witnessed a rabid dog being clubbed to death by a policeman, which, he recalled fifty years later, 'made a terrible effect on me'.[72] Steven Connor points out that animals feature frequently in Beckett's writing,[73] and *How It Is* is no different. The novel is inhabited by rats, butterflies, a llama, insects, a dog, sheep, horses, an albatross, prawns, sprat, a lamb, a pigeon, snakes, a worm, crabs, flies, herring, a humming bird, sardines, slime-worms and blackbirds. Bom says that he 'never disapproved anything really not even cruelty to animals' (*HII*, 34); this statement is at once a denial of compassion towards animals

---

69 Haeckel, *The Riddle Of The Universe*, pp. 289–290.
70 Haeckel, *The Riddle Of The Universe*, p. 290.
71 Knowlson, pp. 162, 338.
72 Knowlson, pp. 35–6.
73 Steven Connor, 'Beckett's Animals', *Journal of Beckett Studies*, 8 (1982), 29–44.

and also an admission—in 'not even'—that such compassion comes naturally to most people. Elsewhere, the question of animal consciousness is briefly touched on when Bom likens a dog to 'Malebranche' (*HII*, 24), the Occasionalist philosopher who inherited Descartes' belief that animals were mindless automata. Bom thinks differently, however: 'animals know', he says of the horses and sheep watching him from the 'granite outcrops' (*HII*, 25). Later on, he says that 'even beasts observe each other' (*HII*, 47). In addition to these musings on animal minds, Bom also contemplates their theological status, when he recalls the llama:

> she would not come to me I would go to her huddle in her fleece but they add no a beast here no the soul is de rigueur the mind too a minimum of each otherwise too great an honour (*HII*, 9)

As Terry points out, the infernal setting of *How It Is* is the probable reason why the llama is excluded from 'here.'[74] In Christian and Cartesian paradigms, animals lack both soul and mind and are therefore ineligible for admission to the afterlife.

Haeckel describes the mistreatment of animals in Ceylon at length, and it is possible that Beckett borrowed certain details of this behaviour for use in *How It Is*. 'The wretched oxen,' Haeckel writes, 'are always marked with their owners' names in large letters cut quite through the skin.' This resembles the cruelty inflicted on Pim by Bom: 'bloody him all over with Roman capitals' (*HII*, 53). Using his nails, Bom carves Pim's name, his own name and various other words into Pim's skin (61, 65). Bom's continual infliction of pain on Pim's backside, including 'fire in the rectum' (31), may owe something to Haeckel's description of colt-breakers in Ceylon, who tie up a horse and 'belabour him from behind, sometimes even scorching the hapless brute with torches', until it submits (*VC*, 159). Bom says he is cruel to Pim in order to 'train him up' (*HII*, 53), just as the colt-breakers train

---

74 Terry, p. 352.

their horses. Haeckel calls the colt-breakers 'tormentors' in several places (*VC*, 159–161), the same word Bom uses later for the aggressors in the abusive relationships of *How It Is* (93). The French word 'bourreaux' (*CC*, III.31) means both torturer and executioner (*TLFi*). Finally, Haeckel says that the horse 'goes through every torment that the "Holy Office" ever devised for the conversion of heretics and infidels' (159). This may be why Bom's violent training of Pim is meted out like the readings in a church service—'end of first lesson' (*HII*, 54)—and why he later refers to the tormentor-victim relationship as a process of 'martyring and being martyred' (*HII*, 110).

Haeckel suggests that religious ideas are often responsible for the mistreatment of animals. In *Riddle of the Universe*, he attacks Christianity for its 'anthropistic illusion', and laments that it

> has no place for that well-known love of animals, that sympathy with the nearly related and friendly mammals (dogs, horses, cattle, etc.), which is urged in the ethical teaching of many of the older religions, especially Buddhism.[75]

Similarly, in *A Visit to Ceylon*, he blames Hinduism for the way in which the colt-breakers treat their horses:

> the black coachman and stable lads [...] are most of them worshippers of Siva, and believe in the transmigration of the soul. Perhaps they imagine that by these brutalities they are avenging their wrongs on the degraded souls of those cruel princes and warriors who were the former tyrants of their race. (*VC*, 150)

The ethical logic in this passage is the same as that of *How It Is*: torturer becomes tortured, and tortured becomes torturer, in a cyclical existence that is seemingly impossible to escape from. Schopenhauer also explains the 'myth of the transmigration of the soul' in similar terms: 'anyone who kills even an animal will have to be born at some point

---

75 Haeckel, *The Riddle Of The Universe*, pp. 289–290.

in the infinity of time as precisely this sort of animal, and suffer the same death' (*WWR*, I.4.63, 376–7). This time, however, Buddhism does not get off so easily. In the midst of his discussion of the colt-breakers, the scarred oxen and the vengeful ethics of 'transmigration', Haeckel points an accusing finger at the Buddha:

> Great Buddha! you who strove so earnestly to diminish the miseries of this miserable life and mitigate the torments of suffering creation, what mistakes you made! What a blessing you would have conferred on men and beasts if, instead of the foolish prohibition to take the life of any creature, you had laid down the merciful law: Thou shalt torture no living thing. (*VC*, 161)

Haeckel sees Singhalese Buddhists scrupulously avoiding *killing* any animals, but treating them badly nonetheless. Similarly, Bom, who aspires to be like the Buddha, who wants to 'renounce' and 'have no more desires', deliberately avoids killing the being he torments. He stops short of gouging Pim in 'the eye the glands', saying, 'no only confuse him fatal thing avoid at all costs' (*HII*, 54). Later on, Bom calls Pim his 'unbutcherable brother' / 'increvable frère' (*HII*, 64; *CC*, II.140). Both 'unbutcherable' and 'increvable' suggest that there is something animalistic about Pim: the French verb 'crever' can mean to die like an animal; it can also, appropriately enough, refer to the exhaustion of a horse through mistreatment (*TLFi*). But Bom cannot butcher Pim, for then he would be left with a 'true corpse untorturable' (*HII*, 80).

Elsewhere in Beckett's work, the suffering of animals is closely connected with that of human beings, particularly those deemed to be outside the sphere of everyday moral concern, such as the damned, the mentally ill or the criminal. The clearest example is in 'Dante and the Lobster', from *More Pricks than Kicks*. Belacqua has been contemplating Canto 20 of the *Inferno* in which Dante's pilgrim makes one of his 'rare movements of compassion in Hell'.[76] The pilgrim's moral feeling is condemned by Virgil as impious pity, but it moves Belacqua to two instances of transgressive compassion, first towards the condemned murderer McCabe—'poor McCabe, he would get it in the neck at dawn. What was he doing now, how was he feeling? He would relish one more meal, one more night'—and second to the titular lobster, boiled alive by Belacqua's aunt at the close of the story (*MPTK*, 18). In *How It Is*, Beckett evokes Canto 20 again when Bom thinks of praying for the damned:

> when I think of the souls in torment true torment true souls who have no right to it no right ever to sleep we're talking of sleep I prayed for them once (*HII*, 29)

The problem is that neither Belacqua nor Bom are moved to substantive action by their Dantean contemplations. Even though their compassion is transgressive, neither of them is brave enough to 'trouble the peace' (*HII*, 129) and put a stop to patterns of suffering that are deeply woven into their worlds. Belacqua's aunt is said to be astonished and angry at his suggestion that she cannot boil the lobster alive, and her 'sharp' response silences Belacqua for the remainder of the story. The aunt says that 'lobsters are always boiled alive. They must be', and Belacqua absorbs the inevitability of this fate into his thoughts: 'Now it was going alive into scalding water. It had to.' (*MPTK*, 19) In other words, this is just 'how it is': a theodicy of social and gastronomic convention that is just as unconvincing and cruel as the one that Virgil foists on the pilgrim in Canto 20. Likewise, Bom, although capable of thinking kind thoughts to some hypothetical damned, still goes on to torment Pim. When explaining the arrangement of tormentor and victim in his world he stresses its scientific and moral inevitability—'it's mathematical it's our justice' (*HII*, 97)—and imagines an 'intelligence somewhere a love' (120) watching over and

---

76 Samuel Beckett, *More Pricks Than Kicks* (London: Picador, 1977), p. 16. Hereafter, *MPTK*.

controlling it all. Imagining that suffering is predetermined and divinely ordained is, it seems, far easier than having to confront it and do anything to alleviate it.

The End of Suffering?

Bom's theodicy of inevitability, justice and love absolves him of responsibility for Pim's suffering. At least, that seems to be idea. Towards the end of the novel, however, Bom's Buddhist aspirations catch up with him, and he has to retract his explanation for how the universe works as soon as it becomes apparent that holding such knowledge more or less obliges him to bring the cycles of suffering to a close.

For both Schopenhauer and the Buddha, salvation from the world of suffering comes about through an insight into the way the world really is. Insight, knowledge and understanding are tantamount to liberation, while illusion—whether the Buddhist *samsāra* or Schopenhauer's 'veil of Maya'—traps us in suffering. Schopenhauer explains that one of the highest realisations in Buddhism is the 'Pradschna-Paramita'—that is, *prajñāpāramitā*, a Sanskrit term from Mahāyāna Buddhism meaning the 'perfection of wisdom'.[77] Schopenhauer glosses it in his own Kantian terms as 'cognition of things in themselves' (*WWR*, II.2.22, 288). While Beckett, as we have seen, was suspicious of both 'oriental philosophers' and indeed Schopenhauer, for offering a 'way out', he actually wrote something strikingly similar to their understanding of the unity of insight and salvation. This is from his Clare Street notebook, from August 1936:

> Es gibt Augenblicke, wo der Hoffnungsschleier endgültig weggerissen wird und die plötzlich befreiten Augen ihre Welt anblicken, wie sie ist, wie sie sein muss. (UoR MS5003, 17r–18r)

---

77 See Paul Williams, *Mahayana Buddhism: The Doctrinal Foundations*, 2nd edn (London: Routledge, 2008), p. 52.

> [There are moments when the veil of hope is finally torn apart and the suddenly liberated eyes see their world, how it is, how it must be.[78]]

Nixon says that Beckett is 'paraphrasing the Schopenhauerian act of achieving a state of being where the veil of Maya is torn aside to reveal the authentic world, the deeper level of reality'.[79] The eyes are 'liberated': freed, saved. This passage also anticipates Bom's insight into 'how it is' when he realises that his existence is driven by a cycle of tormentors and victims.

Schopenhauer says that the Buddha has the unique 'privilege of clearly recognizing his own earlier births and those of other people'; for everyone else, a past life is 'a memory that cannot be made clearly conscious' (*WWR*, II.4.41, 520). Bom has a similar ability: he can, as we have seen, remember living, dying and being born again in a hospital, and is aware of previous 'formulations', that is, lives lived elsewhere. And whereas any other inhabitant of his world has 'long since forgotten' their role as a victim by the time they become a tormentor, and vice versa (*HII*, 105), Bom alone is able to see 'all along the chain in both directions' (*HII*, 123). For the Buddha, however, such knowledge has consequences, as Schopenhauer explains:

> These constant rebirths make up the succession of life dreams of a will that is in itself indestructible until, informed and improved by traversing so many and various successive cognitions, always in a new form, it abolishes itself. (*WWR*, II.4.41, 519)

The abolition of the will is, according to Schopenhauer, *nirvāna*, salvation. It brings an end to 'hatred', 'wickedness', 'egoism', 'evil', and rebirth, and brings about 'loving kindness', 'justice', 'tranquillity', and 'peace' (*WWR*, II.4.41, 625). Beckett makes the connection explicit in his philosophy notebooks:

---

78 Translation modified from Nixon, p. 170.
79 Nixon, p. 170.

> Deliverance from misery only possible through repudiation of the will. But how shall the will, the ἓν καὶ πᾶν [=] one & all, only Real, TII [Thing-in-Itself] by its very nature self-affirmation, repudiate itself? Yet is present in asceticism etc., peace of soul & absence of wishes. Here Sch[openhauer] found confirmation in the Indian philosophy, called the world of idea the veil of Maia & repudiation of will entrance to Nirvana. (TCD MS10967, 253r)

This 'peace of soul' comes at a seemingly high price, however. Schopenhauer says that he who wishes to be saved must 'willingly leave his individuality behind' and renounce any attachment to the idea that he is a self separate from the rest of the world (*WWR*, II.4.41, 507). Although the Buddha was quite adamant that the achievement of *nirvāna* is expressible neither in terms of annihilation or eternal life—largely because 'when all phenomena have been uprooted, all pathways of speech are also uprooted'[80]— nineteenth-century interpreters of Buddhism did see *nirvāna* as tantamount to a kind of nihilistic obliteration: Plümacher, as I mentioned, was quite explicit about this, and Beckett underlined her account of *nirvāna* as self-extinction and blissful nothingness.[81]

Extinction of the self is precisely what Bom contemplates and what causes him to repudiate his theodicy. He begins by considering the 'advantage of stopping' the 'procession which seemed as if it must be eternal' (*HII*, 123), but worries that such an ending would be unjust, with tormentors left without victims, and victims left without tormentors. Of course, this is only unjust to someone with a crudely retributive attitude, the kind which Schopenhauer called 'senseless', 'utterly groundless and wrong-headed' (*WWR*, I.4.62, 375). It would be far better for all concerned if the procession stopped as soon as possible, regardless of any unsettled scores. Bom, however, suspects that none of his peers have the stomach to bring the suffering to an end: 'to have done with this not one of us' (*HII*, 124). But then he imagines what such a one would be like, and even offers him advice:

---

80 *The Suttanipāta: An Ancient Collection of Buddha's Discourses*, trans. by Bhikkhu Bodhi (Somerville, MA: Wisdom Publications, 2017), V.6, p. 335
81 Plümacher, p. 24; Nixon and Van Hulle, p. 154.

> this is not one of us harping harping mad too with weariness to have done with him
>
> has he not staring him in the face I quote a solution more simple by far and by far more radical
>
> a formulation that would eliminate him completely and so admit him to that peace at least (*HII*, 126)

Given that 'new formulation' is glossed a few pages earlier as 'namely this new life' (*HII*, 124), it would seem that what Bom is proposing to this 'one of us' is a new lifetime that is not a lifetime at all: in other words, the end of rebirth, *nirvāna*. But self-extinction is a hard thing to accept, as Beckett noted thirty years earlier in *Proust*, the 'old ego dies hard' (*PTD*, 21). Habit, argues Beckett, is what the ego wants to preserve. But when it is exposed, as Bom is, to the 'suffering of being' this cuts through the *ennui*, the 'boredom of living' that otherwise paralyses our attention (*PTD*, 20).

Ruby Cohn argues that Bom 'experiences a kind of relief in his forthcoming death.'[82] This conclusion, however, is based on a rather selective quotation. Cohn cites 'JE VAIS CREVER hurlements bon' ('I SHALL DIE screams good'). But the whole passage says something slightly different:

> so things may change no answer end no answer I may choke no answer sink no answer sully the mud no answer the dark no answer trouble the peace no more no answer the silence no answer die no answer DIE screams I MAY DIE screams I SHALL DIE screams good (*HII*, 129)

Given the separation of the narrator from the 'voice' coming at him from without, we could read this paragraph as a kind of call-and-response:

---

82 Cohn, p. 256.

Call	Response
so things may change	no answer
end	no answer
I may choke	no answer
sink	no answer
sully the mud	no answer
the dark	no answer
trouble the peace no more	no answer
the silence	no answer
die	no answer
DIE	screams
I MAY DIE	screams
I SHALL DIE	screams

Bom is trying to provoke the voice—which he also says is 'my voice'—to respond. Like most of us, the voice is unmoved by the usual clichés about aging and death: 'things may change' and 'trouble the peace no more' get no response. Even 'die' fails to do anything. We all know that we must die, but rarely do we think of this in terms of what Heidegger called our 'ownmost death'.[83] As the philosopher Mark Johnston explains:

> I [...], that is, the human being Johnston, will die. A particular human being, one of the teeming horde, the one who has just used the first person pronoun to pick himself out, will die. His mental and bodily life will cease to exist. When I think of this outcome in that way, my special concern for myself need not be engaged. The shutting down of the mental and bodily life of a human being has happened billions of times before, and it will continue to happen, as part of the natural life of our species. Biological death, the death of the human being I pick out by the first-person pronoun, is thus not even a prima facie object of the intense self-concern that the threat of death provokes. But in thus holding Johnston at such a distance, I am forgetting something. That human being is ME, the one at the center of this arena of presence and action. When that human

---

83 Martin Heidegger, *Being and Time*, trans. by John Macquarrie and E.S. Robinson (Oxford: Blackwell, 1978), p. 294ff.

being dies this arena of presence and action will come to an end. That is my subjective death, my *ownmost* death is terrifying, it is the end of this arena of presence and action, and *thus the end of the frame in which the fundamental distinction of value, the distinction between the value of what is* HERE *and of what is* THERE, *appears.*

This is why it appears, *madly I know, but nonetheless it does so appear*, that a world in which no one is ME is in a certain way defective: the very frame in which the fundamental distinction of value appears is missing from such a world.

And yet I find nothing obviously defective in the myriad possible worlds and actual times that are without Johnston.[84]

Like Johnston, Beckett resorts to capitals to spell out the difference between imagining biological death—'die'—and imagining *ownmost* death—'I SHALL DIE'. It is only the latter which manages to transcend platitude and provoke a sense of horror. But given that Bom has rejected the idea of making an end in the sense of *nirvāna*, is it not contradictory that he should recall his ownmost death with such approval ('good')? This is where I think Cohn misreads the line. The 'good' does not refer to the prospect of death, but rather the 'screams'. After eliciting three screams with the threat of death, Bom is satisfied and the call-and-response exercise can come to an end. He is satisfied with the screams because they reassure him that he is still alive. And not just alive, but still *willing* in Schopenhauer's terms. When Schopenhauer seeks to illustrate to his reader what exactly he means by the 'will-to-live', he points to the 'terrified alarm and wild uproar' and 'unbelievable anxiety' of a being threatened with death (*WWR*, II.2.28, 366). To reach *nirvāna*, Bom would have to deny his will-to-live, that self-centred striving that Schopenhauer sees as the source of suffering.

---

84 Mark Johnston, *Surviving Death* (Princeton, NJ: Princeton University Press, 2010), p. 159.

Reasserting it, through his screams, through his solipsism, is therefore a rejection of salvation.

Cioran's final essay in *La Tentation d'exister*, which bears the same title, is also instructive here. Our fear of death, he writes, 'replaces space, welling up until it substitutes itself for death. All experience is suddenly reduced to an exchange between the self and this fear' (*TE*, 208). Beckett dramatizes Cioran's 'exchange' in Bom's frantic dialogue with his 'voice'. It is surely relevant that Cioran mentions the Buddha, and indeed purports to quote him, in this same paragraph:

> "We live in fear, and therefore do not live." Buddha's words may be taken to mean that instead of keeping ourselves at the stage of being where fear opens out onto the world, we make it an end of itself, a closed universe, a substitute for space. (*TE*, 209)

The fear of death, according to Schopenhauer and Cioran, provokes an absurd and claustrophilic solipsism which is incompatible with the teachings of the Buddha and with entry into *nirvāna*. Both these texts seem to be touchstones for Beckett in the final pages of *How It Is*.

Like the Buddha, Schopenhauer believed that salvation has ethical implications. In Schopenhauer's soteriology, what goes extinct through salvation is not exactly the self—since it never really existed—but rather the *'principium individuationis'*, according to which someone sees 'his own person as utterly distinct and separated from everyone else by a wide gulf', a 'cognition that he firmly embraces, because it is the only viewpoint that will serve and support his egoism' (*WWR*, I.4.65, 392). Seeing through the illusion of separateness is, according to Schopenhauer, the seed of compassion for all living creatures. Bom has some ethical feeling—he imagines praying for the damned—and even an inkling of this Schopenhauerian monism—'in reality we are one', 'each one of us is at the same time Bom and Pim tormentor and tormented' (*HII*, 122, 123). This is what prompts Alain Badiou to suggest that the violence in *How It Is* is ultimately ethical. Badiou reads *How It Is* as a work preoccupied with 'alterity', in which the encounter with the Other 'fissures and displaces the solipsistic interment of the *cogito*'.⁸⁵ This kind of release from solipsism is certainly what Beckett has in mind, drawing on Schopenhauer and the fragments of Buddhism that I have been exploring in this chapter, but crucially it is also what Bom rejects. He actually prefers the solipsistic internment of the self—the *principium individuationis*—to the ethical consequences of liberation from this solipsism. He clings to a rigid sense of self and therefore *nirvāna* remains impossible for him.

It quickly becomes apparent that in addressing the hypothetical 'one of us', the one who would bring an end to it all, Bom is really talking to himself: 'in the familiar form of questions I am said to ask myself' (*HII*, 126). And if everything he says is true, then he cannot refuse his own radical solution of 'elimination': 'if all that all that yes if all that is not how shall I say no answer if all that is not false yes' (*HII*, 126). He cynically adopted the theodicy as a justification for his cruelty to Pim, but now that it impinges upon him, ethically and ontologically, it must be forthrightly denied: 'all these calculations yes explanations yes the whole story from beginning to end yes completely false yes' (*HII*, 126). He denies all his dreams, the procession, the existence of Pim, everything except the existence of himself 'alone in the mud' (*HII*, 128). He is, quite literally, interred in his solipsism. In *La Tentation d'exister*, Cioran suggests that while the 'Orient advances toward a Void of its own [...] and triumphs there', we Europeans 'bog down in ours and lose our last resources' (63). This is precisely what happens to Bom. All that remains at the end of the novel is that bare sense of himself existing, that illusory yet dearly cherished thing which 'screams' when he contemplates death (*HII*, 129). Bom is the aspiring Buddha who rejects his *nirvāna*, the European man who cannot assimilate the 'oriental' hope for annihilation and void, and being so, he takes his place in Beckett's pantheon of failed sages.

---

85 Alain Badiou, *On Beckett*, trans. by Alberto Toscano and Nina Power (Manchester: Clinamen Press, 2003), p. 16.

Conclusion

> Having already seen that arrow onto which human beings hang and cling—'*I know! I see! That's just how it is!*'—the Tathagatas [= Buddhas] hang onto nothing.
>
> —The Buddha[86]

Bom's failure to reach salvation and to find a way out, would seem to fit with what Beckett rejected in Buddhism, in his comments to the puppeteer's wife about *Act Without Words I* and to Charles Juliet about the 'oriental philosophers'. Schopenhauer and even Leopardi perhaps 'still have some hope of an answer, of a solution,' Beckett told Juliet, 'But I haven't.'[87] We might conclude that *How It Is* ultimately affirms this pessimism: the novel becomes Beckett's disavowal of the possibility of salvation and with it the possibility of an ethics based on compassion rather than retribution. This reading is certainly open to us, but in closing this chapter I want to present two cases for not insisting on it. The first relies on Beckett's comments to the theologian Tom Driver in 1961, just after he had finished writing *Comment c'est*, during an interview for the *Columbia University Forum*. Beckett told Driver that he admired the 'dramatic qualities' of 'Augustine's doctrine of grace given and grace withheld':

> Two thieves are crucified with Christ, one saved and the other damned. How can we make sense of this division? In classical drama, such problems do not arise. The destiny of Racine's *Phèdre* is sealed from the beginning: she will proceed into the dark. [...] Within this notion clarity is possible, but for us who are neither Greek nor Jansenist there is not such clarity. The question would also be removed if we believed in the contrary—total salvation. But where we have both dark and light we have also the inexplicable.[88]

---

86 Anguttara Nikāya 4:24; translation from Rob Burbea, *Seeing That Frees: Meditations on Emptiness and Dependent Arising* (West Ogwell: Hermes Amāra Publications, 2014), p. 218.
87 Juliet, p. 49.
88 Tom Driver, 'Interview with Beckett', in *Samuel Beckett: The Critical Heritage*, ed. by Lawrence Graver and Raymond Federman (London: Routledge, 2005), pp. 241–48 (p. 244).

Beckett places both his work and twentieth-century human beings in a situation where neither salvation nor damnation are predetermined, where such clarity is not available to us. *How It Is*, as I mentioned above, is a deliberately unclear text in which different accounts of 'how it is', of how the universe works, jostle for the attention of the reader. If we were to insist on the pessimistic reading, that would force Bom, and perhaps us as readers, into the mould of the Racinian protagonist. We would be doomed from the start. As I have shown, the possibility of salvation and its rejection remain open to Bom until the very last moment, preserving the crepuscular balance between light and dark, between grace and doom, that Beckett preferred.

The second reason to reject the wholly pessimistic reading is that if we held onto it, we would be committing the same error as the colt-breakers, Bom, Belacqua's aunt, and Virgil in Canto 20. That error is to take a just-so story, a story that claims to describe 'how it is', and insist on its truthfulness and inevitability. It does not matter whether we choose to explain away the suffering of the world as part of the godless 'natural order' or as the inscrutable operations of a 'regimen of grace' (*HII*, 108), or whether our chosen theodicy offers tyrants and criminals an afterlife in hell or a rebirth as an ox. When such justifications relieve us of responsibility for the suffering of others and foster retributive attitudes, they need to be questioned and critiqued. If we read *How It Is* as the revelation of some pessimistic truth about the world, we are choosing yet another theodicy, which will result in the same moral apathy and unwillingness to 'trouble the peace' that afflicts Bom. The solution to this impasse is to read the pessimistic aspects of *How It Is*—the violence, the failure to end violence, the religious and metaphysical justifications for violence—as ethical challenges, rather than as truth claims on Beckett's part. That challenge is to question all the just-so stories, whether religious, scientific, or political, and replace retributive ethics with transgressive compassion, and then, crucially, to act on that ethical feeling.

What does this mean for Beckett's relationship to quietism? I started this chapter with Nordau's argument that Buddhism and quietism amounted to much the same thing. Beckett's engagement with

Buddhist ethics in *How It Is* would suggest that he has developed an understanding of Buddhism that does not conform to the navel-gazing, solipsistic stereotype that he had so often resorted to in his early writing, such as 'Le Concentrisme' and *Murphy*. But whether this constitutes a rejection of quietism is a different matter. Schopenhauer saw no contradiction between quietism and the ethics of compassion: quite the opposite, the two go hand in hand. Liberation from the *principium individuationis* can bring about feelings of compassion, because the liberated saint is no longer held hostage by self-concern. And the same is true the other way around: ethical behaviour and feeling can bring about salvation. As Schopenhauer put it, 'from the same source that gives rise to all goodness, love, virtue and nobility there ultimately emerges also what I call the negation of the will to life' (*WWR*, I.4.68, 405) and 'to be just, noble, and humane is simply to translate my metaphysics into action' (*WWR*, II.4.47, 616). *How It Is* would appear to fit this model insofar as it presents a cosmology in which a quietist solution to life's ills is also the most ethical option: had Bom resigned the will and abandoned the self he would have, in doing so, rejected the principal of revenge. His individual salvation would also have broken the cycle of suffering in which he, and many others, have been trapped. Ethics and soteriology—the two aspects of Buddhism that Beckett underlined in his copy of *Der Pessimismus*—turn out to be interconnected in this novel. In *Murphy* and *Molloy* quietism and ethics are at odds. In *Murphy*, the search for the little world proves to be incompatible with a deeper need for companionship and brotherhood, a conclusion which reflects Beckett's own anxieties about 'baroque solipsism' at the time of writing. In *Molloy*, the commitment to the contradictory aesthetics of Gide and Dostoevsky, against those of Balzac, meant that ethics had to be sidelined. With *How It Is*, Beckett finds a way to maintain his loyalty to the aesthetic of incoherence while also imagining a cosmology in which quietism and ethics are reconcilable. As I have suggested in this chapter, it seems likely that the ethical substance of this novel emerged from Beckett's engagement with two 'quietists' whose teachings were profoundly ethical—the Buddha and Schopenhauer—and with the ethical questions that emerge in Haeckel's memoir.

Chapter 5
so much short of blessed nothing:
Salvation, rebirth and the late prose

> we too seek "salvation", if only by wanting nothing to do with it.
>
> —E.M. Cioran, A Short History of Decay (36)

> Paradise is locked and bolted, and the cherubim stands behind us. We have to go on and make the journey round the world to see if it is perhaps open somewhere at the back.
>
> —Heinrich von Kleist,
> 'On the Marionette Theatre'[1]

Writing in *The Independent* shortly after Beckett's death in December 1989, Eric Griffiths pointed out how Beckett's

> late work often imagines places of calm, of cool or chill refreshment, lit with an inexplicably constant light, with a "light that makes all so white no visible source, all shines with the same white shine" (*Imagination Dead Imagine*).[2]

For Griffiths, this was evidence of a 'paradisiacal' side to Beckett, beyond the more familiar infernal and purgatorial flavours of his writing. Griffiths compared Beckett's 'Oh all to end' from *Stirrings Still* to Dante's 'end of all desires' (*Paradiso*, 33.46), and drew his description of the late texts from the Catholic prayer that the dead may be granted 'refrigerii sedem, quietis beatitudinem, et luminis claritatem' [a place of cool refreshment, the blessing of calm, and radiant light]. He was not alone in evaluating the late prose from this perspective: Thomas

---

1 Quoted in Boxall, p. 75.
2 Eric Griffiths, 'At Odds with Ends', *The Independent* (London, 27 December 1989), Arts Section, p. 11.

Merton, the American Trappist monk and writer, was similarly captivated by Beckett's 'quite perfect' *Ping*, another vision of light and repose.[3] Beckett admitted that *Ping* was an attempt to create a 'refuge', and that it emerged out of writing *The Lost Ones*, one of his more infernal works.[4] As Beckett told a friend, *Ping* is 'all whiteness and silence and finishedness', and all the more 'outrageous' for being so (SB to JHe, 18/8/66).[5]

The outrage, of course, is that the crepuscular, purgatorial Samuel Beckett could write anything approaching paradise or ultimate beatitude. Three decades earlier, Beckett had dismissed paradise as a 'static lifelessness of unrelieved immaculation' (*Dis*, 33). He insisted to Juliet that unlike certain 'oriental thinkers', and unlike Schopenhauer, he did not 'propose a way out [*issue*]' or 'hope for an answer, a solution': 'One solution, which is death.'[6] And as we saw in the last chapter, Beckett quietly refused the suggestion that the protagonist of *Act Without Words I* might be 'liberated' by his ordeal. And yet, *Ping* really does seem immaculate: its principal figure stands in a 'shining white infinite' which is 'known not' (*CSP*, 194). Here at last is an ineffable that is not to be effed (*W*, 52–3).

In Beckett's earlier fictions, we meet characters who strive for lasting beatitude and never quite get there. Murphy's quest for a quiet body and mind is realised only ironically in the quiet of his sudden and gruesome death. Watt's 'ataraxy' and 'utmost serenity' last only as long as it takes him to walk from Mr Knott's house to the garden gate: 'no sooner in the public road than he burst into tears' (*W*, 180). Molloy and Malone have their moments of respite and relief but these are short-lived, and unreliable. And Bom turns away from his radical 'solution' which would break through the illusion of the self and admit

---

3   Thomas Merton, *The Hidden Ground of Love: The Letters of Thomas Merton on Religious Experience and Social Concerns*, ed. by William Henry Shannon (San Diego, CA: Harcourt Brace Jovanovich, 1993), p. 636.
4   Beckett, quoted in Knowlson, p. 564.
5   Quoted in Knowlson, p. 542.
6   Juliet, pp. 17, 49.

him to peace. A fifty per cent chance of salvation was deemed a 'reasonable percentage' in *Waiting for Godot* (*CDW*, 13), but more often than not the odds in Beckett's cosmos are stacked far less favourably. If Griffiths is right about the late prose breaking with this trend, it is worth asking why this might be and how exactly this new 'paradisiacal' side to Beckett's work operates. Griffiths admits that his own Catholic hope for post-mortem calm sits rather uneasily beside the way Beckett's writing 'eloquently often seems to long for absolute cessation, the pulse dropped away to nought'. In this chapter, I argue that understanding Beckett's soteriological turn in the late prose demands that we look beyond the familiar orthodox Christian paradigm of salvation as a heavenly afterlife. Instead, I want to turn to the paradoxical soteriologies that are found in the writings of the Christian Quietists, as well as the teachings of Schopenhauer, Buddhism, and Pyrrhonism. In all these schools of thought, salvation is thought of not as a place where the soul ends up after death, but as a state of mind achieved through a process of resignation or giving up: an 'absolute cessation' not of the pulse, but of desire, will, striving, hope, and, in many cases, self. I also want to think about this 'paradisiacal' late style as a necessary movement in the structure of Beckett's prose canon, particularly when it is thought of as a kind of series. The enduring influence of Marcel Proust will be important here, as will E.M. Cioran's reflections on the state of the novel in Proust's wake.

Beckett's novel 'series'

> to go on means going from here, means finding me, losing me, vanishing and beginning again, a stranger first, then little by little the same as always, in another place
>
> —The Unnamable (13)

In May 1947, Beckett wrote to his friend George Reavey about *Watt*. It was, he said, an 'unsatisfactory book,' but 'has its place in the series, as will perhaps appear in time' (14/5/47; *LSB2*, 55). At this point in his life, Beckett had completed several works of prose fiction: *Dream*,

More Pricks than Kicks, *Murphy*, the *Nouvelles*—'La Fin', 'L'Expulsé', 'Le Calmant', and 'Premier amour'—and *Mercier et Camier*. He was also just starting work on *Molloy*. If these books constituted a 'series' it was a rather unorthodox one. Not only were its volumes written in different languages, only two of them were published at the time. *Molloy* was also at odds with its predecessors, as Beckett had shifted his narration from the third to first person. And while *Dream*, *More Pricks than Kicks*, and *Murphy* were set in Dublin and London, the novels from *Watt* onwards abandon geographical specificity in favour of anonymous, composite landscapes. There is little that would tie these disparate books together, at least at first glance, and yet Beckett still thought they could be taken as a whole. The following year, with *Molloy* finished and *Malone meurt* just begun, Beckett wrote to MacGreevy:

> The French Murphy fell stillborn from the press as I think Dr J[ohnson] said. Molloy is a long book, the second last of the series, begun with Murphy, if it can be said to be a series. The last is begun and then I hope I'll hear no more of him. (4/1/48; *LSB2*, 71)

Six months later, he wrote to Reavey again:

> I am now retyping, for rejection by the publishers, Malone Meurt, the last I hope of the series Murphy, Watt, Mercier & Camier, Molloy, not to mention the 4 Nouvelles & Eleuthéria. A young publisher here is interested, I forget his name, Editions K I think, and I am preparing him for burial. All that will see in time the sorry light of the domaine public. (8/7/48; *LSB2*, 80)

The Belacqua books are out, but the novellas and the unpublished, unperformed play *Eleuthéria* might be in. Can this really be 'said to be a series'?

Although Beckett equivocates, these letters do provide a few clues as to what he might have meant when he called these books a series. The first thing to notice is that Beckett attributes these novels to 'him': some sort of voice or entity that animates all the books from *Murphy* onwards. The narrators of the trilogy suggest something similar by assuming responsibility for the characters that preceded them. Moran tells us that Murphy, Watt, and Mercier are a 'rabble in my head' (*Mo*, 143). Malone says that when he dies, 'it will all be over with the Murphys, Merciers, Molloys, Morans, and Malones, unless it goes beyond the grave' (*MD*, 63). And finally the Unnamable complains that instead of talking about himself, he has wasted his time 'with these bran-dips, beginning with Murphy, who wasn't even the first' (*U*, 108). Belacqua is hereby reinstated into the series, fitting with a comment that Beckett made about the character in a 1958 letter to Con Leventhal: 'There are a good many degrees between him and l'Innommable, but it's the same engeance' (21/4/58).[7] This last word means 'species', 'kind' or 'race', and calls to mind Haeckel's definition of palingenesis as the recapitulation of older births, of the forms of one's ancestors. Indeed birth and death appear prominently in these letters about the series: Beckett mentions how the French *Murphy* is stillborn, while *Malone meurt* is both about to see the light of day and being prepared for burial. Each novel might be thought of as both a birth and a death of whatever voice or being follows its dogged path through all of them. But Beckett is very clear that he does not want the voice to return: 'I hope I'll hear no more of him', he says to MacGreevy. *Malone meurt* will be 'the last I hope of the series', he tells Reavey. Writing to MacGreevy again, he says: 'I have finished typing Malone meurt (may he never come back) and am now happily doing nothing' (26/9/48; *LSB2*, 105). So we have the idea in these letters of a residue of narratorial identity—perhaps merely *will*—that keeps coming back after successive deaths and births, but which ideally should never come back at all. This would correspond quite closely to the doctrines of rebirth and *nirvāna* that I explored in the last chapter. In *How It Is*, reincarnation was explored thematically as a means of grappling with Buddhist ethics and metaphysics. But in these comments to Reavey

---

7   Nixon, p. 222.

and MacGreevy, the concern is about the process of writing. This suggests that we need to look beyond Beckett's philosophical and Indological sources for rebirth, such as Zimmer, Plümacher, Schopenhauer, and Haeckel, to a more explicitly literary model, one which I believe Beckett found in Marcel Proust's *À la recherche du temps perdu*.

Proustian Rebirth

Eve Kosofsky Sedgwick was rare among Proust's readers in picking up on his interest in what she dubs a 'Venn diagram of concepts' that includes 'Rebirth, transmigration, metempsychosis, metamorphosis, reincarnation, and […] resurrection' and to which we could also add the palingenesis of Schopenhauer and Haeckel. While Sedgwick admits that she comes to the texts 'with something of a Buddhist eye', she rightly points out that 'it would be no more surprising to find [these doctrines] in Proust's very Orientalizing cultural context than our own'.[8] Indeed, as a reader of Schopenhauer, Proust would have encountered these ideas just as Beckett did, and they had their place in the Platonist and Pythagorean schools of European antiquity. Proust even suggests in *Du Côté de chez-Swann* that reincarnation is a 'Celtic belief'.[9] Roger Shattuck also notes Proust's concern with rebirth when he likens the novel to Platonic reminiscence or 'anamnesis', outlined by Socrates in the *Meno* and the *Phaedo*.[10] Beckett made a note of this term while he was reading Alfred Adler's *Practice and Theory of Individual Psychology* in the early 1930s and glossed it in parentheses. In psychotherapy, the word signifies a patient's personal account of their own medical history, but Beckett gives the Platonic definition as a 'doctrine of recollection of previous existence' (TCD MS10971/7–8, 32).[11]

---

8   Eve Kosofsky Sedgwick, *The Weather in Proust*, ed. by Jonathan Goldberg (Durham, NC: Duke University Press, 2011), p. 6.
9   Proust, *The Way by Swann's*, p. 47.
10 Roger Shattuck, *Proust* (London: Fontana, 1974), p. 144.
11 Dominic Scott, 'Platonic Anamnesis Revisited', *The Classical Quarterly (New Series)*, 37 (1987), 346–66.

The fact that there has been little critical commentary on Proust and reincarnation is all the more surprising given that Proust himself refers to it on the very first page of *À la recherche du temps perdu*. Marcel describes how, when he wakes up, his sleep-addled mind confuses his own sense of identity with the subject of whatever book he was reading as he fell asleep. After a few moments of wakefulness, however, this belief 'began to grow unintelligible, as after metempsychosis do the thoughts of an earlier existence.'[12] Similarly, Beckett's narrators mingle their identities with the stories that they tell, and with the subjects of earlier novels. Beckett also takes Proust's comparison between sleep and transmigration and turns it around in *How It Is*, where falling asleep and waking up are metaphorical substitutes for dying and being born again (*HII*, 17). Proust himself returns to the correspondence in his second volume, where he includes 'the transmigration of souls' as one of the mysteries to 'which we are admitted almost every night, just as we are to the other great mystery of annihilation and resurrection' that occurs in falling asleep and waking up again.[13] Another metaphorical interpretation of rebirth is at work when Marcel describes how the 'self of mine that had once loved' Gilberte has died.[14] He finds this realisation troubling—not because it means the end of a relationship, but because after such a dramatic shift in feeling

> our actual self [would be] changed [...] it would amount to a death of our self, albeit followed by a resurrection, but a resurrection in the form of a different self, whose love will remain for ever beyond the reach of those parts of the former self which have gone down to death.[15]

---

12   Proust, *The Way by Swann's*, p. 7.
13   Marcel Proust, *In Search of Lost Time, Vol. 2: In the Shadow of Young Girls in Flower*, trans. by James Grieve (London: Penguin, 2003), p. 400.
14   Proust, *In the Shadow of Young Girls in Flower*, p. 221.
15   Proust, *In the Shadow of Young Girls in Flower*, p. 250.

As Beckett says in *Proust*, Marcel mounts a 'long and desperate and daily resistance before the perpetual exfoliation of personality' (*PTD*, 25).

Based on their reading of these and other passages, both Shattuck and Sedgwick conclude that although Proust was tempted by the post-mortem understanding of rebirth, he appealed to the doctrine 'only in highly poetic terms and generally confined memory to the dimensions of a single human life'.[16] Even when a literal post-mortem reincarnation is proposed, Proust uses it to make the same point as when he applies the doctrine metaphorically to one lifetime. In *Sodome et Gomorrhe*, Marcel and an unnamed 'Norwegian philosopher' discuss rebirth in connection with the philosophy of Henri Bergson. According to Bergson, we are steeped in our memories of three decades past, even if we cannot recall them. The philosopher then asks: 'why then stop at thirty years, why not continue this previous existence back beyond our birth?'[17] He clearly hopes that Bergson's theory might lend support to a belief in the immortality of the soul, but as Marcel points out, the doctrine of transmigration is hardly a guarantee of personal continuity. It actually reveals a self that is fragmented and disrupted by the passage of time. Marcel says: 'The person that I shall be after death has no more reason to remember the man that I have been since my birth than this latter remembers what I was before it.'[18] If we are reborn as a completely different person, who has no memory of our current existence, in what sense can this be thought of as immortality?[19] So whether rebirth is understood as a metaphor for the changes that a person undergoes in this present life, or as a theory of the afterlife, Proust uses the doctrine to undermine the otherwise intractable

---

16 Shattuck, p. 145.
17 Marcel Proust, *In Search of Lost Time, Vol. 4: Sodom and Gomorrah*, trans. by John Sturrock (London: Penguin, 2003), p. 380.
18 Proust, *Sodom and Gomorrah*, p. 381.
19 On Buddhism's seemingly contradictory notions of an impermanent, contingent self and post-mortem rebirth see Johnston, pp. 234, 316–7; On Proust's theory of selfhood, see Joshua Landy, *Philosophy As Fiction: Self, Deception, and Knowledge in Proust* (Oxford: Oxford University Press, 2009), chap. 3.

belief in 'an individual, identical and permanent self.'[20] Even without future lives after death, rebirth happens moment to moment: as Schopenhauer says, human life is an 'unchecked flight of the present into the past' and therefore 'a continuous passage into death, a constant dying' (*WWR*, I.4.57, 337).

Beckett was clearly interested in this aspect of Proust's writing and its Schopenhauerian origins. One of Proust's chief insights for Beckett is that, over time, there are 'countless subjects that constitute the individual' (19):

> The aspirations of yesterday were valid for yesterday's ego, not for today's. [...] The subject has died—and perhaps many times—on the way. For subject B to be disappointed by the banality of an object [of desire] chosen by subject A is as illogical as to expect one's hunger to be dissipated by the spectacle of Uncle eating his dinner. (*PTD*, 13–14)

For Proust, Beckett says, the 'creation of the world did not take place once and for all time, but takes place every day':

> the individual is a succession of individuals; the world being a projection of the individual's consciousness (an objectification of the individual's will, Schopenhauer would say). (19)

Proust's subject, like all subjects, undergoes

> an unceasing modification of his personality, whose permanent reality, if any, can only be apprehended as a retrospective hypothesis. The individual is the seat of a constant process of decantation, decantation from the vessel containing the fluid of future time, sluggish, pale and monochrome, to the vessel containing the fluid of past time. (15)

---

20 Proust, *The Prisoner and The Fugitive*, p. 558.

In this metaphor of vessels and fluids, it is striking that the individual is identified with neither. The individual is not a substance being decanted, nor the container of that substance, but merely the 'seat' of this process: an oddly passive and empty noun. No wonder that Beckett denies the individual's reality outside of retrospective storytelling.

Beckett never explicitly references reincarnation in his discussion of Proust, but he does make several nods in that direction. For instance, he stresses that between each of the 'countless subjects that constitute the individual' there is inevitably a 'perilous' period of transition, 'because by no expedient of macabre transubstantiation can the grave-sheets serve as swaddling-clothes' (*PTD*, 19). As in the passage about the Uncle's dinner, it seems he thought of Proust's decantation of the subject as a series of deaths and births. Beckett also mentions Schopenhauer a number of times, and quotes Calderón's anti-natalist maxim—'el delito major / Del hombre es haber nacido' [man's greatest sin is to have been born]—that Schopenhauer uses in the middle of his discussion of transmigration in *The World as Will and Representation*. There is also, as I suggested in the last chapter, that commemoration of 'the wisdom of all the sages, from Brahma to Leopardi' (*PTD*, 18), which may well be a mangled reference to the Buddha.

Rebirth in the Trilogy

At one point in the essay, Beckett notes how Proust's narrator makes a 'series of identifications'. This phrase might be usefully applied to Beckett's own novel 'series' from *Murphy* (or perhaps *Dream*) through to the otherworldly *How It Is* and possibly beyond. Rather than needing a coherent collection of stories, characters, and settings, this 'series' might be thought of as something closer to metempsychosis: a rebirth, not of personality, but of something much sparser and more fundamental, like will, delusion, pensum, or desire, or what Malone calls 'a stratum, a strata, without debris or vestiges' (*MD*, 53). As well as taking responsibility for the creation of earlier characters, the narrators of *Malone Dies* and *The Unnamable* refer to reincarnation quite explicitly, but equivocate, as Proust does, between a post-mortem and a single-lifetime understanding of it. 'After the fiasco, the solace, the repose,' says Malone, 'I began again, to try and live, cause to live, be another, in myself, in another' (*MD*, 20). This 'fiasco' appears to be life, and Malone is thrown back into it, it would seem, after a few moments of post-mortem rest. On the previous page, he had mentioned how 'on the threshold of being no more I succeed in being another' (19). Now, he wants to live again 'but with a different aim, no longer in order to succeed, but in order to fail' (20). If 'success' is 'being another', then failure would be something like Bom's radical solution: the end of rebirth. Malone describes this end as 'the relapse to darkness, to nothingness' (20). A more explicit reference to rebirth comes later when Malone says that there are times 'you begin to wonder if you have not died without knowing and gone to hell or been born again into an even worse place than before' (54).

While Malone's mentions of rebirth are fleeting and mostly isolated from the rest of the narration, the narrator of *The Unnamable* is less reticent about the matter. He imagines having 'died, all on my own' and then 'come back to earth again, by way of the vagina like a real live baby' (*U*, 43). He blames his unseen tormentors for this new life: 'To saddle me with a lifetime is probably not enough for them, I have to be given a taste of two or three generations'. 'But it's not certain,' he adds. Perhaps all this 'has reference to a single existence, the confusion of identities being merely apparent and due to my inaptitude to assume any'. He concludes that he 'may therefore perhaps legitimately suppose' that the two roles he has played in the novel so far—that of the 'wayfarer' coming home to his family, and that of Mahood, the limbless man confined to a jar festooned with Chinese lanterns—are 'simply two phases of the same carnal envelope, the soul being notoriously immune to deterioration and dismemberment' (43). The passage resembles a rewriting of Marcel's conversation with the Norwegian philosopher in *Sodome et Gomorrhe* in which the interlocutors have been removed or combined. In fact, even in Proust's passage, it is never quite clear who is speaking: the text almost seems to hedge its own assertions in a way that anticipates the epanorthosis of

Beckett's trilogy (also a common feature of Dostoevsky's prose).[21] In *The Unnamable*, the narrator contemplates a theory of post-mortem rebirth, then retracts it in favour of a single life version, and then turns back to logic of the afterlife at the end with his claim that the soul is 'immune to deterioration'. Whereas Marcel saw post-mortem reincarnation as little comfort to those people who want to believe in an immortal and immutable soul, the Unnamable decides, rather perversely, that the dramatically shifting identities of his present lifetime—the 'confusion of identities' in 'the same carnal envelope'—*prove* the existence of such a soul. Once again, Beckett seems to want to literalise Proust's metaphor, but never completely commits to its reality. We need not press these texts for too much metaphysical coherence, however. What matters for Beckett, I suspect, is less the precise mechanics of the process of rebirth than the way the doctrine fragments the personality while stretching out an impersonal substrate across different times, lives, and novels. The Unnamable's suggestion that rebirth of one kind or another explains his relationship to Mahood and the wayfarer implies that the same is true of his relationship to the previous characters of Beckett's novels—'these Murphys, Molloys and Malones' (*U*, 14). Indeed, towards the end of the novel, the Unnamable says that 'the two old buffers here present' are the 'last but not least' in the line that began with Murphy (109). Yet another confirmation that Beckett was thinking along these lines can be found in the second typescript of *Comment c'est*. At the end of the paragraph that I examined in the last chapter about being 'somewhere alive vast stretch of time then it's over you are there no more alive no more then again you are there again alive again' and 'com[ing] to in a hospital in the dark' (*HII*, 16) Beckett handwrites and then crosses out the words 'Molloy Malone je ne suis plus dans la chambre de ma mère'.[22] The words following 'Malone' are, of course, the first words of *Molloy*. Here Beckett is not only connecting the narrator of *How It Is* with Molloy and Malone, he is doing so with explicit reference to reincarnation.

---

21 Bruno Clément, *L'Oeuvre sans qualités: Rhétorique de Samuel Beckett* (Paris: Éditions de Seuil, 1994); Moore, p. 53.
22 Beckett, *Comment c'est*, p. 301.

Being alive again is, in Beckett's world, the same as narrating a new novel.

The fact that Beckett, following Proust's lead, saw his novels as a series of narratorial rebirths might account for the sustained interest in soteriology in the late prose that follows them. Beckett quotes from Leopardi's 'A se stesso' in his comment on the asceticism of *À la recherche du temps perdu*—'In noi di cari inganni / non che la speme, il desiderio è spento' [not only hope, but the desire for loved illusions is spent for us] (*PTD*, 18). This suggests that he was thinking of Proust's novel as pointing the way to a quietistic soteriology that sees salvation in the end of desire, hope, and illusion. E.M. Cioran makes a similar point in an essay entitled 'Beyond the Novel' that Beckett read in *La Tentation d'exister*. Like Beckett, Cioran concludes that Proust has revealed the contingency of the inner life, and the fleeting, evanescent nature of the self: 'an emotional meteorology whose variations furnish no meaning'. After reading *Le Temps retrouvé*, any 'appeal to self' is impossible, according to Cioran: 'Take away those functions of our memory by which it attempts to triumph over time, and nothing is left inside us save the rhythm marking the degrees of our deliquescence' (*TE*, 139). A novelist like Proust, he says, is like a mystic who has transcended God: both have taken their practice to such extremes as to make the practice itself impossible to sustain. Meister Eckhart, Cioran suggests, discovered a 'metaphysical void', and Proust encountered a psychological one. Neither prayer nor novel writing makes much sense after these discoveries. While Cioran thinks that what Proust has done is 'disastrous' for the novel, he claims that it has a spiritual import in that it obliges us to take our nothingness seriously. 'At this point,' he writes, referring once again to the end of *À la recherche du temps perdu*, 'to refuse our annihilation is a kind of bad manners'. Cioran sees Proust's novel as something which should bring the reader—not to mention the aspiring novelist—to the point of ascetic abandon: a soteriology not of redemption, but of resignation in the face of one's own nothingness. Elsewhere in Cioran's book, 'annihilation' [*anéantissement*] is almost always aligned with a mystical version of salvation, whether that of Eckhart, the Buddha, Angelus Silesius or

Lao-Tzu, whereby the soul is left 'unfettered, [...] indifferent and void' (*TE*, 39, 155). This is a variety of salvation that Beckett might have been more sympathetic to, and which I think is more likely to be at work in his late prose, rather than the more traditional Christian paradigm that Eric Griffiths invokes. Salvation as an annihilation of the self or soul would also fit with Beckett's wish that the voice or being that animated his novels would not come back, a wish that suggests the end of rebirth, the 'nothingness' and absolute cessation of *nirvāna*.

The Mystic Paradox

> Thinking of one's salvation: egotism.
>
> —André Gide[23]

Griffiths made his observations about Beckett's late prose within the context of Catholic theology and the locales of the Christian afterlife as imagined by Dante. But he also expressed his appreciation of Beckett's paradisiacal turn in the language of affect and atmosphere, noting how the late prose texts demonstrate a newfound 'quietude of tone' and 'a perfected acquiescence at life and its end'. Christian Quietism favoured such states of mind over and above otherworldly salvation, often regarding the traditional heavenly afterlife as a kind of snare or temptation for the devout soul. Miguel de Molinos thought that the soul of an advanced contemplative has 'so imbibed the divine love, and remains so resigned in divine consent, that it would very gladly go into hell if it knew that was the will of the Most High'.[24] William Inge quotes these words in *Christian Mysticism*, and provides other examples of the phenomenon, which he dubs the 'mystic paradox'. He notes that Fénelon was accused by his critics of 'really preach[ing] indifference to salvation' (*CM*, 240) and also claims that Thomas à Kempis 'wrote and then erased in his manuscript' the statement that 'it would

---

23 André Gide, *The Journals of André Gide*, trans. by Justin O'Brien, 4 vols. (Champaign, IL: University of Illinois Press, 2000), vol. 1, p. 8. (End of November 1890).

24 Molinos, p. 167.

be better to be with Christ in hell than without Him in heaven' (9). This last example is particularly striking given Beckett's familiarity with the *Imitation* and also his own writing and erasure of different versions of salvation from the manuscripts of the late prose. La Bruyère's parodic prayer sounds another note of indifference to heaven: 'if thou wouldst rather punish me by damnation, then so much the better, since it is thy pleasure'. And Beckett would have also seen a quotation from St Francis of Sales in Léon Brunschvicg's chapter on Fénelon in *Spinoza et ses contemporains*: 'If it there were more [...] of God's good pleasure in hell, the saints would leave paradise to go there.'[25] It would seem that the Quietists believed that accepting the will of God and remaining indifferent to one's own well-being was far more important than entering heaven. Ronald Knox goes as far as to say that such indifference was the 'keynote' of Quietism.[26] In the eyes of the Quietists, this blessed resignation and holy indifference constituted a more perfect salvation than any celestial afterlife.

This kind of ambivalence would have surely appealed to Beckett, who, as we saw in the last chapter, preferred the 'inexplicable' suspension between Greek darkness and Jansenist light. Indeed, several critics have found in Beckett's own writing something similar to the mystic paradox. 'Suppose,' writes Stanley Cavell of *Endgame*, 'what Hamm sees is that salvation lies in the ending of endgames, the final renunciation of all final solutions'.[27] 'We can be redeemed only by ending the demand for redemption,' writes Martha Nussbaum of *Molloy*, 'by ceasing to use the concepts of redemption.'[28] Simon Critchley similarly argues that Beckett's texts should leave us 'saved from salvation, redeemed from redemption'.[29] And for David Wheatley, Beckett's

---

25 Léon Brunschvicg, *Spinoza et ses contemporains* (Paris: Presses universitaires de France, 1971), p. 233.
26 Knox, p. 238.
27 Stanley Cavell, 'Ending the Waiting Game: A Reading of *Endgame*', in *Must We Mean What We Say?* (Cambridge: Cambridge University Press, 2002), pp. 115–62 (p. 148).
28 Nussbaum, p. 305.
29 Critchley, p. 180.

'ability to ricochet between heaven and hell without succumbing to either is [...] what gives his work its capacity for unearthly, one might almost say religious, moments of calm and release'.[30] There is a salvation, of sorts, in eschewing salvation, just as there was for the Quietists.

The Quietists' tendency to understand salvation in terms of indifference and resignation was no doubt one of the reasons why Schopenhauer was so attracted to their thinking. His salvation is not about reaching heaven or being absolved of sin, but rather about seeing everything 'in a different light': the saint will 'find the world consonant, if not with his wishes, then at least with his views' (*WWR*, II.4.49, 651). Put more positively, it is a state of 'inner joy and true heavenly peace' and 'profound calm and inner serenity' (*WWR*, I.4.68, 416–7). As Gerard Mannion points out, descriptions of such states of peace are found again and again in *The World as Will and Representation* and Schopenhauer has no qualms about borrowing from completely different philosophies and religions in creating them. He variously describes the blessed state of salvation as a Buddhist *nirvāna*, a Hellenistic *ataraxia*, a quietist indifference, and union with God. Mannion is surely right to suggest that Schopenhauer's invocation of the 'peace that is higher than all reason' is borrowed from Philippians 4:7: 'And the peace of God, which passeth all understanding, shall keep your hearts and minds through Christ Jesus'.[31] It is worth stressing here just how important this state of salvation is to Schopenhauer: as Neil Jordan argues, it stands 'at the very summit' of his thought.[32] Beckett could hardly have failed to notice this. And for all his insistence that there was 'no way out', Beckett was, like Schopenhauer, drawn to descriptions of beatitude. We saw in Chapter 1 how he copied out various

---

30 David Wheatley, '"Sweet Thing Theology": Beckett, E.M. Cioran and the Lives of the Saints', in *Samuel Beckett: Debts and Legacies*, ed. by Peter Fifield and David Addyman (London: Bloomsbury, 2013), pp. 39–62 (p. 54).
31 Mannion, p. 269.
32 Neil Jordan, *Schopenhauer's Ethics of Patience: Virtue, Salvation, and Value* (Lewiston, NY: Edwin Mellen Press, 2009), p. 119.

examples from the writings of Hölderlin, Thomas à Kempis, Augustine, Grillparzer, and others. He also wrote many beautiful versions of his own: none more poignant nor more quietist than Malone's belief that 'beyond this tumult there is a great calm, and a great indifference, never really to be troubled by anything again' (*MD*, 24). Like Schopenhauer, however, Beckett sees no need to settle on the vocabulary and imagery of any particular philosophy or religion. While I am arguing that the soteriological question in the late prose arises from Beckett's implicit comparison between his novel series and reincarnation, these late texts create their vision of salvation by appropriating the language of Pyrrhonism, Christian mysticism, and, inevitably, Dante's *Commedia*, as well as the Buddhism and Vedantism that Beckett inherits from Schopenhauer.

It was the Quietists' insistence on indifference that forced them into this paradox whereby the traditional Christian virtue of hoping for salvation becomes something to be shunned. Many other quietist philosophies—in Schopenhauer's more expansive understanding of that term—also found themselves in similar quandaries. Buddhism, for instance, teaches that suffering is caused by desire, and therefore salvation—*nirvāna*—is the absence of desire. But this might suggest that a Buddhist cannot legitimately desire salvation.[33] Schopenhauer, who agrees with the Buddhists about desire and its end, talks in terms of will: salvation is brought about by the denial of the will. But even if we have thoroughly absorbed Schopenhauer's message that 'it must be a ballsaching world'—in Beckett's colourful summary (TCD MS10967 252v)—we cannot, it would seem, choose to resign the will and thereby gain liberation from life's vicissitudes. Schopenhauer was aware of this paradox:[34] even though he thought that salvation could be approached through ascetic practices, compassionate behaviour, and other deliberate activity, he insisted that the ultimate step of renouncing the will to live has to be a kind of accident:

---

33 For a solution, see David Webster, *The Philosophy of Desire in the Buddhist Pali Canon* (Abingdon: RoutledgeCurzon, 2005).
34 Jordan, pp. 125–6.

> the *self-abolition* of the will begins with cognition, but cognition and insight as such are independent of free choice; consequently, that negation of the will, that entrance into freedom cannot be forced by any intention or resolution, but rather emerges from the innermost relation of cognition to willing in human beings, and thus arrives suddenly, as if flying in from outside. That is precisely why the church calls it the *effect of divine grace*. (*WWR*, I.4.70, 432)

Beckett's interest in such soteriological riddles is apparent from the first pages of *The Unnamable*, where he approaches the mystic paradox through the technical terms of ancient Greek Pyrrhonism:[35]

> What am I to do, what shall I do, in my situation, how proceed? By aporia pure and simple? Or by affirmations and negations invalidated as uttered, or sooner or later? Generally speaking. There must be other shifts. Otherwise it would be quite hopeless. But it is quite hopeless. I should mention before going any further, any further on, that I say aporia without knowing what it means. Can one be ephectic otherwise than unawares? (*U*, 1)

Sextus Empiricus defines Pyrrhonism as the 'ability to set out oppositions among things,'[36] which is precisely what Beckett's narrator is doing through his 'affirmations and negations'. After weighing up the equally compelling oppositions, the Pyrrhonist reaches a position of radical unknowing, called *aporia*. This is 'an obstacle, a roadblock,' a position of 'debilitating poverty', a helpless state of 'epistemic frustration'.[37] (Appropriately enough, the Unnamable uses the word *aporia*

---

35 For a fuller reading of Beckett's trilogy through the lens of Pyrrhonism, see Landy, *How to Do Things with Fictions*, chap. 5.
36 Sextus Empiricus, *Outlines of Scepticism*, trans. by Julia Annas and Jonathan Barnes (Cambridge: Cambridge University Press, 2000), p. 4 (I.iv).
37 Paul Woodruff, 'Aporetic Pyrrhonism', in *Oxford Studies in Ancient Philosophy: Volume VI: 1988*, ed. by Julia Annas (Oxford: Oxford University Press, 1988), pp. 139–68 (p. 141).

'without knowing what it means'.) For the skilled Pyrrhonist practitioner, this state of helplessness will naturally give way to *epochē*. This word, which is related to Beckett's adjective *ephectic*, indicates the suspension of judgment and detachment from belief that leads to the Pyrrhonist salvation of tranquillity or *ataraxia*. As Filip Grgic points out, the Pyrrhonist's tranquillity is the result of an epistemological constraint, and therefore something which is not voluntarily chosen but forcibly imposed.[38] Like Schopenhauer's 'grace', it comes from without. It is a by-product of sceptical inquiry and yet it is also the goal of the Pyrrhonist path. This is the paradox to which Beckett is referring when his narrator asks: 'Can one be ephectic otherwise than unawares?'

Sextus famously draws an analogy between the Pyrrhonist's path to tranquillity and the frustrations of a painter at work:

> A story told of the painter Apelles applies to the Skeptics. They say that he was painting a horse and wanted to represent in his picture the lather on the horse's mouth; but he was so unsuccessful that he gave up, took the sponge on which he had been wiping off the colours from his brush, and flung it at the picture. And when it hit the picture, it produced a representation of the horse's lather.[39]

For Sextus, we cannot aim directly at *ataraxia*.[40] We have to aim at something else—namely, the resolution of the anomalies between phenomena and noumena—and then, in failing to achieve it, we are forced to give up, suspend judgment, and hence come to tranquillity. Beckett would have surely appreciated Sextus's analogy between *ataraxia* and aesthetic failure. According to Patrick Bowles, Beckett preferred those of Hölderlin's poems which 'go on, falter, stammer, and

---

38 Filip Grgic, 'Sextus Empiricus on the Goal of Skepticism', *Ancient Philosophy*, 26 (2006), 141–60 (p. 142).
39 Sextus Empiricus, p. 10.
40 Benson Mates, *The Skeptic Way: Sextus Empiricus's Outlines of Pyrrhonism* (Oxford: Oxford University Press, 1996), p. 61.

then admit failure, and are abandoned', rather than those which strove for 'spurious magnificence'.[41] We also saw in Chapter 3 that Beckett distanced his own work from novelists who he felt were too successful in their aims, whether the well-regulated clockwork of Balzac, the powerful heroics of Joyce, or the purposeful steamroller of Kafka. In the *Three Dialogues*, 'B' proclaims that 'to be an artist is to fail, as no other dare fail [...] failure is his world' (*PTD*, 125). And then there are the famous and widely misappropriated words from *Worstward Ho*: 'Ever tried. Ever failed. No matter. Try again. Fail again. Fail better.'[42] Despite their bewildering appearance on motivational posters and in books devoted to self-help and career advancement, these six sentences are far from advocating a melioristic attitude that would have us learn from our mistakes.[43] What Beckett wants is surely a more spectacular failure: a poem that collapses, a novel that contradicts itself, a painting that is a mess, a life resigned at last. And as Malone suggests, this failure might itself be a kind of salvation.

There is an aesthetic version of the mystic paradox in Beckett's early writing when, as we saw in Chapter 3, he sets his literary project against Balzacian realism. In describing how the novels of Balzac and Jane Austen are preoccupied with the 'centripetal backwash that checks the rot', the narrator of *Dream of Fair to Middling Women* likens this backwash to 'odd periods of recueillement' (119). This French word and its Spanish equivalent *recogimiento* were used frequently by the Christian Quietists and other mystics to describe the interior recollection that takes place during contemplative prayer.[44] In

---

41 Patrick Bowles, 'How to Fail: Notes on Talks with Samuel Beckett', *PN Review*, 96 (March–April), 24–38 (p. 31).
42 Samuel Beckett, *Company / Ill Seen Ill Said / Worstward Ho / Stirrings Still*, ed. by Dirk Van Hulle (London: Faber and Faber, 2009), p. 81. Hereafter, *C*, *ISIS*, *WH*, or *SS*, depending on the text cited.
43 Ned Beauman, 'Fail Worse', *The New Inquiry*, 2012 <http://thenewinquiry.com/essays/fail-worse/> [accessed 8 July 2014].
44 McGinn, 'Miguel de Molinos and the *Spiritual Guide*', p. 30; Hermann-Josef Sieben and Saturnino Lopez Santidrían, 'Recueillement', ed. by Marcel Villier, *Dictionnaire de Spiritualité: Ascétique et mystique, doctrine et histoire* (Paris: Gabriel Beauchesne, 1988), 247–67.

this section of *Dream*, Beckett had clearly wanted to ally himself with the quietist aesthetic of Gide and Dostoevsky, and yet he assigns the term of quietist repose to their antagonists, the classical realists. Similarly, Beckett contrasts Proust's quietism with Albert Feuillerat's desire to erase the 'perturbations' of *À la recherche du temps perdu* in a Balzacian manner (*Dis*, 64). This anticipates the way he felt 'disturbed by the imperturbable aspect' of Kafka's approach to novel writing (SB to HN, 17/2/54; *LSB2*, 464–5), another writer who he felt was 'classical' in form.[45] In both instances Beckett takes a quietist word—the Hellenistic philosophers' mental imperturbability (*ataraxia*)—and associates it not with the quietist aesthetic, but with its opposite: classicism. Beckett's quietist aesthetic demanded that even the quietist goals of *recueillement*, imperturbability, and composure had to be rejected if they came through the artificial immobilisation of classical realism and at the expense of that Gidean integrity of incoherence. This resembles the way in which the Christian Quietists, in their pursuit of total indifference and through zeal for renunciation, came to distrust even the pleasant states of mind that were encountered in prayer, as Knox explains:

> The soul of the Quietist has [...] been progressively stripped. It has renounced considerations of the intellect; it has renounced sensible affections; it has renounced acts of the will; it has renounced all preferences in time and in eternity. What remains for it to lose or to abjure? Only those 'consolations' from above which are given to the contemplative, at certain stages in his course, to compensate for the earthly privileges he has abandoned. These, too, must figure in the holocaust of Quietism.[46]

Beckett's quietist aesthetic also demanded renunciation and sacrifice, even of quiet itself. As he wrote to Mary Manning Howe, 'There is an end to the temptation of light, its polite scorchings & consolations' (30/8/37; *LSB1*, 546).

---

45 Beckett, quoted in Shenker, p. 148.
46 Knox, p. 274.

True refuge: from *Ping* to *Lessness*

> I said to my soul, be still, and wait without hope
> For hope would be hope for the wrong thing
>
> —T.S. Eliot, 'East Coker', *The Four Quartets*[47]

In 1967, Beckett discovered another version of the mystic paradox when he became interested in a 'memorable comment' on the subject of hope in Nicolas Chamfort's *Maximes*. He told the bookseller Henry Wenning that the little verse would stand as an answer to all those readers and audiences who had found 'affirmations of expressions of hope' in his work.[48] Beckett then inscribed the maxim from memory in Wenning's copy of *Fin de partie*, and again, this time translating it himself, in another copy of the play for John and Evelyn Kobler in 1969. The translation was then slightly revised and published in *Hermathena: A Dublin University Review* in 1973, where it appeared as follows:

> Hope is a knave befools us evermore
> Which till I lost no happiness was mine.
> I strike from hell's to grave on heaven's door
> All hope abandon ye who enter in.[49]

Chamfort's words were therefore in the background of Beckett's mind for at least six years, during which he wrote both *Ping* and *Lessness*. Like those two texts, and much of Beckett's other late prose, Chamfort's lines evoke the imagery of Christian salvation but subvert their meaning. It is worth noting that although Beckett quoted them to Wenning in order to counter 'those hope fellows' who had sought an optimistic message in his work, the only casualty of Chamfort's erasure and re-engraving is hope. Happiness and even heaven are, remarkably, left intact. Chamfort was merely saying that, in order to reach happiness

---

47 T.S. Eliot, *Collected Poems 1909–1962* (London: Faber and Faber, 2002), p. 188.
48 Beckett, *Collected Poems*, p. 437.
49 Beckett, *Collected Poems*, p. 199.

or heaven, we must abandon hope for them through resignation and giving up. Or put another way, resignation of hope is the only happiness and heaven we are likely to attain. This is largely the same message that is preached by the Christian Quietists, Sextus Empiricus, and Schopenhauer. It also fits with the lines that Beckett quoted from Leopardi's 'A se stesso' in *Proust*—'non che la speme, il desiderio è spento' [not only hope, but desire is spent] (*PTD*, 18)—and with the homespun soteriology that Beckett imagined in the Clare Street notebook in 1936: 'the veil of hope is finally torn apart and the suddenly liberated eyes see their world, how it is, how it must be.'[50]

A similar line of thought can be found in *Ping*, and its sequel *Lessness*. In both texts, we find the terms 'issue' or 'way out', which were for Beckett euphemisms for salvation. In *The Lost Ones*, the narrator dismisses talk of a 'way out' as a 'rumour' and the object of arcane debate for 'sects' and 'partisans' (*CSP*, 206–7). It is an object of 'belief', 'credence' and 'loyalty' which has 'possessed' its adherents. The narrator seems to think it fortunate for all involved that the most popular account of the 'way out' posits an unreachable and therefore unfalsifiable trapdoor in the ceiling of their cylindrical world. As Schopenhauer said, life shows us plenty of paradises through the 'magic of distance' (*WWR*, II.4.46, 588). The 'outrageous' *Ping*, however, departs from this Beckettian orthodoxy and entertains the possibility that there is 'perhaps a way out': 'peut-être une issue'.[51] It simply leaves it at that: there is no hurry to find this way out, or to create elaborate theories about it. In fact, it hardly seems necessary since the protagonist is, as Beckett stated, already in a kind of refuge. Most importantly he has 'silence within' (*CSP*, 193): perhaps he has already reached a quietist 'solution' of a mind at rest that renders the possibility of physical or metaphysical escape irrelevant. As in the maxims of Chamfort and Molinos, paradise is found by not bothering about paradise.

---

50 Translation modified from Nixon, p. 170.
51 Samuel Beckett, *Têtes-Mortes* (Paris: Éditions de Minuit, 1967), p. 62.

Lessness takes things further still by adopting an iconoclastic attitude towards *Ping*'s comforts, much in the same way as the Christian Quietists renounced even the consolations afforded by their prayerful resignation. Beckett admitted that *Lessness*, written first as *Sans* in 1968, was a direct response to *Ping*, written two years earlier.[52] As he put it in the blurb he wrote for the Calder edition of the text, *Lessness* had

> to do with the collapse of some such refuge as that last attempt in *Ping* and with the ensuing situation of the refugee. Ruin, exposure, wilderness, mindlessness, past and future denied and affirmed, are the categories, formally distinguishable, through which the writing winds, first in one disorder, then another.[53]

Whereas *Ping* provides a rumour of God in the phrase 'shining white infinite' and the suspicion or hope of not being alone, *Lessness* is a Promethean rebellion against that God: 'He will curse God again as in the blessed days' (*CSP*, 197). In *Ping*, the signs of life are imperceptible—'invisible heart breath no sound' (*CSP*, 194)—perhaps because it takes place in a heavenly afterlife or because the protagonist has stilled both body and mind in a triumph of ascetic control. Whatever the case, in *Lessness* the 'heart will beat again' and the protagonist will 'live again'. Everything about *Ping* has been erased in *Lessness*: 'calm long last all gone from mind' (197), 'all light white calm all gone from mind' (199). The crepuscular atmosphere of purgatory returns too in the grey of *Lessness*'s dusk and dawn. The *Ping*-like 'Four square all light sheer white blank planes' are now 'all gone from mind' (197) and ruins remain: 'Blacked out fallen open four walls over backwards [...] Scattered ruins same grey as the sand ash grey' (197). Whereas *Ping* suggests, as Beckett said, 'finishedness' with its final word 'over', *Lessness* is about putting one's 'face to endlessness' (197). *Ping* imagined the possibility of a way out, or 'issue' in the original French, and now the

---

52   Knowlson, p. 542.
53   Quoted in Knowlson, p. 564.

world of *Lessness* is 'issueless' (198). If *Ping* was a relief from suffering with its 'silence within' (194), *Lessness* is a return to misery: 'unhappiness will reign again' (198).

And yet, the paradoxical nature of quietist salvation intrudes again. The landscape and mind state of *Lessness* might be grey, godforsaken, and miserable, but this is likened to 'the blessed days', and described as a 'true refuge long last'. Both 'blessed' and 'refuge' are words of salvation, as in Psalm 62:7: 'In God is my salvation and my glory: the rock of my strength, and my refuge, is in God.' There is also something pleasingly resolute about it all: 'he will make it' (198). Perhaps the refuge of *Ping* was too constricted, and now there is a sense of liberation arising from its broken walls. The protagonist has his 'face to the open sky' (197). But the most important thing about *Lessness* is its iconoclasm: the comforts of *Ping* are deemed not to be true beatitude, but merely the products of a deluded mind and therefore the results of desire and hope. They were 'figments' and 'wild imagining' (199). Although the whiteness and calm seemed heavenly, these things were but a 'celeste of poesy' (198) and therefore not a 'true refuge'. Again, Beckett seems to adhere to the quietist insistence that the only salvation worth having is one in which any remnant of self-serving desire and hopeful delusion is eradicated. Such is the rejection of consolation in Molinos's *Spiritual Guide* that Ronald Knox wryly notes that reading it makes 'you feel as if you had strayed, not into the *Obscure Night* [of St John of the Cross], but into the *Anatomy of Melancholy*.'[54] The transition from *Ping* to *Lessness* is Beckett's version of the way that the soul is progressively stripped of its comforts along the quietist journey. The French title *Sans* and the English *Lessness* suggest an ongoing deprivation and renunciation. The English title *Lessness* also evokes the awkward Schopenhauerian term 'will-lessness', mentioned way back in *Murphy*, which translates the German word *Willenslosigkeit*. The original French title *Sans* performs the same allusive feat with the equivalent phrase from French translations of *The World as Will and*

---

54 Knox, p. 291.

Representation: 'sans volonté'. Even though Schopenhauer had a fondness for descriptions of bliss and beatitude, he also recognised that such will-lessness was unlikely to be a permanent state, but rather one which 'must constantly be regained by steady struggle' (*WWR*, I.4.68, 418). In the efforts to define 'true refuge', Beckett's *Lessness* engages in this struggle.

The manner in which Beckett composed *Sans* gives further evidence of his priorities.[55] The text is made up of sixty unique sentences, each repeated twice. As Ruby Cohn explains, Beckett chose an aleatory method for structuring the text:

> Beckett wrote each of these sixty sentences on a separate piece of paper, mixed them all in a container, and then drew them out in random order twice. This became the order of the hundred twenty sentences in *Sans*. Beckett then wrote the number 3 on four separate pieces of paper, the number 4 on six pieces of paper, the number 5 on four pieces, the number 6 on six pieces, and the number 7 on four pieces of paper. Again drawing randomly, he ordered the sentences into paragraphs according to the number drawn, finally totaling one hundred twenty.[56]

It was, Beckett said to Cohn, 'the only honest thing to do'.[57] Beckett's appeal to honesty in formal matters harkens back to his admiration for 'integrity of incoherence' in the work of Gide and Dostoevsky. Furthermore, the 'honest' form of *Sans / Lessness* is appropriate for the speaker's wish to abandon 'figments' and 'wild imaginings' (*CSP*, 199). Rosemary Pountney adds that 'the shuffled arrangement of sentences' introduces 'the element of chance into formal patterning and, by emphasizing the cyclic nature of the piece, gives it its particular quality of

---

55 My thanks to Paul Stewart for drawing my attention to this.
56 Ruby Cohn, *Back to Beckett* (Princeton, NJ: Princeton University Press, 1973), p. 265.
57 Quoted in Rosemary Pountney, *Theatre of Shadows: Samuel Beckett's Drama, 1956–76* (Gerrard's Cross: Colin Smythe, 1988), p. 16.

endlessness. Instead of a prose statement in which certain themes evolve and some kind of progression [...] may be deduced, the themes become linked in paragraphs that lead nowhere'.⁵⁸ This, then, is a 'samsaric' text if ever there was one: a text that gets trapped in its own eddies and loops, a text that cannot bring itself to a close. Indeed, Pountney herself notes that in *Lessness* 'Beckett's thought seems to tend [...] towards physical generation, in the manner of the phoenix'⁵⁹ and compares it to a passage in *The Unnamable*:

> It will be the same silence, the same as ever, murmurous with muted lamentation: panting and exhaling of impossible sorrow, like distant laughter. And brief spells of hush, as of one buried before his time. Long or short, the same silence. Then I resurrect and begin again. That's what I'll have got for my pains. Unless this time it's the real silence at last! (*U*, 111–112)

The textual rebirth that occurs in *Lessness*, thanks to Beckett's unusual method of composition, is precisely what the 'engeance', the voice, the unnamable creator of all of Beckett's fiction is worried about when it talks about coming back or beginning again. Narrating again *is* being born again. *Ping*—a creation, a 'poesy'—could therefore never have been true salvation.

Unhappily no: *Company*

Aspects of the mystic paradox, and the framework of Proustian rebirth, recur in *Company*, begun in 1977. Beckett told Laurence Harvey that *Company* was concerned with 'a presence, embryonic, undeveloped, of a self that might have been but never got born, an *être manqué*'.⁶⁰ H. Porter Abbott proposes that these comments and several moments in the text itself encourage us—'irresistibly'—to think of a

---

58 Pountney, p. 17.
59 Pountney, p. 21.
60 Lawrence E. Harvey, *Samuel Beckett: Poet and Critic* (Princeton, NJ: Princeton University Press, 1970), p. 247.

foetus in the dark of the womb.[61] But it could equally be argued that *Company* is situated in some sort of afterlife. There are references to Belacqua, to the 'darkness visible' of hell in Milton's *Paradise Lost* (11), and, in the phrase 'bourneless dark' (33), to Hamlet's 'dread of something after death / (The undiscovered country from whose bourn / No traveller returns)' (III.i.77–79).[62] I see no reason to press in favour of one interpretation or another: as with *How It Is*, Beckett seems less concerned about precise setting than he is with affective resonance and the shapes of the ideas in the text. Nevertheless, it is worth noting that Abbott's womb and my suggestion of an afterlife can be reconciled if we think again in terms of reincarnation. Indeed, both a previous existence and a being that is yet to be born are suggested in the following short sentences: 'You were once. You were never. Were you ever? Oh never to have been! Be again' (12). As with Beckett's comment on his novel 'series', there is the hope that this voice or substrate of being will not come back, will not have to be again, and yet it seems unable to truly fail and never return. Of the 'voice' that is heard in *Company*, the narrator says:

> Another trait its long silences when he dare almost hope it is at an end [...] At each slow ebb hope slowly dawns that it is dying. He must know it will flow again. And yet at each slow ebb hope slowly dawns that it is dying (10)

The hope is undermined by the text itself, which does not ebb or die but repeats itself almost word for word. Repetition also operates at the intertextual level as *Company* borrows words and phrases from a litany of previous work that includes *Texts for Nothing*, *The Unnamable*, *All Strange Away*, *How It Is*, and *Murphy*.[63] This is a level of self-plagiarism that is unprecedented even for Beckett, but it all serves to connect the

---

61   Abbott, p. 11.
62   William Shakespeare, *Hamlet*, ed. by Ann Thompson and Neil Taylor (London: Arden, 2005), p. 286.
63   John Pilling, 'Review of Company by Samuel Beckett', *Journal of Beckett Studies*, 7 (1982), 49–70.

voice of *Company* to the voice that animates Beckett's earlier prose work. Daniella Caselli usefully points out that these echoes of previous texts are one of the ways in which *Company* aims to 'win credence' for its memories: not only does it authenticate itself through the use of popular pre-existing (and arguably sentimental) cultural tropes about childhood, it also does so via a sense of déjà vu created by its intertextual allusions.[64]

Beckett had said that the Unnamable was of the same 'engeance' as Belacqua Shuah. In *Company*, that early character's Dantean namesake makes a number of appearances that once again suggest continuation of the same voice from the earlier novels. The father in the story (who resembles Beckett's own father) is shown 'looking out to sea from the lee of a great rock on the first summit scaled', much like Belacqua's outpost in the ante-purgatory (7). Later on, the 'deviser' is imagined in Belacqua's foetal position, 'huddled with his legs drawn up within the semicircle of his arms and his head on knees' (17). Just before the close of the text, this pose is explicitly compared to Belacqua's:

> So sat waiting to be purged the old lutist cause of Dante's first quarter-smile now perhaps singing praises with some section of the blest at last. To whom here in any case farewell. (40)

Like *Ping* before it, *Company* contravenes Beckettian orthodoxy to consider the possibility of salvation. Although the allusion is to Dante's Christian soteriology, with its traditional promise of heaven after several years in purgatory, the deeper point is that this 'engeance'—which has carried its pensum from *Dream* through *The Unnamable* and right into these late texts with its Belacqua-like deviser—is now, finally, on its way out. To bid farewell to Belacqua might also bring the narration of Beckett's whole canon to a close. For a text that is so concerned about the 'deviser'—that is, the ultimate creator of the text itself—this is a question of the utmost importance. But in keeping with Beckett's

---

64 Daniela Caselli, 'Tiny Little Things in Beckett's Company', *Samuel Beckett Today / Aujourd'hui*, 15 (2005), 217–80 (p. 278).

own ambivalence about salvation—as well as his ambivalence about the end of writing—a 'perhaps' intrudes in this passage and prevents total closure.

The spectre of salvation is summoned again, however, by *Company*'s borrowing from *The Unnamable*. It comes, appropriately, before that Schopenhauerian anti-natalist wish 'never to have been'. There, the voice is said to speak in 'affirmations' and 'negations' (12): the same Pyrrhonist vocabulary that began *The Unnamable*. But while such oppositions should, as I explained earlier, bring the mind to *aporia*, then *epochē*, and finally *ataraxia*, the mind in *Company* is unable to come to rest:

> But as the eye dwells it grows obscure. Indeed the longer the eye dwells the obscurer it grows. Till the eye closes and freed from pore the mind inquires, What does this mean? What finally does this mean that at first seemed clear? Till it the mind too closes as it were. As the window might close of a dark empty room. The single window giving on outer dark. Then nothing more. No. Unhappily no. Pangs of faint light and stirrings still. Unformulable gropings of the mind. Unstillable. (*C*, 13–14)

This passage describes the search for truth, for clarity, and for discernment. After a failed attempt to focus the eye on something in the impenetrable dark, the eye closes and the mind takes its place as the seat of seeking. Beckett uses the word 'pore' as a noun here, in the sense of close examination, but might also have been thinking of a verb sense given by the *OED*:

> To bring or put (oneself) into some state by poring. Chiefly in **to pore one's eyes out**: to blind oneself, ruin one's eyesight, or tire one's eyes by close reading or overstudy. *Obs.*

It is worth noting here that when Beckett contrasted the patient outward turn of Arnold Geulincx with the *Schwärmerei* of quietism, he connected the latter with putting one's eyes out 'as Heraclites did &

Rimbaud began to' (SB to TM, 5 March 1936; *LSB1*, 319). In *Company*, the eyes have pored themselves out—exhausted themselves—in the darkness, and now the mind tries to understand and draw out meaning. But just as the eye fails to see in the dark, the mind fails to 'see', that is to understand, and somehow 'closes' like a blinking eye. And then: 'nothing more'. Or at least that is the idea. But 'unhappily' the mind has not completely failed and closed: it is still 'stirring' and 'groping', that is, feeling its way in the darkness, continuing to investigate. This is in spite of the fact that its gropings are 'unformulable', a word which sounds like an Anglicisation of the French *informulable*, meaning something that cannot be reduced to comprehensible signs (*TLFi*). In other words, it is something which should lead to *aporia*. But the mind in *Company* has not reached this point and therefore continues to suffer: a 'pang' is a spasm of physical or emotional pain which recalls the 'miserable erethisms' of Belacqua's mind in *Dream of Fair to Middling Women* (44). This mind is, unfortunately, 'Unstillable'.

Erik Tonning[65] has shown that the presence of eyes in Beckett's work around 1980 owes a debt to Inge's account of German medieval mysticism, which Beckett read fifty years earlier. In his *Dream* notebook, Beckett recorded a list of three organs of spiritual sense: '[Meister] Eckhart's Fünkelein [spark], [Johannes] Tauler's Image and the Right Eye of the Theologica [*sic*] Germanica' (*DN*, 100). Inge explains that all three represent the ground or image of the Godhead contained within the human being, which enables a person to perceive God. For the anonymous author of the *Theologia Germanica*, the 'Right Eye' is able to contemplate God, while the left eye is only able to see the created and temporal world. Tonning convincingly argues that despite the half-century gap Beckett remembered the dichotomy of the left and right eyes, and incorporated it into *Mal vu mal dit*, written between 1979 and 1980. The protagonist is said to see 'Nor by the eye of flesh nor by the other' (*ISIS*, 51). The narrator exclaims: 'Close it for good this filthy eye of flesh' (59). Tonning does not mention *Company*,

---

65 Erik Tonning, 'Nor by the Eye of Flesh Nor by the Other: Fleshly, Creative and Mystical Vision in Late Beckett', *Samuel Beckett Today / Aujourd'hui*, 22 (2010), 223–39.

but it seems likely that its description of the eye closing so that the mind can begin to 'see' has a similar provenance to the phrase in *Ill Seen Ill Said*. And it's important that in both texts the eye of flesh and the inner eye—whether that of the mind or some spiritual faculty—are equally blind. Rather than aiming at spiritual or psychological insight, *Company* desires total blindness, darkness, and nothingness: something more like Schopenhauer's *nirvāna*, which is 'for our eyes, *nothing*' (*WWR*, II.4.41, 525). As with Molloy's erasure of Christian iconography to abide in darkness, this closing of the mystical eye suggests something of the iconoclastic one-upmanship found in quietist thinking.

Inge describes how as 'the tendency towards quietism and introspection increased among [the Neo-Platonists], another derivation for "Mysticism" was found—it was explained to mean deliberately shutting the eyes to all external things' (*CM*, 4). Belacqua, in *Dream of Fair to Middling Women*, achieves his 'dark gulf' of self-elimination by closing the 'lids of the hard aching mind' (44), or by 'forc[ing] the lids of the brain down against the flaring bric-à-brac' (123). Reworking the Alexandrine warning that was once printed inside the doors of Paris Metro carriages, Beckett writes: 'Le train ne peut partir que les paupières fermées' [The train can only leave if the eyelids are closed] (*Dream*, 45). Similarly, when Malone talks about 'coming to the point, the abandoning' (*MD*, 107; 'venir au fait, à l'abandon'[66]), he also talks about eyes:

> The horror-worn eyes linger abject on all they have beseeched so long, in a last prayer, the true prayer at last, the one that asks for nothing. (*MD*, 107)

Malone's beseeching and abjection correspond to *Company*'s pore and obscurity, but in Malone's case it becomes recognisably quietistic. Malone's 'abandon' borrows Madame Guyon's term for the soul's final surrender before God,[67] while his prayer echoes what Molinos

---

66 Samuel Beckett, *Malone meurt* (Paris: Éditions de Minuit, 2004), p. 171.
67 Parish, 'Introduction', p. 15; Guyon, *The Complete Madame Guyon*, p. 228.

dubbed the 'best kind of prayer': 'the prayer of silence: and there are three silences, that of words, that of desires, and that of thought,' in Inge's paraphrase (*CM*, 223). And when Inge describes the *alumbrados* of Toledo—the spiritual ancestors of the Quietists[68]—'true prayer' is described as 'a kind of ecstasy, without words or mental images' (*CM*, 217). Malone, however, like the creature of *Company*, fails to remain in this prayerful state for long:

> And then a little breath of fulfilment revives the dead longings and a murmur is born in the silent world, reproaching you affectionately with having despaired too late. (*MD*, 107)

The sense of achievement from attaining this 'true prayer' brings back all the desires, the words and the thoughts that the quietist is supposed to abandon. It is, he says, 'hard to leave everything' (*MD*, 107). Malone is a kind of quietist Belacqua, despairing—rather than repenting—too late. This same movement is repeated in *Company*: the eyes close, and then the mind closes, leaving only 'nothing', but then this is negated with 'No. Unhappily no.'

As well as revisiting the predicaments of Belacqua, Malone and the Unnamable, *Company* also touches on the soteriological challenge that Beckett investigated in *How It Is*, and which Cioran felt was the spiritual dividend left by Proust's 'death-blow' to the novel (*SHD*, 146): the revelation that the self is an illusion masking a void. Caselli proposes that '*Company* plays with the confessional mode and with the deceptive directedness of childhood memories in order to question [...] the assumption of the stable self.'[69] As we have seen, Schopenhauer and his Buddhist precursors would see this questioning as a stepping stone to salvation whereby the illusion of self is dissolved. Something similar is true for the Christian Quietists—'Happy is the state of that soul which has slain and annihilated itself', says Molinos

---

68 Knox, pp. 241–2.
69 Caselli, *Beckett's Dantes*, p. 203.

(*CM*, 232)—and Dostoevsky, according to Gide, believed in a 'beatitude [...] which is only reached by renouncing the individual self and sinking deep in a solidarity without distinctions' (*Dost*, 217).

But as for Bom in *How It Is* and Marcel in *À la recherche du temps perdu*, piercing the illusion of the *principium individuationis* remains too terrifying a prospect to properly consider for the narrator of *Company*. After introducing the voice and the hearer in the dark, the narrator remarks off-hand in the second paragraph that there might be 'another' who is 'devising it all for company', but then appears to change his mind and hurriedly distracts us from this other deviser: 'Quick leave him' (*C*, 3). Ten pages in, and the narrator wonders again: 'In another dark or in the same another devising it all for company' (*C*, 13). But now the suspicion about the unseen deviser prompts a thought about the narratorial voice itself. It asks:

> Why in another dark or the same? And whose voice asking this? Who asks, Whose voice asking this? And answers, His soever who devises it all. In the same dark as his creature or in another. For company. Who asks in the end, Who asks? And in the end who answers as above? And adds long after to himself, Unless another still. Nowhere to be found. Nowhere to be sought. The unthinkable last of all. Unnamable. Last person. I. Quick leave him. (*C*, 15)

Company sets up a process of infinite regression in search of a fundamental narrative voice that is just as elusive as that 'ideal core of the onion' that Beckett posited in *Proust* (29). There is no fundamental voice that speaks 'in the end': each is merely another mask. The movement of these passages in *Company* bears a strong resemblance to a passage from the first volume of *The World as Will and Representation*:

> as soon as we try for once to understand ourselves, and to do so by turning in on ourselves and directing our cognition inwardly, we lose ourselves in a bottomless void and find ourselves like hollow, transparent spheres from whose void a voice

is speaking, while the cause of it is not to be found within, and in wanting to grasp ourselves we shudder as we catch nothing but an insubstantial phantom. (*WWR*, I.4.54, 304)

For Beckett's narrator, the shudder comes when that 'Last person. I' is 'Nowhere to be sought'. A page later, the narrator comes up with a solution:

> Deviser of the voice and of its hearer and of himself. Deviser of himself for company. Leave it at that. He speaks of himself as of another. He says speaking of himself, He speaks of himself as of another. Himself he devises too for company. Leave it at that. Confusion too is company up to a point. Better hope deferred than none. Up to a point. Till the heart starts to sicken. Company too up to a point. Better a sick heart than none. Till it starts to break. (*C*, 16)

In *How It Is*, Bom evaded the consequences of his thinking about the illusion of self and its dissolution by considering it in the third person: 'has he not staring him in the face I quote a solution more simple by far and by far more radical' (*HII*, 126). The narrator of *Company* does the same thing by talking about the deviser as someone else. Even when admitting his ploy, he cannot bear to use the first person: 'He speaks of himself as of another'. This is no doubt because the implication—that the stable story-telling self is an auto-generating fiction—is too disturbing. He prefers to 'Leave it at that' and move on. When the deviser, 'Of whom nothing' can be said, is seen to be 'Devising figments to temper his nothingness', the distraction becomes more urgent: 'Quick leave him. Pause and again in panic to himself, Quick leave him.' (*C*, 30). The narrator is comfortable discussing the 'Devised deviser devising it all for company' (*C*, 30) so long as the conversation does not impinge upon the first person. As Cioran says in his discussion of Proust, '[t]he "self" constitutes the privilege only of those who do not follow themselves as far as they can go' (*TE*, 139).

Company, like *How It Is*, concludes with solipsistic internment rather than salvation, ending on a one-word sentence: 'Alone.' But the text comes closer to seeing through the veil of Maya and the illusion of self by turning its attention to the nature of its own deviser. This deviser is identified with the narrator of Beckett's previous novels through the comparison with Belacqua and its blessed end is entertained briefly through the possibility of Belacqua's entrance to paradise. But the impetus of the writing itself seems to will this deviser back into life and into fiction. Proust's narrator had decided, in his conversation with the Norwegian philosopher, that we have little reason to identify with the person we once were in a former life because they seem too remote from us. Likewise, in *Company*, the voice has to press the listener—that is, the deviser has to press himself—into accepting the memories, which otherwise seem too much like 'figments' or 'imaginings'. The text is 'willing him by this dint to make it his. To confess, Yes I remember' (9). There is an onus on the hearer to identify himself with the person he once was: 'In the end you will utter again. Yes I remember. That was I. That was I then.' (13) It might be, however, that truth is less important than it seems: imagining has its own philoprogenitiveness, to borrow *Company*'s term (33). In Beckett's world of textual rebirth, fiction itself is the *conatus* that drives future texts, and therefore future lives for this deviser of it all. To quote Cioran again: 'The poet would betray himself if he aspired to be saved: salvation is the death of song, the negation of art and of the mind' (*SHD*, 28).

The One True End to Time and Grief: *Stirrings Still*

> Salvation ends everything; and ends us. Who, once *saved*, dares still to call himself alive?
>
> —E.M. Cioran, A Short History of Decay (27)

Stirrings Still describes a man waiting for the end, and 'seeking a way out' (*SS*, 108). Beckett even toyed with calling the text 'End': he wrote this word at the top of one of the typescript versions of Section 1 (MS-UoR-2935-3-5, p. 1r). The question is what kind of 'end' or 'way out' he desires. As we have seen, 'way out'—or *'issue'* in French—meant both death and salvation to Beckett. In his introduction to *Beckett and Death*, Matthew Feldman presumes that Beckett meant the first, and that *Stirrings Still* 'remind[s] us [...] that death is not such a foreign country after all.'[70] I want to argue that this is not necessarily the case, and that remnants of that other end and other 'issue'—salvation—is present in the text and lurking in its genetic history.

Beckett described *Stirrings Still* as an attempt to 'eff' the 'Ineffable departure' (SB to AA, 27/4/84).[71] Like Feldman, Dirk Van Hulle concludes that this departure refers to death, particularly the recent deaths of Roger Blin and Alan Schneider, Beckett's friends and theatrical collaborators of many years.[72] Certainly the departure of dear friends was on his mind as he was writing: the allusion to the death of 'Darly' (*SS*, 108) harks back to Beckett's experience in the 1940s. Arthur Darley was a doctor who worked alongside Beckett for the Irish Red Cross in Saint-Lô, in the aftermath of the Second World War. A photocopy of the typescript of Section 1 has a note in Beckett's hand in the margin: 'Dr. Arthur Darden [*sic*] St. Lô' (MS-UoR-2859). In 1948 Darley died from tuberculosis—the very disease that he was in France to treat. Beckett was deeply upset by his death and wrote the poem 'Mort de A.D.' shortly after.[73] In *Stirrings Still*, Darley seems to stand for all those friends who have died before or since. Nevertheless, the use of the word 'ineffable' to describe this 'departure' suggests something altogether more mystical. In the last section I argued, via Tonning, that the blinking eye and mind in *Company* was related to the German mystics' spiritual eye and it is from this very passage that *Stirrings Still* takes its title. The 'stirrings still' were, in *Company*, the detritus

---

70 Matthew Feldman, '"Strange Exalted Death!" Disinterring Beckett and Death', in *Beckett and Death*, ed. by Philip Tew, Steven Barfield, and Matthew Feldman (London: Continuum, 2009), pp. 9–22 (p. 18).
71 Quoted in Knowlson, p. 697.
72 Dirk Van Hulle, '"(Hiatus in MS.)": *Watt* and the Textual Genesis of *Stirrings Still*', *Samuel Beckett Today / Aujourd'hui*, 14 (2004), 483–94 (p. 484).
73 Knowlson, pp. 348–9.

of thought and suffering left over after the mind failed to close. This already suggests that the 'end' or 'way out' being sought by the protagonist is a quietist extinction of mind and self, will and desire, pensum and suffering. In the mid-eighties, Beckett revealingly told Lawrence Shainberg how he was 'haunted' by a sentence that eventually made its way into *Stirrings Still*: 'One night, as he sat, with his head on his hands, he saw himself rise, and go'. Beckett added: 'It's like the situation I spoke of in my book on Proust. "Not just hope is gone, but desire."'[74]

As with *Company*, *Stirrings Still* looks back to some of the ideas explored in *How It Is*, particularly reincarnation. As the protagonist of *Stirrings Still* sits imagining himself 'rise and go', he both hopes and fears that this departure will be his final one.

> he disappeared only to reappear later at another place. Then disappeared again only to reappear again later at another place again. So again and again disappeared again only to reappear again at another place again. Another place in the place where he sat at his table head on hands. [...] Head on hands half hoping when he disappeared again that he would not reappear again and half fearing that he would not. (*SS*, 108)

This passage, and ambivalence about a final disappearance, recalls the treatment of reincarnation and *nirvāna* in *How It Is*. Compare the use of the words 'place' and 'again' with this passage that I discussed in Chapter 4:

> you are there somewhere alive somewhere vast stretch of time then it's over you are there no more alive no more then again you are there again alive again it wasn't an error you begin again all over more or less in the same place (*HII* 16; *CC* I.116)

Although the explicit reference to death and rebirth is missing from *Stirrings Still*, there is evidence from the manuscripts that afterlives of

---

74 Shainberg, p. 132.

various sorts were on Beckett's mind as he wrote. A hand-annotated typescript from the summer of 1984, which contained an earlier, abandoned version of Section 3 of *Stirring Still*, describes how people have come to read to the protagonist in his bed. The narrator says how 'eerily familiar' the words of these texts feel to the protagonist, who has 'heard it somewhere before and most likely ~~in the course of some~~ in a previous ~~incarnation~~ ~~existence~~ life' (MS-UoR-2935-2-3). They will be eerily familiar to Beckett's readers as well:

> Fragments of what he heard when he ~~paind peided~~ paid heed[ed] what he heard he seemed to have heard before. For example~~,~~ Mr Knott turned the corb[n]er and saw his seat. Example chosen for its frequency. Rare the session when ~~it did not~~ sooner or later it did not occur once or more. (MS-UoR-2935-2-3)

Beckett is, of course, reworking the opening sentence of *Watt*, albeit with another of the novel's characters in place of Hackett:

> Mr Hackett turned the corner and saw, in the failing light, at some little distance, his seat. (*W*, 3)

Further down the page of the abandoned manuscript, Beckett corrects the name of the character, crossing out 'Knott' and writing 'Hackett'. It is worth remembering that *Watt* was the novel that Beckett first mentioned in connection with the 'series' when he wrote to Reavey in 1947. This series, as I have argued, corresponds to the process of rebirth or reincarnation, and here we have more or less explicit confirmation of the analogy when the protagonist is said to have heard the stories of Knott and Hackett in a 'previous ~~incarnation~~ ~~existence~~ life'. Beckett may have been remembering Proust's narrator at the start of *À la recherche du temps perdu* and the comparison Marcel made between metempsychosis and bedtime reading. Although the *Watt* reference is erased in the final text, the passage concerning how 'he disappeared only to reappear later at another place' clearly grew out of Beckett's experimentation with this textual rebirth since a draft passage on the following page of the manuscript corresponds closely to it.

As with *How It Is* and *Company*, Beckett clearly felt no compulsion to keep his cosmologies unmixed, and in drafts of *Stirrings Still* we find references to other forms of afterlife. A note on the second verso of the first handwritten manuscript reads:

> ~~serait-il au paradis et~~
> ~~transfiguré à l'aberrant?~~
> souvenir du purgatoire effacé
> Temps mort n'était-ce l'alternance
> jour nuit .. tuer
> ~~Evenements de jadis~~ (MS-UoR-2933-1, p. 2v)

A fragment like this is difficult to translate but it might go as follows: 'would he be in paradise and / absurdly transfigured? / memory of purgatory effaced / Time dead was it not the alternation / day night .. to kill / Events of time past'. This suggests that Beckett was still thinking of the fate of his old friend Belacqua, that not quite permanent resident of purgatory who was (perhaps) finally granted salvation in *Company*. As in that earlier text, Belacqua is only tentatively admitted to paradise through the uncertainty of the question marks and the intimations of the absurdity of his transfiguration.

Over the course of multiple drafts and revisions, Beckett slowly erased or muted mentions of an afterlife and kept the 'Dantesque analogy out of sight', just as he had done with *Murphy* (UoR MS3000, 2r). In a later manuscript, which is recognisably a draft of Section 1 of *Stirrings Still* since it features the protagonist wondering what is outside his window, the explicit allusions to purgatory and paradise have shrunk to a description of the text's setting as 'this afterlife'. (MS-UoR-2935-1-4). What survives in the final text is merely a sense of world-weariness and longing for an end that Beckett drew from the *Purgatorio*, Schopenhauer's quietism, and rebirth filtered through Buddhism and Proust. Rather than expressing the repetitive nature of existence in terms of countless births, lives, and deaths, *Stirrings Still* evokes the Proustian antagonist of time eking itself out slowly in 'hours and half-hours' (*SS*, 108) and the pitiless procession of 'days and nights when day followed hard on night and night on day' (*SS*, 107). To 'Disappear and reappear at another place' does not need to refer to a literal death and rebirth, but simply to what Beckett suggested over fifty years earlier in *Proust*, namely that the individual personality is subject to 'unceasing modification' and the 'constant process of decantation' as time wears on (15). In *Stirrings Still*, the 'strokes' and 'chimes' of the clock are accompanied by 'cries': time plays a 'poisonous' role in the 'science of affliction' (*PTD*, 15). The word 'strokes' also recalls those mental and cardiac erethisms that Beckett had first worried about in *Dream* and the 'pangs' in the mind in *Company*.

If Buddhist and Christian afterlives merely continue this cycle, then death cannot be the solution to this torturous existence. It cannot be 'the one true end to time and grief and self and second self his own' (*SS*, 108, 110). Rather what is needed is the radical solution of *nirvāna* or self-elimination that Bom entertained in *How It Is*. Take the following passage, for example:

> Such and much more such the hubbub of his mind so-called till nothing left from deep within but only ever fainter oh to end. No matter how no matter where. Time and grief and self so-called. Oh all to end. (*SS*, 115)

As Van Hulle has shown, the word 'faint' had an interesting journey through Beckett's manuscript. This passage first appeared on p. 11r of the *super conquérant* notebook (MS-UoR-2934), after which Beckett decisively writes 'June 87' in the middle of the page as if to mark the text complete. It comes two pages after Beckett jotted down a line from Dante's *Inferno*—'per lungo silenzio fioco' (I.63)—the pilgrim's first description of Virgil. Beckett tussled with the translation of this line, opting initially for 'faint from long silence', then crossed it out, and replaced 'faint' with 'hoarse', and then went back to 'faint' again. The word 'faint' had appeared in the manuscript long before Beckett decided, like the Ottelenghi, to 'look it up in [his] big Dante' (*MPTK*, 11), but when the *Inferno* is consulted it is in order to decide how to describe the inner world of the protagonist of *Stirrings Still*, to describe what is going on 'far within'. And this inner world is evoked again in the closing paragraph of the final text: 'called till nothing left from deep within but only ever fainter' (*SS*, 115). For my purposes, it is significant that this waning of mental noise is the result of a long-held silence. As Molinos says in the *Spiritual Guide* in words quoted by Inge, the first silence is the silence of words and the final silence is the silence of thoughts.[75] For Schopenhauer, salvation is brought about by the 'silencing of the will' (*WWR*, I.3.44, 244): metaphysical insight acts as a *Quietiv*—quieter, sedative or tranquillizer—of the will, and this brings about salvation. All this suggests that what is being longed for in *Stirrings Still* is not death precisely, but the permanent quietening of mental chatter, or what Beckett calls 'the hubbub of the mind'. The manuscript provides further evidence of this. On a loose page, which contains abandoned versions of Section 3 of *Stirrings Still*, the following paragraph has been written and then crossed out:

> [If] Between the strokes the cries were to cease ~~and he~~ and to at the same time he as second seen to disappear then there would be nothing in his head. That nothing so hardly dearly won. (MS-UoR-2935-1-2, p. 1r)

In this abandoned fragment, 'nothing' is tantamount to the end of suffering (the cries have ceased), mental quiet ('nothing in his head') and some sort of final *telos* ('That nothing so hardly dearly won'). Schopenhauer imagines salvation as the 'peace of blissful nothingness' (*WWR*, II.4.50, 657) which Beckett may be alluding to in an early draft of Section 1, where the narrator laments that the protagonist is still 'somehow ~~short~~ so much short of blessed nothing' (MS-UoR-2935-1-5, 1r). One of the abandoned French fragments reads:

---

75 Molinos, p. 98.

Autre raison de douter de son retour ~~une~~ ~~un allègement de sensibilité~~ ~~une xxx sorte de~~ simple quiétude sans exemple dans son souvenir. (MS-UoR-2933-1, p. 3r)

[Other reason to doubt his return ~~a~~ ~~a relief of sensibility~~ a sort of simple calm unexampled in his memory]

This is later redrafted as:

Autre motif de douter de sa réapparition une quasi-quiétude sans exemple dans son souvenir. (MS-UoR-2933-5, p. 1r)

[Other motive for doubting his reappearance a quasi-calm unexampled in his memory]

It seems the narrator is interpreting the protagonist's newfound quietude as a reason for suspecting that he will not 'reappear again later' (*SS*, 108). Peace of mind means *nirvāna*, salvation, not returning, never coming back, as Beckett had long hoped 'he' would.

Conclusion

Eric Griffiths was, I think, right to suggest that Beckett's late texts bear the traces of a sustained interest in salvation. My analysis in this chapter, however, has shown that this soteriological turn is far removed from the most familiar Christian paradigms of what salvation might entail. For the late texts, salvation is mainly about being done with it all, about finding that final end to all the rebirths of narration through the series of novels from *Dream* and *Murphy* onwards. And yet even as Beckett sets up a kind of structural necessity for this end to arrive, he remains stubbornly aware of the conceptual and formal obstacles inherent to this aim.

The conceptual obstacle is the core of the mystic paradox: the fact that salvation cannot be aimed at, desired, or hoped for if it is to be true salvation. Even though the Christian Quietists were supposedly concerned with leading the soul to ultimate beatitude, their exaltation of indifference caused them to look on any form of hope, consolation, or pleasure with extreme suspicion. In the eyes of a Quietist, Knox writes, 'every kind of respite from the hard discipline of naked faith is something to be regretted'.[76] Beckett's late prose has the same tendency. Even as he investigates the possibility of salvation, each refuge and source of solace has to be subjected to the same distrust and the same ruthless iconoclasm. This is what we find in *Lessness*, where *Ping*'s calm and whiteness are rejected as 'figments'. The precedent for this attitude was set much earlier in Beckett's career when he concludes that even the explicit goals of quietism—whether the *recueillement* of the Christian mystics or the imperturbability of the Hellenistic philosophers—have to be forsaken in the name of a quietist aesthetic. The corollary of this is that the 'one true end' must forever remain hypothetical. Any version of rest or quietude that comes within reach is automatically something which it is possible to renounce and reject.

This brings us to the formal obstacle to salvation. If each text is a rebirth, then the end can only be found outside of the text. It can never be represented by the writer because that representation would be both a new life and also necessarily a figment. Even after Proust has slain the novel, and robbed it, as Cioran contended, of plot and characters and even causality, 'a self still survives, recalling that it once existed, a self *without a future*' (TE, 146). This is what we find in Beckett's late prose: narrators and protagonists that have the bad manners to refuse their own annihilation, even as they profess to wanting blessed nothing. In the last reckoning, their inability to make an end is not surprising: their position has been compromised all along. As narrators of fiction, they cannot be expected to let go of imagining, figments, and poesy. Quietist salvation is, perhaps, ultimately unrepresentable. In *Tears and Saints*, Cioran wrote that for 'an ancient philosopher or medieval monk, "there is no way out" would make a constant theme for meditation.'[77] The same was true of his friend Samuel Beckett, a writer who inevitably found it hard to leave everything.

---

76 Knox, p. 274.
77 Cioran, *Tears and Saints*, p. 34.

Afterword

In his essay 'Inside the Whale', published in 1940, George Orwell remarked how Henry Miller's *Tropic of Cancer* presents its reader with 'a sort of mystical acceptance of the thing-as-it-is'.[1] Orwell saw Miller as a latter-day Walt Whitman, whose motto of 'I accept' had taken on a much darker and more pessimistic tone once transplanted from the background of prosperous and democratic mid-nineteenth-century America to the shrinking and decaying world seen from the vantage point of Paris in the 1930s. Orwell's suspicions are confirmed by a passage in *Max and the White Phagocytes* in which Miller favourably compares the experience of reading Anaïs Nin's poetry to being stuck, like Jonah, inside a whale. For Miller, Orwell alleges, 'being inside a whale is a very comfortable, cosy, homelike thought':

> The whale's belly is simply a womb big enough for an adult. There you are, in the dark, cushioned space that exactly fits you, with yards of blubber between yourself and reality, able to keep up an attitude of indifference, no matter *what* happens. A storm that would sink all the battleships in the world would hardly reach you as an echo. [...] It will be seen what this amounts to. It is a species of quietism, implying either complete unbelief or else a degree of belief amounting to mysticism. The attitude is *'Je m'en fous'* or 'Though He slay me, yet will I trust Him,' [Job 13:15] whichever way you like to look at it; for practical purposes both are identical, the moral in either case being 'Sit on your bum'.[2]

There is no doubt that Beckett would have come in for similar censure, had Orwell known his work. Belacqua's 'wombtomb' (*Dream*, 5), Murphy's 'embryonal repose', and Celia's 'amnion about her own disquiet' (*Mu*, 51, 44) are symptoms of the same malaise that Orwell is

---

[1] George Orwell, 'Inside the Whale', in *Essays*, ed. by John Carey (London: Everyman, 2002), pp. 211–49 (p. 219).
[2] Orwell, pp. 242–3.

discussing. Belacqua's 'enwombing' is even called 'our old friend the whale of miracle' (*Dream*, 181). Beckett's quietism was, to conflate Orwell's two options, unbelief that almost amounted to mysticism: Belacqua is a 'dud mystic' and a 'John [...] of the Crossroads' (186). In the *Dream* notebook, Beckett recorded a variation on 'sit on your bum': 'sedendo et quiescendo anima efficitur sapiens' [sitting and being quiet the soul gains wisdom]. The phrase came to Beckett via the entry for Belacqua in Paget Toynbee's *Dictionary of Proper Names and Notable Matters in the Works of Dante*,[3] and is bestowed on the homonymous protagonist of *Dream* itself (122). And as we saw at the start of this book, Beckett had even said 'je m'en fous' in the context of quietism, as he contemplated the very quietistic life of his cousin's serenely despairing horse.

But as I have argued, Beckett's quietism was not a comfortable, cosy place where he could settle down like La Fontaine's 'catawampus' and not give a damn about anything (*Dream*, 122). It became instead the site of several artistic and personal struggles, and the starting point for investigation. Through *Dream of Fair to Middling Women*, *Murphy*, *Molloy*, *How It Is*, *Company*, and *Stirrings Still*, Beckett eked out a lifelong conversation with quietism by inquiring into its suitability as a personal solution, its potential for aesthetic direction, its perspective on ethics and justice, and finally its ambivalence about soteriology and endings. We have also seen how Beckett's sustained interest in quietism did not preclude him from parting ways with it at important junctures, or from using one variety of quietism to critique another. This is what we find in the early critical writing where the quietism of Gide and MacGreevy is deemed to be superior to the self-absorption of Rilke. Or when, in *Murphy*, Dostoevsky's vision of human brotherhood is used to temper the isolationism of *The Imitation of Christ*. In that novel, Beckett subjects what Orwell calls the 'yards of blubber' to careful scrutiny and comedic caricature as Murphy, re-

---

3   Daniela Caselli, "'Looking It Up in My Big Dante'": A Note on "Sedendo and Quiescendo"', *Journal of Beckett Studies*, 6 (1997), 85–93.

searching how better to cut himself off from the big world, inadvertently transcends the gulf separating him from the patients at the MMM and finds out that such companionship was what he wanted all along. In *How It Is*, Beckett explores how quietism, in Schopenhauer's Buddhist-inspired version, actually seeks to dissolve the whale's sides: removing the boundary between self and other, tearing up the cushioned ego, and bringing about altruistic compassion. The attitude of indifference, in this case, is only towards oneself, that disregard of oneself that Beckett found so attractive in Geulincx's *Ethics*. Rather than bringing about carelessness, quietism became one of Beckett's 'ancient cares', to borrow Molloy's expression, reverted to with 'renewed vigour' over the course of a lifetime (*Mo*, 64).

Rather surprisingly, Orwell does not condemn Miller for his sojourn inside the whale. He wonders whether such a position is defensible 'in times like ours' but concludes that for the 'sensitive novelist' there may be no alternative. 'Seemingly there is nothing left but quietism [...] A novel on more positive, "constructive" lines, and not emotionally spurious, is at present very difficult to imagine.'[4] Miller's quietism is, Orwell decides, symptomatic of the state of Europe stumbling between wars, and that it cannot be otherwise 'until the world has shaken itself into its new shape'. This raises the fascinating question of how far Beckett's own quietism was determined by the times in which he lived. One novel which I have left out of my analysis is *Watt*, written while Beckett was on the run from the Gestapo after being betrayed by a member of his resistance cell in occupied France. Watt himself is unwilling to resist anything, not even a stone aimed at his head by Lady McCann. Instead he remains 'faithful to his rule' (25), which Ackerley interprets as referring to the quietism that Beckett had drawn from Thomas à Kempis.[5] Watt's own *imitatio christi* is so thorough that he is said to resemble the figure of Jesus in Hieronymus Bosch's *Christ Mocked* (*W*, 136), which Beckett saw in the National Gallery in London. In this painting, Jesus inclines his head towards the crown of thorns and folds his hands as the soldiers tear his clothes.

---

4   Orwell, p. 248.
5   Ackerley, *Obscure Locks*, p. 53.

Mr Nixon says that Watt 'would literally turn the other cheek, I honestly believe, if he had the energy' (*W*, 14). Whether Watt's Christ-like passivity emerged in spite or because of Beckett's encounter with the ills of his time is a matter worth exploring in future research.[6]

What is certain is that Beckett would have agreed with Orwell about the impossibility of writing in any other way. As I have argued, Beckett's quietism was tied up with his efforts to distinguish himself as an artist and to free himself from certain shackles of literary influence and tradition. What Orwell alludes to in his discussion of the sensitive novelist is not so far from what Beckett, in his lectures on André Gide, called 'integrity' (TCD MIC60, 37). Quietism, as Gide describes it, is the capacity to look at oneself with honesty and humility. It is to discern that the self is not a stable thing, but rather riddled with lacunae. It is to see that our mental life is full of discord and that we entertain many inconsistent thoughts and feelings. The so-called realism of Balzac and other nineteenth-century authors was fundamentally dishonest, in Gide's eyes, because it did not acknowledge these inner antagonisms. Beckett concurred and saw in Gide's own novels the 'integrity of incoherence'. He later criticised Kafka for not writing characters who were 'spiritually precarious'. And although Joyce's *Ulysses* and *Finnegans Wake* demonstrated discord and deliquescence, they did so from a position of power that was untenable for Beckett. 'I think anyone nowadays who pays the slightest attention to his own experience,' Beckett told Israel Shenker, 'finds it the experience of a non-knower, a non-can-er'.[7] Here Beckett insinuates that

---

6   Laura Salisbury, 'Gloria SMH and Beckett's Linguistic Encryptions', in *The Edinburgh Companion to Samuel Beckett and the Arts*, ed. by S.E. Gontarski (Edinburgh: Edinburgh University Press, 2014); and Marjorie Perloff, 'Witt-Watt: The Language of Resistance / The Resistance of Language', in *Wittgenstein's Ladder: Poetic Language and the Strangeness of the Ordinary* (Chicago, IL: University of Chicago Press, 1999), pp. 115–43, both demonstrate how the novel's shadowy figures, coded messages, and missed meetings arose from Beckett's resistance experience. I discuss Beckett's use of the Bosch painting and his interest in the figure of Jesus more generally in Andy Wimbush, 'Hey prestos and Humilities: Two of Beckett's Christs'. *The Journal of Beckett Studies*, 25: 1 (2016), 78–95.

7   Shenker, p. 162.

Joyce's 'omnipotence' and 'omniscience' were as much of a betrayal of integrity as Balzac's assurance. Beckett's own commitment to the inner gaze could only lead to a literature of disintegration and powerlessness. Quietist interiority brings quietist resignation.

So while the image of Jonah inside the whale seems apposite for Belacqua's quiet cerebration in *Dream*, it fails to convey how Beckett's quietism developed over the course of his life and work. Beckett's relationship to quietism is better captured by a single word he often used, and which I have chosen for the title of this book: 'still'. To say that something is still going on is to register surprise, or perhaps exasperation. Given the small handful of references to quietism in Beckett's writing from the 1930s, it is indeed surprising that quietism should come to be a fundamental concern of his life and work. But what emerges when we consider Beckett's turn to quietist questions in the novels and late prose is the pertinence of another aspect of the word 'still': the sense of persistence and 'going on' that is central to Beckett's work and which is indebted to the patient suffering of the Quietist devotee and the Schopenhauerian ascetic working off his pensum. Beckett's quietism turned literature itself into a kind of *áskesis*: a task that needed to be dispensed with but which could never quite be finished. And then, of course, 'still' invokes the promise of the end of that pensum, which I explored in the last chapter: the mind at rest, or at least appeased. Such stillness is a perennial aspiration in Beckett's work, but also a hope-riddled delusion, a dangerous temptation, and an impossible dream. Whereas Orwell saw in Miller's whale something closed, cosy, and final, Beckett's 'still' has that 'quality of inconclusiveness' that he admired so much in Gide's writing (TCD MIC60, 43). The word presents several incommensurable faces: peace and suffering, stillness and endurance, ending and persisting. They are all at work in the paradoxes of quietist resignation, summed up by a phrase from *The Imitation of Christ* that Beckett recorded in the *Dream* notebook (85), drew a box around, and later confessed 'seemed to be made for me' (SB to TM, 10/3/35; *LSB1*, 257): 'Qui melius scit pati majorem tenebris pacem', he that can well suffer shall find the most peace.

Bibliography

Published works by Samuel Beckett

Beckett, Samuel, *Comment c'est, How It Is and / et L'Image: A Critical-Genetic Edition / Une edition critic-genetique*, ed. by Édouard Magessa O'Reilly (London: Routledge, 2001)

———, *Company / Ill Seen Ill Said / Worstward Ho / Stirrings Still*, ed. by Dirk Van Hulle (London: Faber and Faber, 2009)

———, *Disjecta: Miscellaneous Writings and a Dramatic Fragment*, ed. by Ruby Cohn (New York, NY: Grove Press, 1984)

———, *Dream of Fair to Middling Women* (New York, NY: Arcade Publishing, 1993)

———, *Echo's Bones*, ed. by Mark Nixon (London: Faber and Faber, 2014)

———, *How It Is*, ed. by Édouard Magessa O'Reilly (London: Faber and Faber, 2009)

———, '"Le Concentrisme" and "Jean Du Chas": Two Extracts', trans. by John Pilling, *Modernism / modernity*, 18 (2011), 883–86

———, *Malone Dies*, ed. by Peter Boxall (London: Faber and Faber, 2010)

———, *Malone meurt* (Paris: Éditions de Minuit, 2004)

———, *Molloy*, ed. by Shane Weller (London: Faber and Faber, 2009)

———, *Molloy* (Paris: Éditions de Minuit, 1982)

———, *More Pricks Than Kicks* (London: Picador, 1977)

———, *Murphy*, ed. by J.C.C. Mays (London: Faber and Faber, 2009)

———, 'Notes on Geulincx', in *Arnold Geulincx' Ethics: With Samuel Beckett's Notes*, by Arnold Geulincx, ed. by Han Van Ruler and Anthony Uhlmann, trans. by Martin Wilson (Leiden: Brill, 2006), pp. 311–54

———, *Proust and Three Dialogues with Georges Duthuit* (London: Calder Publications, 1969)

———, *Têtes-Mortes* (Paris: Éditions de Minuit, 1967)

———, *The Collected Poems of Samuel Beckett*, ed. by John Pilling and Seán Lawlor (London: Faber and Faber, 2012)

———, *The Complete Dramatic Works* (London: Faber and Faber, 1986)

———, *The Complete Short Prose, 1929–1989*, ed. by S.E. Gontarski (New York, NY: Grove Books, 1995)

———, *The Letters of Samuel Beckett: Volume 1, 1929–1940*, ed. by Martha Dow Fehsenfeld, Lois More Overbeck, Dan Gunn, and George Craig (Cambridge: Cambridge University Press, 2009)

———, *The Letters of Samuel Beckett: Volume 2, 1941–1956*, ed. by George Craig, Martha Dow Fehsenfeld, Dan Gunn, and Lois More Overbeck (Cambridge: Cambridge University Press, 2011)

———, *The Letters of Samuel Beckett: Volume 3, 1957–1965*, ed. by George Craig, Martha Dow Fehsenfeld, Dan Gunn, and Lois More Overbeck (Cambridge: Cambridge University Press, 2014)

———, *The Letters of Samuel Beckett: Volume 4, 1966–1989*, ed. by George Craig, Martha Dow Fehsenfeld, Dan Gunn, and Lois More Overbeck (Cambridge: Cambridge University Press, 2016)

———, *The Unnamable*, ed. by Steven Connor (London: Faber and Faber, 2010)

———, *Watt*, ed. by C.J. Ackerley (London: Faber and Faber, 2009)

Pilling, John, ed., *Beckett's Dream Notebook* (Reading: Beckett International Foundation, 1999)

Unpublished work by Samuel Beckett

Beckett, Samuel, 'Clare Street Notebook', MS5003, Beckett International Foundation, Reading University Library

———, 'German Diaries', Unnumbered MS, Beckett International Foundation, Reading University Library

———, 'Notes on Augustine of Hippo and Porphyry on Plotinus', MS10968, Trinity College Dublin

———, 'Notes on German Literature', MS10971/1, Trinity College Dublin

———, 'Philosophy Notes', MS10967, Trinity College Dublin

——, 'Psychology Notes', MS10971/7–8, Trinity College Dublin

——, '*Whoroscope* Notebook', MS3000, Beckett International Foundation, Reading University Library

Secondary material on Beckett

Abbott, H. Porter, *Beckett Writing Beckett: The Author in the Autograph* (Ithaca, NY: Cornell University Press, 1996)

Ackerley, C.J., *Demented Particulars: The Annotated Murphy* (Edinburgh: Edinburgh University Press, 2010)

——, *Obscure Locks, Simple Keys: The Annotated Watt* (Edinburgh: Edinburgh University Press, 2010)

——, '"Primeval Mud Impenetrable Dark": Towards an Annotation of *Comment C'est / How It Is*', *Modernism / modernity*, 18 (2011), 789–800

——, 'Samuel Beckett and Max Nordau: Degeneration, Sausage-Poisoning, the Bloody Rafflesia, Coenaesthesia, and the Not-I', in *Beckett after Beckett*, by S.E. Gontarski and Anthony Uhlmann (Gainesville, FL: University Press of Florida, 2006), pp. 167–76

——, 'Samuel Beckett and Thomas à Kempis: The Roots of Quietism', *Samuel Beckett Today / Aujourd'hui*, 9 (2000), 81–92

Atik, Anne, *How It Was: A Memoir of Samuel Beckett* (London: Faber and Faber, 2001)

D' Aubarède, Gabriel, 'Interview with Beckett', in *Samuel Beckett: The Critical Heritage*, ed. by Lawrence Graver and Raymond Federman (London: Routledge, 2005), pp. 238–40

Badiou, Alain, *On Beckett*, trans. by Alberto Toscano and Nina Power (Manchester: Clinamen Press, 2003)

Bailey, Iain, *Samuel Beckett and The Bible* (London: Bloomsbury, 2014)

Baker, Phil, *Beckett and the Mythology of Psychoanalysis* (London: Palgrave Macmillan, 1997)

——, 'Beckett's Bilingualism and a Possible Source for the Name of Moran in *Molloy*', *Journal of Beckett Studies*, 3 (1994), 81–84

Baldwin, Hélène L., *Samuel Beckett's Real Silence* (London: Pennsylvania State University Press, 1981)

Beauman, Ned, 'Fail Worse', *The New Inquiry*, 2012 <http://thenewinquiry.com/essays/fail-worse/> [accessed 8 July 2014]

Bolin, John, *Beckett and the Modern Novel* (Cambridge: Cambridge University Press, 2012)

Bowles, Patrick, 'How to Fail: Notes on Talks with Samuel Beckett', *PN Review*, 96 (March–April), 24–38

Boxall, Peter, *Since Beckett: Contemporary Writing in the Wake of Modernism* (London: Continuum, 2009)

Bryden, Mary, *Samuel Beckett and the Idea of God* (Basingstoke: Macmillan, 1998)

Buning, Marius, 'Samuel Beckett's Negative Way: Intimations of the *Via Negativa* in His Late Plays.', in *European Literature and Theology in the Twentieth Century: Ends of Time*, ed. by David Jasper and Colin Crowder (London: Macmillan, 1990), pp. 129–42

———, 'The "*Via Negativa*" and Its First Stirrings in *Eleutheria*', *Samuel Beckett Today / Aujourd'hui*, 9 (2000), 43–54

Burrows, Rachel, 'Notes on Beckett's Lectures at Trinity College Dublin', MIC60, Trinity College Dublin

Calder, John, *The Philosophy of Samuel Beckett* (London: Calder Publications, 2001)

Caselli, Daniela, *Beckett's Dantes: Intertextuality in the Fiction and Criticism* (Manchester: Manchester University Press, 2005)

———, '"Looking It Up in My Big Dante": A Note on "Sedendo and Quiescendo"', *Journal of Beckett Studies*, 6 (1997), 85–93

———, 'Tiny Little Things in Beckett's *Company*', *Samuel Beckett Today / Aujourd'hui*, 15 (2005), 217–80

Cavell, Stanley, 'Ending the Waiting Game: A Reading of *Endgame*', in *Must We Mean What We Say?* (Cambridge: Cambridge University Press, 2002), pp. 115–62

Clément, Bruno, *L'Oeuvre sans qualités: Rhétorique de Samuel Beckett* (Paris: Éditions de Seuil, 1994)

Cohn, Ruby, *Back to Beckett* (Princeton: Princeton University Press, 1973)

———, *A Beckett Canon* (Ann Arbor, MI: University of Michigan Press, 2001)

Connor, Steven, *Beckett, Modernism and the Material Imagination* (Cambridge: Cambridge University Press, 2014)

———, 'Beckett's Animals', *Journal of Beckett Studies*, 8 (1982), 29–44

Cordingley, Anthony, 'Beckett and "L'ordre Naturel": The Universal Grammar of *Comment c'est / How It Is*', *Samuel Beckett Today / Aujourd'hui*, 18 (2007), 185–99

———, 'Beckett's Ignorance: Miracles / Memory, Pascal / Proust', *Journal of Modern Literature*, 33 (2010), 129–52

Critchley, Simon, *Very Little ... Almost Nothing: Death, Philosophy and Literature* (London: Taylor & Francis, 2004)

Cronin, Anthony, *Samuel Beckett: The Last Modernist* (London: HarperCollins, 1996)

Davies, Paul, *The Ideal Real: Beckett's Fiction and Imagination* (London: Associated University Presses, 1994)

———, '"Womb of the Great Mother Emptiness": Beckett, the Buddha and the Goddess', *Samuel Beckett Today / Aujourd'hui*, 9 (2000), 119–31

Driver, Tom, 'Interview with Beckett', in *Samuel Beckett: The Critical Heritage*, ed. by Lawrence Graver and Raymond Federman (London: Routledge, 2005), pp. 241–48

Feldman, Matthew, '"Agnostic Quietism" and Samuel Beckett's Early Development', in *Samuel Beckett: History, Memory, Archive*, ed. by Seán Kennedy and Katherine Weiss (New York, NY: Palgrave Macmillan, 2009), pp. 183–200

———, 'Beckett, Sartre and Phenomenology', *Limit(e) Beckett*, 2010 <http://limitebeckett.paris-sorbonne.fr/zero/feldman.html> [accessed 28 October 2011]

———, *Beckett's Books: A Cultural History of Samuel Beckett's 'Interwar Notes'* (London: Continuum, 2006)

———, '"Strange Exalted Death!" Disinterring Beckett and Death', in *Beckett and Death*, ed. by Philip Tew, Steven Barfield, and Matthew Feldman (London: Continuum, 2009), pp. 9–22

Frost, Everett, and Jane Maxwell, 'Catalogues of Beckett's Reading Notes and Other Manuscripts at Trinity College Dublin', *Samuel Beckett Today / Aujourd'hui*, 16 (2006), 15–199

Foster, Paul, *Beckett and Zen: A Study of Dilemma in the Novels of Samuel Beckett* (Somerville, MA: Wisdom, 1989)

Gontarski, S.E., Martha Dow Fehsenfeld and Dougald McMillan, 'Interview with Rachel Burrows (1982)', *Journal of Beckett Studies*, 11–12 (1989), 6–15

Griffiths, Eric, 'At Odds with Ends', *The Independent* (London, 27 December 1989), Arts Section, p. 11

Hamilton, Geoff, 'Annihilating All That's Made: Beckett's *Molloy* and the Pastoral Tradition', *Samuel Beckett Today / Aujourd'hui*, 15 (2005), 325–39

Harvey, Lawrence E., *Samuel Beckett: Poet and Critic* (Princeton, NJ: Princeton University Press, 1970)

Harvey, Robert, *Witnessness: Beckett, Dante, Levi and the Foundations of Responsibility* (London: Continuum, 2010)

Haynes, John, and James Knowlson, *Images of Beckett* (Cambridge: Cambridge University Press, 2003)

Van Hulle, Dirk, 'Accursed Creator: Beckett, Romanticism, and the Modern Prometheus', *Samuel Beckett Today / Aujourd'hui*, 18 (2007), 15–29

———, '"(Hiatus in MS.)": *Watt* and the Textual Genesis of *Stirrings Still*', *Samuel Beckett Today / Aujourd'hui*, 14 (2004), 483–94

———, 'Writers' Libraries and the Extended Mind' (presented at the Writers and their Libraries, Senate House, University of London, 2013)

Le Juez, Brigitte, *Beckett before Beckett*, trans. by Ros Schwartz (London: Souvenir Press, 2008)

Juliet, Charles, *Rencontres avec Samuel Beckett* (Paris: Éditions Fata Morgana, 1986)

Kennedy, Seán, 'Beckett Reviewing MacGreevy: A Reconsideration', *Irish University Review*, 35 (2005), 273–87

Kenner, Hugh, *Samuel Beckett: A Critical Study* (Berkeley, CA: University of California Press, 1968)

Kiely, Robert, 'Beckett and Nordau's Pathologized Mysticism' (presented at the London Beckett Seminar, Birkbeck College, University of London, 2013) <http://www.academia.edu/3409239/Beckett_and_Max_Nordaus_pathologized_mysticism> [accessed 16 July 2013]

Knowlson, Elizabeth, and James Knowlson, eds., *Beckett Remembering, Remembering Beckett: Uncollected Interviews with Samuel Beckett and Memories of Those Who Knew Him* (New York, NY: Arcade Publishing, 2006)

Knowlson, James, *Damned to Fame: The Life of Samuel Beckett* (London: Bloomsbury Publishing, 1997)

Kundert-Gibbs, John L., *No-Thing Is Left to Tell: Zen / Chaos Theory in the Dramatic Art of Samuel Beckett* (London: Associated University Presses, 1999)

Landy, Joshua, *How to Do Things with Fictions* (Oxford: Oxford University Press, 2012)

Laws, Catherine, *Headaches Among the Overtones: Music in Beckett / Beckett in Music* (Amsterdam: Rodopi, 2013)

Marie, Beatrice, 'Beckett's Fathers', *Comparative Literature*, 100 (1985), 1103–9

Mays, J.C.C., 'Preface', in *Murphy*, by Samuel Beckett (London: Faber and Faber, 2009), pp. vii–xix

Mooney, Sinéad, '"Integrity in a Surplice": Beckett's (Post-)Protestant Poetics', *Samuel Beckett Today / Aujourd'hui*, 9 (2000), 223–38

Moorjani, Angela, 'André Gide among the Parisian Ghosts in the "Anglo-Irish" *Murphy*', *Samuel Beckett Today / Aujourd'hui*, 21 (2010), 209–22

——, '"Just Looking": Ne(i)ther-World Icons, Elsheimer Nocturnes, and Other Simultaneities in Beckett's *Play*', in *Beckett at 100: Revolving it*

All, ed. by Angela Moorjani and Linda Ben-Zvi (Oxford: Oxford University Press, 2008), pp. 123–38

Nixon, Mark, *Samuel Beckett's German Diaries 1936–1937* (London: Continuum, 2011)

Nixon, Mark, and Dirk Van Hulle, *Samuel Beckett's Library* (Cambridge: Cambridge University Press, 2013)

Nussbaum, Martha C., *Love's Knowledge: Essays on Philosophy and Literature* (Oxford: Oxford University Press, 1992)

O'Hara, J.D., 'Beckett Backs Down: From Home to *Murphy* via Valéry', *Journal of Beckett Studies*, 3 (1994), 37–55

O'Reilly, Édouard Magessa, '*Molloy*, Part II, Where the Shit Hits the Fan: Ballyba's Economy and the Worth of the World', *Genetic Joyce Studies*, 6 (2006) <http://www.geneticjoycestudies.org/GJS6/GJS6OReilly.htm> [accessed 6 November 2012]

Perloff, Marjorie, 'Witt-Watt: The Language of Resistance / The Resistance of Language', in *Wittgenstein's Ladder: Poetic Language and the Strangeness of the Ordinary* (Chicago, IL: University of Chicago Press, 1999), pp. 115–43

Phillips, K.J., 'Beckett's *Molloy* and *The Odyssey*', *The International Fiction Review*, 11 (1984), 19–24

Pilling, John, *Beckett before Godot* (Cambridge: Cambridge University Press, 2004)

———, 'Dates and Difficulties in Beckett's *Whoroscope* Notebook', *Journal of Beckett Studies*, 13 (2004), 39–48

———, 'Introduction to Samuel Beckett, "Le Concentrisme" and "Jean Du Chas"', *Modernism / modernity*, 18 (2011), 881–881

———, 'Review of *Company* by Samuel Beckett', *Journal of Beckett Studies*, 7 (1982), 49–70

Pothast, Ulrich, *The Metaphysical Vision: Arthur Schopenhauer's Philosophy of Art and Life and Samuel Beckett's Own Way to Make Use of It* (New York, NY: Peter Lang, 2008)

Pountney, Rosemary, *Theatre of Shadows: Samuel Beckett's Drama, 1956–76* (Gerrard's Cross: Colin Smythe, 1988)

Rabinowitz, Rubin, 'Molloy and the Archetypal Traveller', *Journal of Beckett Studies*, 5 (1979), 25–44

———, 'Samuel Beckett's Revised Aphorisms', *Contemporary Literature*, 36 (1995), 203–25

Salisbury, Laura, 'Gloria SMH and Beckett's Linguistic Encryptions', in *The Edinburgh Companion to Samuel Beckett and the Arts*, ed. by S.E. Gontarski (Edinburgh: Edinburgh University Press, 2014)

Shainberg, Lawrence, 'Exorcising Beckett', *Paris Review*, 1987, 100–136

Shenker, Israel, 'Interview with Beckett', in *Samuel Beckett: The Critical Heritage*, ed. by Lawrence Graver and Raymond Federman (London: Routledge, 2005), pp. 160–64

Terry, Philip, 'Waiting for God to Go: *How It Is* and *Inferno* VII–VIII', ed. by Marius Buning, *Samuel Beckett Today / Aujourd'hui*, 7 (1998), 349–60

Thomas, Martin, 'Schopenhauer, Beckett, and the Impoverishment of Knowledge', *Evental Aesthetics*, 2 (2014), 66–91

Tonning, Erik, 'Nor by the Eye of Flesh Nor by the Other: Fleshly, Creative and Mystical Vision in Late Beckett', *Samuel Beckett Today / Aujourd'hui*, 22 (2010), 223–39

Tucker, David, *Samuel Beckett and Arnold Geulincx: Tracing 'a Literary Fantasia'* (London: Continuum, 2012)

Wheatley, David, '"Sweet Thing Theology": Beckett, E.M. Cioran and the Lives of the Saints', in *Samuel Beckett: Debts and Legacies*, ed. by Peter Fifield and David Addyman (London: Bloomsbury, 2013), pp. 39–62

Wimbush, Andy, 'The Buddha, Biology and the Beasts: The Influence of Ernst Haeckel and Arthur Schopenhauer on Samuel Beckett's *How It Is*', in *Encountering Buddhism in Twentieth-Century British and American Literature*, ed. by Lawrence Normand and Alison Winch (London: Bloomsbury, 2013), pp. 123–38

———, 'Humility, Self-Awareness, and Religious Ambivalence: Another Look at Beckett's "Humanistic Quietism"', *Journal of Beckett Studies*, 23: 2 (2014), 202–21

———, 'The Pretty Quietist Pater: Samuel Beckett's *Molloy* and the Aesthetics of Quietism', *Literature and Theology* 30: 4 (2016), 439–455

———, 'Palaeozoic Profounds: Samuel Beckett and Ecological Time' in *Time and Temporality*, ed. by MDRN (Leuven: Peeters Publishing, 2016), pp. 3–14

———, 'Hey prestos and Humilities: Two of Beckett's Christs'. *The Journal of Beckett Studies*, 25: 1 (2016), 78–95

———, '"Omniscience and Omnipotence": *Molloy* and the end of "Joyceology"', in *Beckett and Modernism*, ed. by Olga Beloborodova, Dirk Van Hulle and Pim Verhulst (London: Palgrave, 2018), pp. 95–109

Wolosky, Shira, *Language Mysticism: The Negative Way of Language in Eliot, Beckett, and Celan* (Stanford, CA: Stanford University Press, 1995)

General works

Agamben, Giorgio, *The Highest Poverty: Monastic Rules and Form-of-Life*, trans. by Adam Kotso (Stanford, CA: Stanford University Press, 2013)

Alexander, Archibald, *A Short History of Philosophy* (London: Macmillan, 1922)

Amiel, Henri-Frédéric, *Journal intime*, ed. by Bernard Gagnebin and Philippe M. Monnier, 12 vols. (Paris: Éditions L'Âge d'Homme, 1976)

Baird, Robert P., 'Miguel de Molinos: Life and Controversy', in *The Spiritual Guide*, by Miguel de Molinos, trans. by Robert P. Baird (Mahwah, NJ: Paulist Press, 2010), pp. 1–20

———, ed., 'The Errors of Miguel de Molinos: Apostolic Constitution "Caelestis Pater" Issued by Innocent XI', in *The Spiritual Guide*, by Miguel de Molinos, trans. by Bernard McGinn (Mahwah, NJ: Paulist Press, 2010), pp. 185–93

Bakhtin, Mikhail, *Problems of Dostoevsky's Politics*, trans. by Caryl Emerson (London: University of Minnesota Press, 1984)

Blake, William, *The Complete Poetry and Prose*, ed. by David V. Erdman (New York, NY: Anchor Books, 1988)

Blinderman, Charles S., 'Huxley, Pater, and Protoplasm', *Journal of the History of Ideas*, 43 (1982), 477–86

Bodhi, Bhikkhu, trans., *The Suttanipāta: An Ancient Collection of Buddha's Discourses* (Somerville, MA: Wisdom Publications, 2017)

———, trans., The Connected Discourses of the Buddha: A Translation of the Samyutta Nikāya, (Somerville, MA: Wisdom Publications, 2000)

Brunet, Pierre Gustav, *Curiosités théologiques par un bibliophile* (Paris: Adolphe Delahays, 1861)

Brunschvicg, Léon, *Spinoza et ses contemporains* (Paris: Presses universitaires de France, 1971)

La Bruyère, Jean de, *Dialogues posthumes sur le quiétisme*, ed. by Richard Parish (Grenoble: Éditions Jérôme Millon, 2005)

Burbea, Rob, *Seeing That Frees: Meditations on Emptiness and Dependent Arising* (West Ogwell: Hermes Amāra Publications, 2014)

Cartwright, David E., *Historical Dictionary Of Schopenhauer's Philosophy* (Oxford: Scarecrow Press, 2005)

———, *Schopenhauer: A Biography* (Cambridge: Cambridge University Press, 2010)

Choudhury, Mita, 'A Betrayal of Trust: The Jesuits and Quietism in Eighteenth-Century France', *Common Knowledge*, 15 (2009), 164–80

Cioran, E.M., *A Short History of Decay*, trans. by Richard Howard (Oxford: Basil Blackwell, 1975)

———, *La Tentation d'exister* (Paris: Gallimard, 1956)

———, *Tears and Saints*, trans. by Ilinca Zarifopol-Johnston (London: University Of Chicago Press, 1995)

———, *The Temptation to Exist*, trans. by Richard Howard (New York, NY: Arcade Publishing, 2012)

Coetzee, J. M., *Diary of a Bad Year* (London: Vintage, 2008)

Collins, Steven, *Selfless Persons: Imagery and Thought in Theravāda Buddhism* (Cambridge: Cambridge University Press, 1982), pp. 104–105.

———, *Nirvana: Concept, Imagery, Narrative* (Cambridge: Cambridge University Press, 2010)

Connolly, Thomas E., *The Personal Library of James Joyce: A Descriptive Bibliography* (Buffalo, NY: University of Buffalo Studies, 1955)

Cook, Daniel J., 'Leibniz on Enthusiasm', in *Leibniz, Mysticism and Religion*, ed. by Allison P. Coudert, Richard H. Popkin, and Gordon M. Weiner (Dordrecht: Springer Netherlands, 1998), pp. 107–35

Dalal, Roshen, *Hinduism: An Alphabetical Guide* (London: Penguin, 2011)

Dante Alighieri, *Inferno*, trans. by Robin Kirkpatrick (London: Penguin, 2006)

David-Neel, Alexandra, *With Mystics and Magicians in Tibet* (London: Penguin, 1931)

Donne, John, *Selected Prose*, ed. by Neil Rhodes (Harmondsworth: Penguin, 1987)

Dostoevsky, Fyodor, *The Brothers Karamazov*, trans. by Richard Pevear and Larissa Volokhonsky (London: Vintage, 2004)

Droit, Roger-Pol, *The Cult of Nothingness: The Philosophers and the Buddha*, trans. by Pamela Vohnson (Chapel Hill, NC: The University of North Carolina Press, 2003)

Eliot, George, *The Mill on the Floss*, ed. by Gordon S. Haight (Oxford: Oxford University Press, 2008)

Eliot, T.S., *Collected Poems 1909–1962* (London: Faber and Faber, 2002)

Evans, G. R., '*Sancta Indifferentia* and *Adiaphora*: "Holy Indifference" and "Things Indifferent"', *Common Knowledge*, 15 (2009), 23–38

Faure, Bernard, 'In the Quiet of the Monastery: Buddhist Controversies over Quietism', *Common Knowledge*, 16 (2010), 424–38

La Fontaine, Jean de, *Fables* (Tours: Alfred Mame et fils, 1870)

Frank, Joseph, *Dostoevsky: A Writer in His Time*, ed. by Mary Petrusewicz (Oxford: Princeton University Press, 2010)

Garnier, Pierre, *Onanisme, seul et à deux sous toutes ses formes et leurs conséquences* (Paris: Garnier Frères, 1894)

Garvin, J.L., 'Quietism', ed. by J.L. Garvin, *The Encyclopædia Britannica: A new survey of universal knowledge* (London: The Encyclopædia Britannica Company, Ltd., 1929), 850

Geulincx, Arnold, *Arnold Geulincx' Ethics: With Samuel Beckett's Notes*, ed. by Han Van Ruler and Anthony Uhlmann, trans. by Martin Wilson (Leiden: Brill, 2006)

Gide, André, *Dostoïevsky: articles et causeries* (Paris: Librairie Plon, 1923)

———, 'Feuillets', in *Oeuvres Complètes*, ed. by Louis Martin-Chauffier, 15 vols. (Paris: Nouvelle Revue Française, 1932), 439–40

———, *La Porte étroite* (Paris: Éditions Mercure de France, 1959)

———, *The Journals of André Gide*, trans. by Justin O'Brien, 4 vols. (Champaign, IL: University of Illinois Press, 2000)

Goethe, Johann Wolfgang von, *The Autobiography of Goethe: Truth and Fiction Relating to My Life*, trans. by John Oxenford, 2 vols. (Boston, MA: Estes and Lauriat, 1883), I

Gray, Ronald D., *Goethe: A Critical Introduction* (Cambridge: Cambridge University Press, 1967)

Grgic, Filip, 'Sextus Empiricus on the Goal of Skepticism', *Ancient Philosophy*, 26 (2006), 141–60

Guyon, Jeanne Marie Bouvier de La Mothe, *A Short Method of Prayer and Spiritual Torrents*, trans. by A.W. Marston (London: Sampson Low, Marston, Low & Searle, 1875)

———, *The Complete Madame Guyon*, trans. by Nancy C. James (Brewster, MA: Paraclete Press, 2011)

Haeckel, Ernst, *A Visit to Ceylon*, trans. by Clara Bell (New York, NY: Peter Eckler, 1911)

———, *The Riddle Of The Universe*, trans. by Joseph McCabe (London: Watts & Co., 1934)

Heidegger, Martin, *Being and Time*, trans. by John Macquarrie and E.S. Robinson (Oxford: Blackwell, 1978)

Huxley, Aldous, *Eyeless in Gaza* (London: Vintage, 2004)

———, *The Perennial Philosophy* (New York, NY: Harper Perennial Modern Classics, 2009)

Inge, William Ralph, *Christian Mysticism* (London: Methuen, 1899)

James, Nancy C., 'Introduction', in *The Complete Madame Guyon*, by Jeanne Marie Bouvier de La Motte Guyon, trans. by Nancy C. James (Brewster, MA: Paraclete Press, 2011), pp. 3–35

———, *The Spiritual Teachings of Madame Guyon, Including Translations into English from Her Writings* (Lewiston, NY: Edwin Mellen Press, 2007)

James, William, *The Varieties of Religious Experience: A Study in Human Nature* (London: Routledge, 2008)

Johnson, Samuel, *A Dictionary of the English Language* (London: J & P Knapton, 1755)

———, *Johnsonian Miscellanies*, ed. by George Birkbeck Norman Hill, 2 vols. (Oxford: Clarendon Press, 1897)

Johnston, Mark, *Surviving Death* (Princeton, NJ: Princeton University Press, 2010)

Jordan, Neil, *Schopenhauer's Ethics of Patience: Virtue, Salvation, and Value* (Lewiston, NY: Edwin Mellen Press, 2009)

Joyce, James, *Ulysses*, ed. by Declan Kiberd (London: Penguin, 2008)

Keown, Damien, 'Pu-Tai', *A Dictionary of Buddhism* (Oxford: Oxford University Press, 2004) <http://www.oxfordreference.com/view/10.1093/acref/9780198605607.001.0001/acref-9780198605607-e-1462> [accessed 29 August 2014]

Knox, R. A., *Enthusiasm: A Chapter in the History of Religion* (Oxford: Oxford University Press, 1950)

Landy, Joshua, *Philosophy As Fiction: Self, Deception, and Knowledge in Proust* (Oxford: Oxford University Press, 2009)

Leopardi, Giacomo, *Canti: Bilingual Edition*, trans. by Jonathan Galassi (New York, NY: Farrar Straus Giroux, 2010)

Lernout, Geert, *Help My Unbelief: James Joyce and Religion* (London: Continuum, 2010)

Lewis, Charles T., and Charles Short, *A Latin Dictionary Founded on Andrews' Edition of Freund's Latin Dictionary* (Oxford: Oxford University Press, 1879)

MacGreevy, Thomas, *Poems* (London: William Heinemann, 1934)

———, 'Saint Francis de Sales', *Father Mathew Record*, June 1943, 2

———, *Thomas Stearns Eliot: A Study*, The Dolphin Books (London: Chatto & Windus, 1931)

Magee, Glenn Alexander, 'Quietism in German Mysticism and Philosophy', *Common Knowledge*, 16 (2010), 457–73

Mannion, Gerard, *Schopenhauer, Religion and Morality: The Humble Path to Ethics* (Aldershot: Ashgate Publishing, Ltd., 2003)

Mann, Thomas, *Buddenbrooks: The Decline of a Family*, trans. by H.T. Lowe-Porter (London: Vintage, 1999)

———, *The Magic Mountain*, trans. by S. Fisher Verlag (London: Vintage, 1996)

Marcin, Raymond B., *In Search of Schopenhauer's Cat: Arthur Schopenhauer's Quantum-Mystical Theory of Justice* (Washington, DC: Catholic University of America Press, 2006)

Marcus Aurelius, *Meditations*, ed. by Ernest Rhys, trans. by Méric Casaubon (London: J.M. Dent & Sons Ltd, 1906)

Marvell, Andrew, *The Complete Poems*, ed. by Elizabeth Story Donno (Harmondsworth: Penguin, 1996)

Mates, Benson, *The Skeptic Way: Sextus Empiricus's Outlines of Pyrrhonism* (Oxford: Oxford University Press, 1996)

Mays, J.C.C., 'How Is MacGreevy a Modernist?', in *Modernism and Ireland: The Poetry of the 1930s*, ed. by Patricia Coughlan and Alex Davis (Cork: Cork University Press, 1995), pp. 103–28

McDonnell, Eunan, *The Concept of Freedom in the Writings of St. Francis de Sales* (Bern: Peter Lang, 2009)

McGinn, Bernard, '"Evil-Sounding, Rash, and Suspect of Heresy": Tensions between Mysticism and Magisterium in the History of the Church', *The Catholic Historical Review*, 90 (2004), 193–212

———, 'Miguel de Molinos and the *Spiritual Guide*: A Theological Reappraisal', in *The Spiritual Guide*, by Miguel de Molinos, trans. by Robert P. Baird (Mahwah, NJ: Paulist Press, 2010), pp. 21–39

———, ed., *The Essential Writings of Christian Mysticism* (New York, NY: Modern Library, 2006)

Merton, Thomas, *The Hidden Ground of Love: The Letters of Thomas Merton on Religious Experience and Social Concerns*, ed. by William Henry Shannon (San Diego, CA: Harcourt Brace Jovanovich, 1993)

Molinos, Miguel de, *The Spiritual Guide*, trans. by Robert P. Baird (Mahwah, NJ: Paulist Press, 2010)

Moore, Gene M., 'The Voices of Legion: The Narrator of *The Possessed*', *Dostoevsky Studies*, 6 (1985), 51–65

Mourad, Ronney, and Dianne Guenin-Lelle, *The Prison Narratives of Jeanne Guyon* (Oxford: Oxford University Press, 2012)

Murav, Harriet, *Holy Foolishness: Dostoevsky's Novels & the Poetics of Cultural Critique* (Stanford, CA: Stanford University Press, 1992)

Nicholls, Moira, 'The Influences of Eastern Thought on Schopenhauer's Doctrine of the Thing-in-Itself', in *The Cambridge Companion to Schopenhauer*, ed. by Christopher Janaway (Cambridge: Cambridge University Press, 2006), pp. 171–212

Nordau, Max, *Degeneration* (London: William Heinemann, 1895)

Olendzki, Andrew, *Untangling Self: A Buddhist investigation of who we really are* (Somerville, MA: Wisdom Publications, 2016)

Orwell, George, 'Inside the Whale', in *Essays*, ed. by John Carey (London: Everyman, 2002), pp. 211–49

Parish, Richard, *Catholic Particularity in Seventeenth-Century French Writing: 'Christianity Is Strange'* (Oxford: Oxford University Press, 2011)

———, 'Introduction', in *Dialogues posthumes sur le quiétisme*, by Jean de La Bruyère, ed. by Richard Parish (Grenoble: Éditions Jérôme Millon, 2005), pp. 5–44

Pevear, Richard, 'Foreword', in *Demons*, by Fyodor Dostoevsky, trans. by Richard Pevear and Larissa Volokhonsky (London: Vintage, 1994), pp. vii–xxiii

———, 'Introduction', in *The Brothers Karamazov*, by Fyodor Dostoevsky, trans. by Richard Pevear and Larissa Volokhonsky (London: Vintage, 2004), pp. xi–xviii

Plümacher, Olga, *Der Pessimismus in Vergangenheit und Gegenwart* (Heidelberg: George Weiss, 1888)

Potkay, Adam, *The Story of Joy: From the Bible to Late Romanticism* (Cambridge: Cambridge University Press, 2007)

Pringle-Pattison, Andrew Seth, and Evelyn Underhill, 'Mysticism', ed. by J.L. Garvin, *The Encyclopædia Britannica: A new survey of universal knowledge* (London: The Encyclopædia Britannica Company, Ltd., 1929), 51–55

Proust, Marcel, *À la recherche du temps perdu*, 3 vols. (Paris: Gallimard, 1954)

———, *In Search of Lost Time, Vol. 1: The Way by Swann's*, trans. by Lydia Davis (London: Penguin, 2003)

———, *In Search of Lost Time, Vol. 2: In the Shadow of Young Girls in Flower*, trans. by James Grieve (London: Penguin, 2003)

———, *In Search of Lost Time, Vol. 4: Sodom and Gomorrah*, trans. by John Sturrock (London: Penguin, 2003)

———, *In Search of Lost Time, Vol. 5: The Prisoner and the Fugitive*, trans. by Carol Clark (London: Penguin, 2003)

Radden, Jennifer, ed., *The Nature of Melancholy: From Aristotle to Kristeva* (Oxford: Oxford University Press, 2002)

Radler, Charlotte, 'Actio et Contemplatio / Action and Contemplation', in *The Cambridge Companion to Christian Mysticism*, ed. by Amy Hollywood and Patricia Z. Beckman (Cambridge: Cambridge University Press), pp. 211–22

Raz, Jacob, '"Kill the Buddha": Quietism in Action and Quietism as Action in Zen Buddhist Thought and Practice', *Common Knowledge*, 16 (2010), 439–56

Rehbock, Philip F., 'Huxley, Haeckel, and the Oceanographers: The Case of *Bathybius haeckelii*', *Isis*, 66 (1975), 504–33

Robertson, John G., *A History of German Literature* (London: William Blackwood and Sons, 1902)

Roebuck, Valerie, tran., *Upanishads* (London: Penguin Classics, 2004)

Rouse, W.H.D., 'Introduction', in *Meditations*, by Marcus Aurelius, ed. by Ernest Rhys, trans. by Méric Casaubon (London: J.M. Dent & Sons Ltd, 1906), pp. ix–xxii

Ruffing, Margit, 'The Overcoming of the Individual in Schopenhauer's Ethics of Compassion, Illustrated by the Sanskrit Formula of the "Tat Tvam Asi"', in *Understanding Schopenhauer Through the Prism of Indian Culture*, ed. by Arati Barua, Michael Gerhard, and Matthias Koßler (Berlin: Walter de Gruyter, 2013), pp. 97–108

Sartre, Jean-Paul, 'Existentialism Is a Humanism', in *Existentialism from Dostoevsky to Sartre*, ed. by Walter Kaufmann, Revised and Expanded Edition (London: Penguin, 1975), pp. 345–68

Scholem, Gershom, *On the Kabbalah and Its Symbolism* (New York, NY: Random House, 1996)

Schopenhauer, Arthur, *Aus Arthur Schopenhauer's handschriftlichen Nachlass: Abhandlungen, Anmerkungen, Aphorismen und Fragmente*, ed. by Julius Frauenstädt (Leipzig: F.A. Brockhaus, 1864)

———, *Die Welt als Wille und Vorstellung* (München: Dt. Taschenbuch-Verl., 1998)

———, *Parerga and Paralipomena: Short Philosophical Essays*, trans. by E.F.J. Payne, 2 vols. (Oxford: Oxford University Press, 1974)

———, *Parerga und Paralipomena*, 2 vols. (Leipzig: F.A. Brockhaus, 1874)

———, *Sämtliche Werke*, ed. by Arthur Hübscher (Mannheim: F.A. Brockhaus, 1988)

———, *Studies in Pessimism*, trans. by T. Bailey Saunders (London: Swann Sonnenschein & Co., 1893)

———, *The Two Fundamental Problems of Ethics*, trans. by Christopher Janaway (Cambridge: Cambridge University Press, 2009)

———, *The World as Will and Representation: Volume 1*, ed. by Christopher Janaway, trans. by Judith Norman and Alistair Welchman (Cambridge: Cambridge University Press, 2014)

———, *The World as Will and Representation: Volume 2*, ed. by Christopher Janaway, trans. by Judith Norman and Alistair Welchman (Cambridge: Cambridge University Press, 2018)

Schriebmann, Susan, 'Introduction', in *Collected Poems of Thomas MacGreevy* (Washington, DC: Catholic University of America Press, 1991), pp. ix–xxxviii

Scott, Dominic, 'Platonic Anamnesis Revisited', *The Classical Quarterly (New Series)*, 37 (1987), 346–66

Sedgwick, Eve Kosofsky, *The Weather in Proust*, ed. by Jonathan Goldberg (Durham, NC: Duke University Press, 2011)

Sextus Empiricus, *Outlines of Scepticism*, trans. by Julia Annas and Jonathan Barnes (Cambridge: Cambridge University Press, 2000)

Shakespeare, William, *Hamlet*, ed. by Ann Thompson and Neil Taylor (London: Arden, 2005)

Shattuck, Roger, *Proust* (London: Fontana, 1974)

Siderits, Mark, *Buddhism As Philosophy: An Introduction* (Aldershot: Ashgate Publishing, 2007)

Sieben, Hermann-Josef, and Saturnino Lopez Santidrían, 'Recueillement', ed. by Marcel Villier, *Dictionnaire de Spiritualité: Ascétique et mystique, doctrine et histoire* (Paris: Gabriel Beauchesne, 1988), 247–67

Swift, Jonathan, *A Tale of a Tub and Other Works*, ed. by Angus Ross and David Woolley (Oxford: Oxford University Press, 2008)

Taylor, Charles, *A Secular Age* (London: Belknap Press, 2007)

Thomas à Kempis, *The Earliest English Translation of the First Three Books of the De Imitatione Christi*, ed. by John K. Ingram (London: Kegan Paul, Trench, Trübner & Co. Ltd, 1893)

——, *The Imitation of Christ* (London: J.M. Dent & Sons Ltd, 1910)

Toscano, Alberto, *Fanaticism: On the Uses of an Idea* (London: Verso, 2010)

Ueberweg, Friedrich, *A History of Philosophy from Thales to the Present Time: Vol. 1* (New York, NY: Charles Scribner's Sons, 1889)

Underhill, Evelyn, *Mysticism: A Study in Nature and Development of Spiritual Consciousness* (Mineola, NY: Dover Publications, 2002)

Valéry, Paul, *Monsieur Teste* (Paris: Gallimard, 1946)

Vetlovskaya, Valentina, 'Alyosha Karamazov and the Hagiographic Hero', in *Dostoevsky: New Perspectives*, ed. by Robert Louis Jackson, trans. by Nancy Pollack and Susanne Fusso (Englewood Cliffs, NJ: Prentice-Hall, 1984), pp. 206–26

Virvidakis, Stelios, and Vasso Kindi, 'Quietism', *Oxford Bibliographies Online: Philosophy*, 2013 <http://www.oxfordbibliographies.com/display/id/obo-9780195396577-0184> [accessed 3 September 2014]

Wallace, William, 'Schopenhauer', ed. by J.L. Garvin, *The Encyclopædia Britannica: A new survey of universal knowledge* (London: The Encyclopædia Britannica Company, Ltd., 1929), 102–4

Ward, Patricia A., 'Madame Guyon (1648–1717)', in *The Pietist Theologians: An Introduction to Theology in the Seventeenth and Eighteenth Centuries*, ed. by Carter Lindberg (Oxford: Blackwell, 2008)

Webster, David, *The Philosophy of Desire in the Buddhist Pali Canon* (Abingdon: RoutledgeCurzon, 2005)

Webster, Douglas Raymund, 'The Carthusian Order', *The Catholic Encyclopedia* (New York, NY: Robert Appleton Company, 1908) <http://www.newadvent.org/cathen/03388a.htm> [accessed 3 May 2013]

Wilenski, R.H., *Dutch Painting*, Revised edition. First published 1929. (New York, NY: Beechhurst, 1955)

Williams, Paul, *Mahayana Buddhism: The Doctrinal Foundations*, 2nd edn (London: Routledge, 2008)

Windelband, Wilhelm, *A History Of Philosophy* (New York, NY: Macmillan, 1901)

Wolfe, Phillip, 'La Bruyère Critique de Quiétisme', *Papers on French Seventeenth Century Literature*, 15 (1981), 255–66

Woodruff, Paul, 'Aporetic Pyrrhonism', in *Oxford Studies in Ancient Philosophy: Volume VI: 1988*, ed. by Julia Annas (Oxford: Oxford University Press, 1988), pp. 139–68

Zimmer, Heinrich, *Maya der indische Mythos* (Berlin: Deutsche Verlags-Anstalt, 1936)

Index

A

accidia, 48–49
Amiel, 59, 62–63
animals, 122–123, 126, 186–7, 195–8
   anthropomorphism, 17
   Beckett's attitude towards, 195
   Buddhist attitude towards, 198
   Haeckel's attitude towards, 195–8
   in *How It Is*, 186, 195–196, 198
   rebirth as an animal, 197–198, 209
   suffering of, 195–198
anti-natalism, 72, 220
asceticism, 21, 32–34, 37–39, 81, 102, 125, 188–189, 192, 202, 223, 228, 234, 259
   self-mortification, 188–189
ataraxia, 47–48, 50, 75, 106, 212, 226, 229–231, 240
Augustine, St, 55, 74, 157, 208, 227
Austen, Jane, 139, 152, 153, 230

B

Bacon, Francis, 96
Bakhtin, Mikhail, 142
Balzac, Honoré de, 20, 124, 139–146, 148, 150–154, 159, 164, 165, 166–7, 168, 210, 230–231, 258–259
Beckett, Samuel,
   Act Without Words I, 173, 208, 212
   Company, 237–246, 247, 248, 250, 251, 256
   'Le Concentrisme', 175–176
   Dream of Fair to Middling Women, 20, 40, 41, 45, 54, 55–57, 64, 75, 77, 89, 94, 97, 114, 118, 125, 127–8, 133–135, 139–147, 150–153, 154, 170, 179, 213–214, 220, 230–231, 239, 241–242, 251, 253, 255–256, 259
   Eleuthéria, 214
   Endgame, 124, 173, 225, 232
   How It Is, 21, 87, 168, 169–210, 215, 217, 220, 222, 238, 243–246, 248, 250, 251, 256, 257
   'Humanistic Quietism', 57–64, 69
   Ill Seen Ill Said, 241–242
   Lessness, 232–237, 254
   The Lost Ones, 212, 233,
   Malone Dies, 17, 72, 75, 153, 162, 165, 173, 212, 214, 215, 220–222, 227, 230, 242–243
   Mercier and Camier, 214, 215
   Molloy, 21, 29, 39, 45, 75, 89, 94, 117–168, 210, 212, 214, 215, 222, 224, 242, 256, 257
   More Pricks than Kicks, 114, 198–199, 214, 250
   Murphy, 19, 21, 44, 54, 68, 71, 72, 75, 79–115, 118, 124, 137, 145, 147, 152, 176–177, 185, 210, 212, 214, 215, 220, 235, 238, 250, 254, 255, 256–257
   Ping, 212, 232–237, 239, 254
   Proust, 36, 44, 58, 71, 118, 124, 135, 143, 146, 174–175, 203, 218–220, 223, 233, 244, 248, 251
   Stirrings Still, 21, 50, 211, 246–253, 256
   The Unnamable, 18, 50, 82, 153–4, 165, 213, 215, 220–222, 228, 237–240, 243
   Waiting for Godot, 50, 213
   Watt, 122–123, 124, 143, 212, 213, 214, 249, 257–258
   Worstward Ho, 172, 230
   Clare Street notebook, 49, 53, 56, 132, 200, 233,
   Dream notebook, 39, 41, 45, 55, 63, 64–65, 74, 83, 133, 135, 170, 241, 256, 259
   German diaries, 18, 77, 117, 120, 147
   notes on German literature, 55
   philosophy notes, 24, 36, 47–49, 71, 102, 106, 192–193, 201,
   psychology notes, 53–55, 59, 216,
   Whoroscope notebook, 35, 50, 72, 79–80, 101, 107, 114, 142–143, 176, 250
   Buddhism, knowledge of, 170–181
   failure, view of, 229–230
   heart problems, 51–57, 64, 67, 69, 87, 118, 134
   lectures at Trinity College Dublin, 42–43, 61, 67, 112, 139–140, 151, 166, 167, 175, 176, 258
   mysticism, relation to, 37–41
   novel 'series', 213–223, 227, 238, 249, 253–254
   unheroic aesthetic, 139–149

Bible, 17–18, 24, 39, 46, 53, 55, 95, 108, 119, 128, 135–136, 157–158, 164, 182–183, 190, 226, 235, 255
Blake, William, 164, 166
Bonaventure, St, 28, 127
Bosch, Hieronymus, 257–258
Bossuet, Jacques-Bénigne (Bishop), 28, 78, 122
Brahma, 58, 174, 220
Brahman, 85
Brahmanism, 33, 84–87, 177–178, 187, 188–189, 192,
see also: Hinduism
Buddha, 86–87, 169, 170, 174–176, 178–179, 180, 181, 188, 198, 200, 201–202, 206, 207, 208, 220, 223
Buddhism,
awakening (enlightenment), 169–170, 177, 188, 192, 200–203, 206, 213–214, 226, 227, 243
Beckett's knowledge of, 170–181
bodhi tree (*Ficus religiosa*), 169–170, 188, 194–195
ethics, 177, 198, 209–210, 214, 257
quietism, 33–34, 170–172, 227
rebirth, 189–192, 201, 203, 250–251
see also: reincarnation
self, view of, 178, 206, 218n, 243, 257
Zen, 172–173
Burrows, Rachel, 42, 43, 61, 112, 144, 176
Burton, Robert, 55, 235

C

Calderón, Pedro, 71–72, 220
Catholicism, 59–64, 69, 122, 124–125, 150, 157, 159, 211
Christian Quietism, 25–30
monasticism, 125–126, 155
Chamfort, Nicolas, 232–233
Christ, see: Jesus
Cioran, Emil,
Beckett's reading of, 179
Buddhism, views on, 179–181, 206–207
Proust, views on, 243, 245, 254

salvation, views on, 206–207, 211, 213, 223–224, 246, 254
compassion,
in Buddhism, 86, 177, 181, 198, 201
in Schopenhauer's philosophy, 32, 33, 66, 69, 85–86, 96, 114, 165, 177, 194, 206, 210, 227
towards animals, 195–196, 198
towards Murphy, 83–84, 87, 94, 104–106
transgressive, 198–200, 208–210

D

Dante,
Inferno, 149–150, 182, 187, 198–199, 251
Purgatorio, 189, 239, 250, 256
Paradiso, 211, 224, 227
Darwin, Charles, 184–187, 190, 192–194
David-Neel, Alexandra, 107, 176,
death, 161–163, 189–191, 203–207, 212, 238, 246–247, 252;
see also: reincarnation
decay, 130–139, 144, 150–152, 163–165, 168
Democritus, 47, 50, 110
desire,
ablation of, 23, 38, 46, 49, 56, 58, 71, 118, 119, 124, 161, 174–175, 223
cause of suffering, 32, 58, 175, 188, 191–193, 219, 235, 243
end of all, 188, 198, 211, 213, 223, 243, 248
for knowledge, 83, 150
paradox of, 227–228, 253
sensual, 83, 219
Donne, John, 131
Dostoevsky, Fyodor,
The Brothers Karamazov, 84, 89–94, 97, 99–100, 108–111, 115, 131, 148
Crime and Punishment, 44, 120
Demons, 44, 92
The Eternal Husband, 152
The House of the Dead, 44
The Idiot, 89, 100
Alyosha mistake, 89–94
anti-Catholic attitudes, 61–62

Balzac, compared to, 141–142, 144, 154
Beckett's reading of, 44–45
hagiography, use of, 89–92, 100
humility, 59, 61, 68–69, 258
incoherence, embrace of, 141, 145, 166–168, 210, 236
interpersonal relationships, depiction of, 67, 99–100, 244, 256
narratorial injections, 92–94, 105
quietist novelist, 19, 20, 42–43, 58–59, 84, 62, 64, 73, 77, 124, 140–143, 147, 151–152, 166–168, 231
realism, 142
third zone of being, 97–100, 145, 151–152

Driver, Tom, 208
Duthuit, Georges, 71

E

Eckhart, Meister, 23–24, 33, 38–41, 46, 138, 223, 241
Elsheimer, Adam, 128–130
Empedocles, 192–193
Empiricus, Sextus, 137, 228–229, 233
Epictetus, 49
Epicurus, 47, 50, 81, 102–103, 106

F

Fénelon, François, 28–29, 33, 45–46, 62, 126–127, 135, 224–225
Feuillerat, Albert, 57–58, 143–144, 152, 231
Francis of Sales, St, 46, 62, 225
Franzen, Erich, 149

G

Geulincx, Arnold,
   Beckett's reading of, 68–73, 81, 114, 144
   Murphy, influence on, 101–102
   Molloy, influence on, 147–150, 158–159
   quietists, compared to, 70–73, 240, 257
Gide, André,
   Les Caves du Vatican, 92

Dostoïevsky: articles et causeries, 42, 97–99, 140–142, 151–152, 154, 166, 176, 244
Les Faux-monnayeurs, 43, 44, 144
La Porte étroite, 43, 68, 144, 166
La Symphonie pastorale, 120
Balzac, views on, 154
Beckett's early interest in, 44–45,
Beckett's lectures on, 42–43, 67–68, 139–140, 144, 151
quietist aesthetic, 19–21, 58, 63, 68, 69, 73, 77, 100, 146–148, 166–168, 210, 231, 236, 258
Protestantism, 61–62
Proust, views on, 58, 143–144
God,
   apophatic description of, 137–138, 164
   erasure of, 25, 29, 39, 126, 130, 133, 159, 164, 223, 234
   gaseous vertebrate, 185
   perceived via divine eye, 241–242
   replaced by self, 64, 66–67, 95–96
   surrender to, 23–24, 26, 43, 45–46, 62, 70, 128n, 149, 160–161, 225, 243
   union with, 23, 28, 45, 85, 126–127, 132, 135, 226
Goethe, Johann Wolfgang von, 53, 54n, 74
   Dichtung und Wahrheit, 76–77, 95–97
Grillparzer, Franz, 74
Guyon, Madame,
   La Bruyère's treatment of, 122, 126–127
   language of decay, 131–133, 151–152
   life and legacy, 27–30
   Schopenhauer's admiration of, 33–34, 67
   teachings, 29–30, 39, 45–46, 125, 126–7, 129n, 158, 242

H

Haeckel, Ernst,
   The Riddle of the Universe, 185–186, 192
   A Visit to Ceylon, 187–189, 194–198
   Bathybius haeckelii, 187
   palingenesis, 192, 215
   recapitulation theory, 215
   view of animals, 195–198
heart,
   ascetic control of, 54, 234

Beckett's heart problems, 51–57, 64, 67, 69, 87, 118, 134
  prayer of the, 27–28
  symbol of the will, 57
Heraclitus, 184
Hinduism, 81, 84–85, 102, 174, 187, 189, 190, 197
  reincarnation, 189–192
  see also: Brahmanism
Hölderlin, Friedrich, 74
hope,
  resignation of, 118, 119, 124, 132, 173, 183, 200–201, 213, 223, 228, 232–233, 235, 248, 254
Howe, Mary Manning, 48, 231
humility,
  Dostoevsky, 59–60, 90, 140–142
  Geulincx, 69–71, 114, 159
  Gide, 144, 258
  Madame Guyon, 127
  Protestant exemplars of, 60–61, 69

I

imperturbability, 47, 50, 106
  Kafka, 231
  see also: *ataraxia*
Inge, William,
  apophatic theology, description of, 137–138
  atomists, views on, 47, 50
  Christian Mysticism, 45–46, 77, 127, 133, 137–138, 160–162
  contemplation and action, 126
  German mysticism, 241
  mystic paradox, 224
  Quietism, views on, 46, 62, 103, 126–127, 135, 161, 243

J

Jesus,
  imitation of, 97, 257–258, 134, 182, 189
  quietist neglect of, 25, 123–124, 128–130
  quietist sayings of, 24, 157
  transcendental Christ, 127–128
John of the Cross, St, 26, 29, 46, 136, 162, 125
Joyce, James,

Finnegans Wake, 258
Ulysses, 118, 258, 185
Beckett, influence on, 145, 148
heroic aesthetic, 40, 147–150, 230
omnipotence, 40, 146, 259
'Work in Progress', 147, 149
Juliet, Charles, 138, 155, 161, 174, 208, 212

K

Kafka, Franz,
  Beckett's view of, 166–167, 230–231, 258
Keats, John, 167
Kempis, Thomas à,
  Beckett's personal experiments with, 64–68, 95–97, 113–114, 147
  descriptions of salvation, 65, 94, 224, 259
  influence on *Molloy*, 160–162
  influence on *Murphy*, 80–83, 95–97, 103, 106, 113–114
  mystic paradox, 224
Klopstock, Friedrich, 183
Knox, Ronald, 225, 231, 235, 243, 254

L

La Bruyère, Jean de,
  Dialogues posthumes sur le quiétisme, 120–124, 126, 128n, 131–132, 158, 162–163, 225
Lao Tzu, 180, 224
Leopardi, Giacomo, 24, 31–32, 58, 71, 81, 174, 208, 220
  'A se stesso' 55, 118, 187, 223, 233
Leventhal, A.J. 'Con', 51, 57, 215
listening, 160–161

M

MacGreevy, Thomas, 19, 57–64, 130, 145, 257
  Poems, 56–59, 62, 77
  Beckett's correspondence with, 31, 32, 36, 44, 64–67, 69, 72, 75, 80, 83–84, 87, 89, 94, 95, 101, 118, 134, 176, 186, 214–216
  Catholicism, 59–60, 64

Malebranche, Nicolas, 196
Malraux, André, 101–102, 105
Mann, Thomas,
    Buddenbrooks, 19, 51–52, 75
Marcus Aurelius, 50
Marvell, Andrew, 156–157
Merton, Thomas, 211–212
Miller, Henry, 255, 257, 259
Milton, John, 75, 182–184, 190, 238
Molinos, Miguel de,
    anti-theoretical attitude, 40
    imprisonment, 27, 104
    indifference to hell, 224, 234
    influences on, 28–29, 62, 133
    La Bruyère's treatment of, 122
    life and legacy, 25–29
    prayer, approach to, 45, 133, 161, 230, 242–243, 252
    rejection of consolation, 235
    Schopenhauer's admiration of, 33
    annihilation of self, 25, 26, 243
mystic paradox, 224–232, 237, 253
mysticism,
    German, 241–242
    quietism, compared to, 28–29, 37–41

N

narration,
    breakdown of, 152–153, 164–165
    deviser of Beckett's characters, 215, 220–221, 224–246, 249
    epanorthosis, 137, 221–222
    interjections, 92–93, 97,
    reborn voice throughout the prose, 213–254
    sympathy with characters, 89–94, 104–106, 114–115
Neo-Platonism, 34, 46, 242
nirvāna,
    Buddhism, 177, 188, 202, 206, 226–227,
    Cioran's understanding of, 180
    in *How It Is*, 203, 205–207, 248, 251
    nihilistic interpretation of, 171, 177, 180, 224
    Schopenhauer's understanding of, 201–202, 205–206, 242

    in *Stirrings Still*, 251, 253
Nordau, Max,
    abhorrence of mysticism, 41–42
    Beckett's reading of *Degeneration*, 55, 170–172, 210–211
novel,
    modernist, 144–146, 148, 258–259
    nineteenth-century realist, 140–142, 145–146, 153–154, 167, 230–231, 258–259
    quietist, 19–20, 42–45, 57–58, 67–68, 139–150, 167–168, 257–258
    status after Proust, 223, 244

O

Orwell, George, 255–259

P

pessimism, 32, 36, 71–72, 76, 119, 171, 177, 181, 255
    rejecting pessimistic reading of *How It Is*, 208–209
Plato, 36, 216
Plümacher, Olga, 76, 86–87, 177, 202, 216
prayer, 158, 180, 211, 224
    contemplative, 25–27, 45–46, 125–126, 159–163, 230–231
    of the heart, 27–28
    Lord's prayer, 119–124
    Moran's quietist pater, 119–124, 168, 225
    poetry, compared to, 60, 64
    of quiet, 23, 25–26, 45–46, 77, 133, 161–163, 242–243
    Quietist approach to, 23–30, 45–46, 123, 160–163, 230–231, 243
Prentice, Charles, 44, 145
Protestantism,
    as aesthetic, 58–62
    and humility, 60–61, 69, 73, 231
    rejection of quietism, 33
    similarities to quietism, 29, 159
Proust, Marcel,
    Du côté de chez Swann, 111–112, 216–217
    La Fugitive (Albertine disparue), 112, 218–219

À l'ombre des jeunes filles en fleurs, 217
Sodome et Gomorrhe, 218, 222
Le Temps retrouvé, 223
Balzac, compared to, 144–146, 152
Beckett's essay on, 36, 44, 58, 71, 118, 124, 135, 143, 146, 174–175, 203, 218–220, 223, 233, 244, 248, 251
destroyer of the novel, 223, 234, 254
quietist novelist, 57–59, 143–144, 23
reincarnation, interest in, 216–218, 222, 246, 249–251
self, depiction of, 218–221, 223, 245–246

Pyrrhonism, 24, 47–50, 137, 228–230, 240

Pythagoreanism, 54, 81, 216

Q

Quietism (Christian tradition),
  anti-theoretical attitude, 39–40
  consolation, rejection of, 231, 234, 253–254
  heretical aspects, 29, 122–123, 128n, 130, 134, 135, 158, 159, 224–227, 242
  mysticism, contrasted with, 40–41
  language of decay, 131–133
  origins, 23–30, 133, 243
  pantheistic tendencies, 123
  persecution of, 27–30, 103–104, 122
  prayer, approach to, 23–30, 45–46, 123, 160–163, 230–231, 243
  salvation, indifference to, 26, 224–227, 253–254
  Schopenhauer's admiration of, 33–34, 6
  Stoicism, connections to, 50, 102
  see also: Molinos, Miguel de and Guyon, Madame

quietism (general),
  as aesthetic, 19, 42–45, 57–64, 76–77, 117–168, 230–231
  in Buddhism, 33–34, 170–172, 227
  in Christianity, 28–30, 45–46
  definition of, 20, 23–24, 37–40, 77
  and despair, 17–19
  as ethical system, 209–210
  as failed life philosophy, 51–57, 64–68, 72–3, 76–77, 79–84, 93, 105, 110, 113–114
  Geulincx and, 70–73, 240, 257

Schopenhauer's, 30–34, 37, 80
in Hellenistic philosophy, 47–50, 106
salvation, 200–210, 224–231, 235, 248, 253–254
and violence, 165–168

R

Racine, Jean, 208–209
Reavey, George, 213–215
rebirth, see: reincarnation
reincarnation,
  animal, rebirth as an, 197–198, 209
  Beckett's prose series imagined as, 211–254
  Buddhism, 189–192, 201, 203, 250–251
  end of, 192, 201, 203, 221, 224, 245,
  in *How It Is*, 190–192
  in the late prose, 237–254
  memory of previous lives, 201, 218
  moment-to-moment, 218–220
  palingenesis, 192, 216
  Proust's interest in, 216–218, 222, 246, 249–251
  Schopenhauer's view of, 191–192
  in the Trilogy, 220–223

Rembrandt, 128–129
Rilke, Rainer Maria, 63–64, 66–68, 73, 256
Rivière, Jacques, 140–141, 154
Ruysbroeck, John van, 30, 127, 138

S

salvation,
  as *ataraxia* (Pyrrhonism and Epicureanism), 47–48, 50, 75, 106, 212, 226, 229–231, 240
  Beckett's repudiation of, 208, 213, 225–226, 233
  Bom's rejection of (*How It Is*), 203–210
  as bringing insight, 132, 200–201, 233
  as end of rebirth (Buddhism and Hinduism), 192, 201, 203, 221, 224, 245, 250–253
  as extinction of self, 122, 192, 200–203, 206–207, 221, 223–224, 243, 245–246, 251
  ethical implications of, 201, 206, 210
  failure to reach, 208, 212–213, 245–246

impossibility of representing, 253–254
indifference to, 26, 224–227, 232, 253–254
as mind state, 75, 94, 202, 213, 223, 226–227, 235, 252
as *nirvāna* (Buddhism), 177, 188, 202, 206, 226–227,
Schopenhauer's view of, 32–33, 75, 112, 192, 200–202, 206, 226–227, 252
samsāra, 191, 194, 200; see also: suffering; reincarnation
scepticism, see: Pyrrhonism
Schopenhauer, Arthur,
    Beckett's reading of, 30–31, 34–36, 51, 75–76, 81, 193, 201–202
    Buddhism, view of, 171–172
    on compassion, 32, 33, 66, 69, 85–86, 96, 114, 165, 177, 194, 206, 210, 227
    ethics, see: compassion
    on gardens, 155–157
    pensum, 36, 77, 117–118, 159–160, 168, 220, 259
    principium individuationis, 33, 152, 206–207, 210, 244
    quietism, 30–34, 37, 80
    Quietiv, 32, 80, 252
    reincarnation, view of, 191–192
    revenge, view of, 202
    soteriology, 32–33, 75, 112, 192, 200–202, 206, 226–227, 252
    tat tvam asi, 84–86, 100, 106, 191–192
    Thing-In-Itself, 37, 80, 110, 202
    veil of Maya, 33, 75, 112, 132, 177, 200–202, 246
    will-to-live, 21, 31–32, 34, 47, 80, 100, 202, 205–206, 210, 227–228, 235–236, 252
self,
    annihilation of, 25–26, 28, 38–39, 42, 46, 74, 126–128, 138–139, 152, 162–165, 181, 202–203, 224, 242–246, 248, 251, 257
    ātman, 84–86, 178
    Buddhist view of, 178, 206, 218n, 243, 257
    exploration of, 63, 143
    illusion of, 33, 152, 178, 192, 202, 206–207, 210, 212–213, 223, 243–244
    instability of, 42, 141–142, 217–220, 223, 258

renunciation of, 20–21, 26, 42, 45–46, 70–71, 125, 131–132, 147, 210, 243–246
replacement for God, 64, 66–67, 95–96
self-absorption, 66–67, 71, 82–83, 95–97, 99–100, 102–103, 110–112, 143, 147, 207; see also: solipsism
self-awareness, 59, 63, 114, 132
self-denial, 32, 34, 37, 70–71, 100, 125, 131, 133, 192
self-hatred, 87
Shainberg, Lawrence, 173–174, 248
Shakespeare, William, 238
Shenker, Israel, 146, 151, 167, 231, 258
Sinclair, Morris 'Sonny', 17–18, 57, 60, 67, 77
solipsism, 18, 63–68, 73, 80, 85, 95, 97, 99, 102, 114, 158, 165, 177, 206–207, 210, 246; see also: self-absorption
soteriology, see: salvation
Spinoza, Baruch, 81, 96
Stoicism, 24, 47, 49, 50, 106
suffering,
    acceptance of, 20, 41, 49, 259
    of animals, 195–198
    Beckett's use of his own, 73, 76–77
    caused by dissatisfaction and desire, 32, 58, 175, 188, 205, 227,
    end of, 32–33, 83, 137, 139, 191, 200–210, 235, 248, 252
    in *How It Is*, 182, 191–199
    religious explanations for, 181–184, 198–200, 202, 207, 209
Swift, Jonathan, 102–103

T

Taoism, 24, 173, 180, 224
Tauler, Johannes, 33, 46, 241
Teresa of Ávila, St,
    precursor of Quietists, 26, 28–29, 30, 45, 104, 133, 162
    Great Dereliction, 77, 133, 136, 152, 168
theodicy, 181–184, 199, 200, 207, 209
Theologia Germanica, 241

theology,
    quietist rejection of, 38–41
    apophatic, 38–39, 138
Toynbee, Paget, 256

U

Upanishads, 34, 81
    tat tvam asi, 84–87

V

Valéry, Paul, 87, 96

W

Windelband, Wilhelm, 36, 53, 71, 96,
    101, 106, 192–193
Wordsworth, William, 151

Z

Zimmer, Heinrich, 86–87, 190–191,
    194, 216

ibidem.*eu*